# PLATO'S
# DOCTRINE OF IDEAS

BY

J. A. STEWART, M.A.

WHITE'S PROFESSOR OF MORAL PHILOSOPHY IN THE UNIVERSITY
OF OXFORD; HON. STUDENT OF CHRIST CHURCH
HON. LL.D. EDINBURGH AND ABERDEEN

OXFORD
AT THE CLARENDON PRESS
1909

HENRY FROWDE, M.A.
PUBLISHER TO THE UNIVERSITY OF OXFORD
LONDON, EDINBURGH, NEW YORK
TORONTO AND MELBOURNE

# PREFACE

I have to thank two friends for valuable assistance —the Dean of Christ Church, for kindly reading the proof-sheets, and, especially, for giving me leave to add a Note containing extracts from a very interesting letter which he wrote to me about Musical Experience,[1]—and Mr. McDougall, Wilde Reader in Mental Philosophy, for allowing me to read the Second Part of this Essay to him in manuscript, and for making important suggestions and criticisms which I have tried to give effect to.

I also owe thanks to the Editor of *Mind* for kindly permitting me to embody (in the Introduction) some passages from a Paper which I contributed to that Review.

J. A. S.

Oxford, *Feb.* 1909.

[1] See p. 153, and Note, p. 198.

# CONTENTS

|  | PAGE |
|---|---|
| INTRODUCTION | 1 |

PART I. THE DOCTRINE OF IDEAS AS CONTRIBUTION TO
METHODOLOGY . . . . . 14–127

| The Apology | 16 |
|---|---|
| The Euthyphro | 17 |
| The Crito | 19 |
| The Charmides | 20 |
| The Laches | 22 |
| The Protagoras | 23 |
| The Meno | 24 |
| The Euthydemus | 28 |
| The Gorgias | 29 |
| The Cratylus | 34 |
| The Phaedo | 39 |
| The Republic | 47 |
| The Phaedrus | 62 |
| The Theaetetus | 65 |
| The Parmenides | 68 |
| The Sophistes | 84 |
| The Politicus | 89 |
| The Philebus | 92 |
| The Timaeus | 101 |
| The Laws | 106 |
| Aristotle's Criticism of the Doctrine of Ideas | 107 |
| Summary of Part I | 119 |

PART II. THE DOCTRINE OF IDEAS AS EXPRESSING
AESTHETIC EXPERIENCE . . . . 128–197

| INDEX | 199 |
|---|---|

## PLATO'S DOCTRINE OF IDEAS

THE question which this Essay is concerned to put and find some answer to is : What has present-day Psychology to tell us about the Variety of Experience which expresses itself in Plato's Doctrine of Ideas ? The importance of this question has been gradually brought home to me by my perusal of various expositions of the Doctrine offered by Plato-scholars in recent times. These expositions, however informing and suggestive they may be in parts, in themselves, as expositions, seem to me to fall short of scientific sufficiency because not controlled from the basis of Psychology. The literary evidence contained in Plato's Dialogues and Aristotle's Criticisms [1] is fully taken, but submitted to the judgement of no court. The cardinal question is not asked : What has present-day Psychology to tell us about the Variety of Experience which expresses itself in the Doctrine of Ideas? The Doctrine is treated as if it were a 'past event' in the 'History of Philosophy' for determining the true nature of which there is such and such documentary evidence which, if only marshalled in the right way, is in itself conclusive. It is as if a commentator on Thucydides should think it unnecessary to submit the literary record of the Plague at Athens to the judgement of present-day medical science in order to ascertain from that authority what precisely the disease is which his author is endeavouring to describe.

[1] For Aristotle's Criticisms, M. Robin's extremely elaborate work *La Théorie Platonicienne des Idées et des Nombres d'après Aristote* (1908) may be mentioned. It is one of those recent works which make it evident that the answer to the question, 'What is the meaning of the Doctrine of Ideas?' is not to be looked for in further examination of the literary data.

The result of their neglect of the Psychology of the Experience which expresses itself in the Doctrine of Ideas is that the scholars to whom I refer, going to Plato's text in the dark, lose themselves in it. Having no clue they find themselves in a labyrinth. Because Plato, dealing, at different periods of his life, with different subjects, in Dialogues differently staged, phrases and accentuates the Doctrine of Ideas differently, they tell us that he has altered the Doctrine essentially: they ask us to believe that at one period of his career he held this opinion, and at another period that opinion, while Pupils of the Academy, Pythagoreans, Eleatics, Megarians, not to mention Aristotle himself, held certain other opinions—'about the Ideas'. 'But,' we ask, '*What are the Ideas?* What were Plato and these other people talking about? Surely about the right way of expressing some Experience which they all had in common, and we ourselves still have. Tell us in the language, vernacular or philosophical, of to-day what that Experience is.' To this appeal the textualists have no response to make; in lieu they either offer us empirical judgements suggested by simple inspection of the language employed in various passages, or else ask us to accept the translation of some term or phrase—αὐτὰ καθ' αὑτά, χωρίς, παρεῖναι, μετέχειν, μίμησις, παράδειγμα—as a sufficient interpretation of Plato's Doctrine as it happened to stand when he used the term or phrase in question. Translation, in which, naturally, the expositors agree, offered as interpretation, and empirical judgements, in which they, as naturally, differ—these are the chief constituents of expositions which attempt to interpret the literary evidence for the meaning of the Doctrine of Ideas without seeking the control of Psychology.

It is to Aristotle's version of the Doctrine of Ideas that these recent expositions ultimately go back—to a version vitiated, like most of Aristotle's versions of Plato's doctrines, by the Pupil's inability or unwillingness to enter into the Psychology of the Experience to which the Master was giving expression.

The Experience to which Plato gave expression in his Doctrine of Ideas was a double one—not always, I think, recognized by himself as double: it was the Experience of one keenly interested in, and highly capable of taking, the scientific point of view in all departments of knowledge; and it was also the Experience of one singularly sensitive to aesthetic influences. It was the Experience of one who was a great man of science and connoisseur of scientific method, and also a great artist.

The Doctrine of Ideas, expressing this double Experience, has accordingly its two sides, the methodological and the aesthetic. The former side Aristotle misunderstands, and to the latter is entirely blind. If the Ideas are 'Separate Things', as Aristotle maintains, then the Doctrine of Ideas can have no methodological significance; for methodology must assume that science works with 'concepts', which are not themselves 'things' but general points of view from which things, i.e. sensible things—the only 'separate things' known to science—are regarded. Even a common-sense estimate of the character and extent of Plato's contribution to methodology in the Doctrine of Ideas —an estimate made with the aid of the most elementary psychology of the faculties with which the man of science goes to work—would have brought Aristotle to see that the Ideas, whether as objects or as instruments of scientific thought, are not 'separate things'. But he did not take the trouble to make such an estimate. He has no eye for the wide view of scientific method opened up in the Doctrine of Ideas as set forth in the Sixth Book of the *Republic*, in the *Phaedo*, in the *Philebus*, and in the *Sophistes*. One is tempted to account for this by saying that Aristotle's eminence as man of science and contributor to the logic of the sciences lay, after all, in the regions of departmental research, and that he never rose to the speculative height which his master occupied as methodologist; but if one declines to say this, one must, at any rate, say that he was so puzzled by the aesthetic side of his master's Doctrine that he failed to do even bare justice to its methodological side, mistaking for the Vision of a mere poet the strictly scientific ideal, set forth in the *Republic* and elsewhere, the ideal of getting, by means of dialectic or hard thinking, to see more and more clearly the interconnexion of all branches of knowledge. And there is another reason, I think, for Aristotle's failure to do justice to the methodological side of the Doctrine of Ideas. It is not enough to say that he took Plato's language too literally, in a sense which made it impossible for any one to regard the Doctrine of Ideas as a serious contribution to methodology. Why did he take it so literally? Why did he so harp on the separate thinghood of the Idea? Because, doubtless, as I have just said, the aesthetic element in the Doctrine as expounded by the Master himself puzzled him and made him see the methodological side wrong; but also, I would suggest, because he judged the teaching of Plato by its results in the minds of Plato's pupils rather than on its own merits. For the average pupil the Ideas were mere doubles of sensible objects. They were like the *densum* and *rarum* and other *anticipationes mentis* condemned by Bacon. Without taking trouble to understand the Doctrine as actually held by Plato, Aristotle denounced it as reflected in the attitude of Plato's pupils. The Lyceum was a place where scientific research was systematically pursued; the Academy Aristotle seems to have regarded as a place were there was too much discussion and too little research. I doubt not that his estimate of the Academy and of the influence there of the Doctrine of Ideas in causing weak disciples to acquiesce in thing-like abstractions was pretty correct, although in making it he showed so little understanding of the vast service which the Master rendered, in that Doctrine, to the logic of the sciences.

To the other side of the Doctrine of Ideas—to its aesthetic side, Aristotle, as I have said, was blind; and is mainly responsible for the neglect of this side which has prevailed down to the present time among exponents and critics of the Doctrine as distinguished from practising Platonists or Devotees who have erred in the opposite way — in exaggerating its aesthetic, and neglecting its logical side. I venture to think, however, that, with all their *Schwärmerei*, the practising Platonists—men like Cudworth, and More, and John Smith—got nearer to the heart of the Doctrine than recent textualists have succeeded in getting.

The lack of psychological basis, then, which we have to deplore in recent expositors of the Doctrine of Ideas is a weakness which they have inherited from Aristotle; and this weakness shows itself in them just as it showed itself in him—in very imperfect appreciation of the methodological significance of the Doctrine, and in blindness to its aesthetic significance.

While the Psychology of the aesthetic experience expressed in the Doctrine of Ideas is difficult, and only lately available in useful form, that of the experience of the man of science also expressed in it is comparatively simple and accessible to any one who takes the common-sense view that a Doctrine obviously intended by Plato to be a contribution to methodology or the logic of the sciences is to be interpreted on the supposition that it resembles closely, not that it differs radically from, what a contribution to methodology coming from a modern man of science might be expected to be. But this common-sense view of the Doctrine as contribution to methodology has not been consistently taken by any of the considerable expositors in recent times except by Professor Natorp.

Professor Natorp's exposition [1] of the Doctrine of Ideas I do not class with some other recent expositions as having no psychological basis. Professor Natorp realizes that Plato's Doctrine of Ideas has, at any rate, one side which can be understood only in the light of Psychology—the Psychology of the faculties by which the man of science

[1] *Platos Ideenlehre* (1903).

interprets Nature. These faculties were the same in Plato as they are in the modern man of science, and Plato's account of their operations must, allowance being made for modes of expression peculiar to himself and his age, bear close comparison with the account of them given by a modern psychologist who should make it his business to explain how the man of science to-day goes to work. This Professor Natorp sees clearly. He sees, what their lack of Psychology prevents some other recent expositors from seeing clearly, or at all, that the Doctrine of Ideas has a large significance as Method of Science; and he is very successful in expounding it as such on lines which, I am interested in noticing, are similar to those which I myself, starting from an *aperçu* of Lotze's (an *aperçu* which Professor Natorp hardly appreciates at its true value [1]), indicated a good many years ago.[2] Explained on these lines, the εἴδη, so far as methodology is concerned, are points of view from which the man of science regards his data. They are the right points of view, and, as such, have the 'permanence' which we nowadays ascribe to 'Laws of Nature'. They are indeed 'separate' from phenomena; but only so in the sense that they are the 'explanations' as distinguished from the 'phenomena explained'. They are not 'separate *things*'; the τρίτος ἄνθρωπος refutation in the Tenth Book of the *Republic* and the *Parmenides* disposes of the error, wrongly attributed by Aristotle to Plato, of substantiating them as 'separate *things*'. If we dismiss from our minds the prejudice raised by Aristotle's criticism we find nothing in the Dialogues of Plato to countenance the view that the Ideas, so far as they have methodological significance, are 'known' as statically existent: they are 'known' only as dynamically existent—only as performing their function of making *sensibilia* intelligible. It is as true of Plato's Ideas as of Kant's Categories that without sense they are empty. The Ideas, so far as their methodological signi-

[1] pp. 195 ff.  [2] *Notes on the Nicomachean Ethics* (1892), vol. i, pp. 71 ff.

ficance is concerned, are nothing more than concepts-in-use —the instruments by employing which Human Understanding performs its work of interpreting the world—this sensible world, not another world beyond. This view of the function of Ideas in science Plato holds and enforces throughout the whole series of his Dialogues, and nowhere more plainly than in his earliest Dialogues, where the object is to find the εἴδη of the Moral Virtues, that is, to *explain* the Moral Virtues by exhibiting each in its special context—by assigning to each its special place and use in the Social System, the System of the 'Good'. Sense, and imagination, and desultory thinking, expressing themselves in Rhetoric, present the 'Virtues' separately, taking no account of the System in which they inhere; ἀνάμνησις, described as αἰτίας λογισμός, connected thinking, stirred by Dialectic, works out the special context of each Virtue and the relations of that context to other contexts viewed as parts, along with it, of the whole System. 'Context grasped,' 'scientific point of view taken,' 'εἶδος discovered' —these are equivalent expressions. The εἶδος is not an impression of sense passively received; it is a product of the mind's activity, an instrument constructed by the mind whereby it 'makes nature', 'moulds environment', so as to serve the purposes of human life. It is really in such Dialogues as the *Charmides, Laches, Euthyphro, Crito*, to which may be added the *Meno* and *Cratylus*, that the Doctrine of Ideas, as Method of Science, is best illustrated; and much harm has been done by the quite gratuitous assumption that the εἶδος which holds so important a place in these Dialogues is not the 'Platonic Idea'. The 'Platonic Idea', we are told, is not a concept-in-use, but a 'separate substance', and does not meet us till we come to later Dialogues. But the truth is that wherever there is scientific explanation, wherever 'context' is thought out, the 'Platonic Idea' is there.

This is what, considering the very simple, though quite adequate, Psychology on which it rests, I have called the common-sense view, the acceptance of which seems to me to dispose of Professor Henry Jackson's view,[1] according to which Plato ended by recognizing only Ideas of 'natural kinds'. The Doctrine of Ideas began, Professor Jackson tells us, with the substantiation of concepts: the Eternal Ideas, the products of the substantiation, were at first coextensive with the groups of objects denoted by class-names: thus we had Ideas of Qualities—goodness, beauty, justice; Ideas of Natural Kinds—man, ox; Ideas of Artefacta—bed, house; Ideas of Relations—great, small, equal; and Ideas of Negations—evil, injustice; as well as Ideas of contemptible things—such as dirt. These Ideas were conceived as 'separate' and yet 'immanent': they were 'in', or 'present with' the objects called by the class-names—these objects 'participated in' them. This is the first form of the Doctrine as it appears in the *Phaedrus, Phaedo, Republic*. But in the *Philebus, Parmenides, Theaetetus, Sophist, Politicus,* and *Timaeus,* the Doctrine assumes a different form. The Ideas are still 'separate', but no longer 'immanent'—particulars no longer 'participate in' them, but 'resemble' them—μίμησις takes the place of μέθεξις—the Ideas are now παραδείγματα: and, further, they are reduced in number—Qualities, Relations, Negations, and Artefacta are rejected from the list of objects of knowledge which have Ideas, and we are left with only Ideas ('hypothetically existent') of Natural Kinds. These are αὐτὰ καθ' αὑτά, and are not κοινωνοῦντα, not predicable of one another—man is man, and not ox—and are distinguished from the non-αὐτὰ καθ' αὑτά, the most important of which, the genera or categories of thought (ὄν, ταὐτόν, θάτερον, στάσις, κίνησις), are κοινωνοῦντα, 'communicate with' one another, while the αὐτὰ καθ' αὑτά 'participate in' them.

[1] *The Journal of Philology,* articles on 'Plato's Later Theory of Ideas', vol. x, pp. 253 ff.; xi, pp. 287 ff.; xiii, pp. 1 ff.; xiii, pp. 242 ff.; xiv, pp. 173 ff.; xv, pp. 280 ff.: for criticism of Professor Jackson's view see Mr. R. G. Bury's article on 'The Later Platonism' in *The Journal of Philology,* vol. xxiii, pp. 161 ff., and Mr. J. Llewelyn Davies' article on. ' Plato's Later Theory of Ideas', *J. of Ph.*, vol. xxv, pp. 5 ff.

# INTRODUCTION 9

We shall see, I think, when we examine the Dialogues mentioned by Professor Jackson, that no such radical change occurred in Plato's Doctrine—no change amounting to the emptying it of methodological significance, the search for 'Ideas' in all but one of the divisions of scientific inquiry being finally renounced. We shall see that the Ideas, from first to last throughout the series of the Dialogues, are 'separate' (though not in such a sense as to make their 'immanence' a difficulty), and 'immanent', and 'paradeigmatic'; we shall also see that, from first to last, they are coextensive with the whole list of concepts—i.e. that, from first to last, there are Ideas of Qualities, Relations, Artefacta, and Negations, as well as of Natural Kinds. We shall see, in short, that the history of the Doctrine of Ideas in Plato's Dialogues is not a history of the dropping of old views and the adoption of new ones, but a history of the natural development of what is involved from the first. At the same time we shall see, I think, how really valuable Professor Jackson's *aperçu* of the 'hypothetical existence' of the Ideas is, and what important service he has incidentally rendered by calling pointed attention to the distinction between εἴδη of general applicability—categories of thought—and εἴδη of special applicability, although, in denying the rank of 'Platonic Ideas' to the former, and restricting it to 'Natural Kinds' among the latter, he has, in my judgement, obscured the methodological significance of the Doctrine.

There is no fault more fatal to sound interpretation than that of going through Plato's Dialogues with the eye fixed on what may be called their 'metaphysics' or 'logic', to the neglect of the *subjects* discussed. From such neglect it is an easy step, taken by too many Plato-scholars—even by Professor Natorp at times—to the treatment of a Dialogue as if the subject of it were merely ostensible—as if Plato's real object were the statement and illustration of dialectical method as evolved up to date. Let us always bear in mind that in a Dialogue on Temperance, like the *Charmides*, or on Courage, like the *Laches*, the 'Idea' of that quality, or of Virtue generally, is as naturally dwelt on as the 'Ideas' of Identity and Difference are dwelt on in a Dialogue, like the *Sophistes*, dealing with scientific method *per se*, apart from any particular application of it. Comparison of the *Laches* with the *Sophistes* does not justify us in concluding that, by the time he came to write the latter, Plato had changed his Doctrine of Ideas; but merely gives us the opportunity of noting that he had gone on to discuss new subjects. 'Others hold that the Ideal Theory in Book X [of the *Republic*] is inconsistent with the theory expounded in V-VII, where we do not hear of Ideas corresponding to concrete and artificial objects, but only of Ideas of Qualities (such as Justice) and the like. In reply we may point out that Plato is not bound to give an exhaustive account of the Ideal Theory whenever he has occasion to make use of it. On the previous occasion he confined himself to Ideas of the virtues, &c., because they only were relevant to his immediate purpose, and it is exactly the same reason which makes him cite Ideas of concrete and artificial objects in Book X.'[1] We shall therefore do well, as we go through the Dialogues, if we take careful note of the manner in which the expression of the Doctrine of Ideas is varied to suit the subject in each case, observing that now the methodological side of the Doctrine is prominent, and then again, the aesthetic side, and that each of these sides is presented in various widely differing modes.

While recognizing the service which Professor Natorp has rendered by insisting on the methodological significance of the Doctrine of Ideas ignored by most of the other recent expositors,[2] I have to find fault with him for

[1] Adam, *The Republic of Plato*, vol. ii, p. 387.
[2] Not by Professor A. E. Taylor ('On the interpretation of Plato's *Parmenides*' in *Mind*, July and October, 1896, January, 1897), and not by Mr. R. G. Bury (*The Philebus of Plato*, 1897). Their important contributions to the elucidation of the methodological significance of the Doctrine of Ideas I shall have to take note of afterwards.

assuming that the Doctrine has only that significance. His psychological basis does not include the psychology of that Experience on which Art and Religion depend for their inspiration. For that Experience the 'Idea' is not a 'point of view' taken by the mind in 'Discourse', but a 'real presence' confronting 'Contemplation'. In 'Discourse' the mind is always 'on the move', looking at particulars now from this, now from that, convenient point of view. Wonder does not enter into one's Experience here; rather the sense of 'getting on', of 'removing difficulties', of 'solving new problems'. But in 'Contemplation' the mind 'rests', wondering, in the presence of one 'eternal' object. The 'Eternal Idea' is revealed in some welcome, some familiar or beautiful, object of sense— literally *in* the object of sense: not as another object which the object of sense 'resembles', but as that very object of sense itself transfigured, become a wonder. It is not *a* skylark that Shelley hears and sees, but *the* Skylark. It is as induced and maintained by the representations, the μιμήματα, of the Fine Arts—especially by those of Painting and Poetry—that this Contemplation of the 'Eternal Idea' as a 'real presence' in the object of sense is most accessible to the observation of the Psychologist. It is here, I am convinced, not in further examination of the letter of Plato's text, that the Platonic παρουσία awaits its explanation. Had Professor Natorp's psychology taken account of this Variety of Experience for which the 'Idea' is not a 'point of view' in 'Discourse' but a 'real presence' confronting 'Contemplation', he could not have spoken as if the *Phaedrus* Myth were a regrettable episode in Plato's otherwise steady advance towards a clear doctrine of scientific method. He would have understood, once for all, that Plato is not only a man of science and critic of scientific method, but also a seer. As it is, Professor Natorp shows no appreciation of the masterly ease with which the man of science in Plato keeps the tendencies of the seer in hand where the interests of science would be compromised by their prevalence; and the *abandon* of the seer, where scientific interests are not in question, he mistakes for serious defection from these interests.

I do not underrate the difficulty of the task which I venture to find fault with Professor Natorp for not having attempted. The Variety of Experience which finds expression in that phase of the Doctrine of Ideas where the Ideas are presented, not as 'scientific points of view', but as 'eternal substances' really present in objects of sense, is one which has its roots very deep in Human Nature, as we must conclude from the fact that the expressions of it (and Plato's Doctrine of Ideas is neither the only expression of it, nor even itself reducible to a single formula) are at once so obscure to thought, and so perennially attractive to feeling. Those minds in which, as in Plato's, this deeply-rooted Experience is most vivid, find any expression of it inadequate, and, in their effort to be out with it, try many modes of expression, emotional, sensuous, conceptual. Thus it is just where, as in Plato's mind, the Experience is most vivid, and its influence on its subject's life and thought presumably most profound, that the literary evidence to be submitted for interpretation to the Court of Psychology is likely to be most conflicting. Here, as it seems to me, lies the peculiar difficulty confronting the psychological interpretation of Plato's Doctrine of Ideas regarded, not as Method of Science—the psychological interpretation of that side of the Doctrine is, I have pointed out, comparatively easy—but as expression of the Experience from which Art and Religion draw their inspiration. But it is, after all, only a difficulty of detail, and will certainly be overcome when trained psychologists, especially those in whom the Experience mentioned is vivid, have made that Experience an object of special study in themselves and in others, and have examined the literary evidence for it in Plato critically in the light of their special study. The trend of Criticism is now so steady in the direction of treating 'Philosophical Doctrines' as expressing Varieties of Experience to be explained psychologically—or, to use the most comprehensive term, biologically—that there can be no doubt that, sooner or later, we shall see the Doctrine of Ideas consistently treated in this way. And we may confidently expect that the employment of this intimate method of interpretation upon work so genial, so charged with rich personality, as is Plato's, will discover there treasures of truth and beauty hitherto hidden. For myself I make no claim to have discovered treasures; but I hope that the Second Part of this Essay may lead younger and better psychologists than I am to believe that there are treasures to be discovered.

Reserving the treatment of the aesthetic side of the Doctrine of Ideas for the Second Part, I now proceed to deal, in detail, with its methodological side.

# PART I

## THE DOCTRINE OF IDEAS AS CONTRIBUTION TO METHODOLOGY

I SHALL take the Dialogues important for the Doctrine of Ideas on its methodological side in Dr. Lutoslawski's [1] order. Whether a 'chronological' order can ever be definitely fixed I have great doubt. Of course it would be interesting to have it fixed; but I do not think that the Doctrine of Ideas on its methodological side receives much illumination from 'chronology'; while to go to 'chronology' for illumination of its aesthetic side—the side which finds expression in myth—seems to me to be a most uncritical proceeding. I take Dr. Lutoslawski's order for convenience, since some order must be taken; and, as it seems likely, especially on stylometric grounds—always weighty grounds—that the Dialogues were written in *some such* order as Dr. Lutoslawski's, any light which 'chronology' may have to throw on the Doctrine will not be lost.

Dr. Lutoslawski's order is the following [2]:—

1. Apology
2. Euthyphro
3. Crito
4. Charmides
5. Laches     } Socratic Group.
6. Protagoras
7. Meno
8. Euthydemus
9. Gorgias

---

[1] *The Origin and Growth of Plato's Logic* (1897).

[2] *Plato's Logic*, pp. 162 ff. The problem of the chronological order of the Platonic Dialogues became a scientific one with the application of the

PART I 15

10. Cratylus &#125;
11. Symposium &#125; First Platonic Group.
12. Phaedo
13. Republic I
14. Republic II-IV
15. Republic V-VII
16. Republic VIII-IX
17. Republic X &#125; Middle Platonic Group.
18. Phaedrus
19. Theaetetus
20. Parmenides
21. Sophist
22. Politicus
23. Philebus
24. Timaeus &#125; Latest Group.
25. Critias
26. Laws

Let us take as starting-point for our review of the Doctrine of Ideas on its methodological side, as it appears in the Dialogues of the 'Socratic Group', the words of Aristotle in *Met.* M. 4. 1078 b 27 ff.—δύο γάρ ἐστιν ἅ τις ἂν ἀποδοίη Σωκράτει δικαίως, τούς τ' ἐπακτικοὺς λόγους καὶ τὸ ὁρίζεσθαι καθόλου . . . ἀλλ' ὁ μὲν Σωκράτης τὰ καθόλου οὐ χωριστὰ ἐποίει οὐδὲ τοὺς ὁρισμούς· οἱ δ' ἐχώρισαν, καὶ τὰ τοιαῦτα τῶν ὄντων ἰδέας προσηγόρευσαν.

The *Euthyphro, Crito, Charmides,* and *Laches* are little dramatic pieces in which Socrates is represented as dissatisfied with the current denotation of such terms as 'pious', 'just', 'temperate', 'courageous', and as trying— without much success—to get at their connotation, to get

stylometric test, which will always be especially associated with the name of Lewis Campbell. Besides Campbell's Introduction to the *Sophistes and Politicus,* and his Essay in vol. ii (pp. 1-66) of the Jowett and Campbell *Republic,* the following works dealing with the chronological problem may be consulted :—Constantin Ritter's *Untersuchungen über Plato* (1888), Lutoslawski's *Plato's Logic* (1897), Natorp's *Platos Ideenlehre* (1903), Raeder's *Platons philosophische Entwickelung* (1905), and Horn's *Platonstudien* (1893 and 1904).

the true meaning of the terms fixed. Till that is done the terms, used at random, are worse than useless. In these four Dialogues (I shall return to the *Apology* which heads the group) Plato seems to be concerned to bring out a shortcoming of some sort in the method of ἐπακτικοὶ λόγοι and τὸ ὁρίζεσθαι καθόλου as practised by Socrates. These are all what Grote called 'Dialogues of Search'—we come away from them feeling that popular opinion and popular language in respect of the virtues discussed are, indeed, hopelessly confused, and that exact definitions are imperatively needed if good conduct is to be achieved and a theory or science of conduct *pari passu* evolved; at the same time we feel that the difficulty of finding such definitions is immense, and that hardly any way has been made towards their discovery.

### *The Apology.*

The *Apology* is a fit prelude to these four Dialogues of Search—unsuccessful search so far as positive results are concerned—with its burden 'nobody knows what Virtue is—but Socrates alone knows that he does not know what it is' (*Apol.* 22, 23). He cannot teach it, and has never professed to teach it; nor has he ever found any one who can teach it among those who profess to do so. The Athenians show how far they are from knowing what Virtue is—and unless a man knows what Virtue is he cannot be virtuous—by their pursuit of honour and reputation without heed for knowledge and truth and the soul's welfare (*Apol.* 29 E). Here the thought is: Virtue is knowledge, or cannot exist without knowledge; but this knowledge cannot be acquired and communicated. It is not the man who pleases himself, the man who follows the fashion of the day in pursuing the objects of social and political ambition and is successful in the pursuit, who is 'virtuous': it is the man who is led, not by personal feeling through life, but by reflective thought, who is really 'virtuous'—'Virtue is knowledge: but it cannot be taught.'

This, then, is the *impasse* in which the 'Socrates' of the *Apology* finds himself. The four Dialogues which follow in the list which we are making use of exhibit 'Socrates' as endeavouring, with little success, to open up the *impasse*.

## The Euthyphro.

In the *Euthyphro* he tries to make Piety (τὸ ὅσιον) object of knowledge, to get a concept which shall enable him to see the many different actions indiscriminately called 'pious' in such a light, from such a point of view, that they shall take their proper places in the Good Life—all of them, or some of them, for perhaps there are actions commonly called 'pious' which have no place in that Life. The problem, in other words, is to find the proper connotation of 'pious'; and it is to be noted that in this early Dialogue the word ἰδέα occurs (*Euthyphro* 6 D), and also the word παράδειγμα (6 E), which Professor Jackson and others regard as belonging to the technique of the 'later theory of Ideas'—Σω. μέμνησαι οὖν ὅτι οὐ τοῦτό σοι διεκελευόμην, ἕν τι ἢ δύο με διδάξαι τῶν πολλῶν ὁσίων [Euthyphro has just said that τὸ ὅσιον is that which he is now doing, viz. indicting his own father for homicide], ἀλλ' ἐκεῖνο αὐτὸ τὸ εἶδος ᾧ πάντα τὰ ὅσια ὅσιά ἐστιν; ἔφησθα γάρ που (*supra*, 5 D) μιᾷ ἰδέᾳ τά τε ἀνόσια ἀνόσια εἶναι καὶ τὰ ὅσια ὅσια· ἢ οὐ μνημονεύεις; Ευθ. ἔγωγε. Σω. ταύτην τοίνυν με αὐτὴν δ.δαξον τὴν ἰδέαν τίς ποτέ ἐστιν, ἵνα εἰς ἐκείνην ἀποβλέπων καὶ χρώμενος αὐτῇ παραδείγματι, ὃ μὲν ἂν τοιοῦτον ᾖ ὧν ἂν ἢ σὺ ἢ ἄλλος τις πράττῃ φῶ ὅσιον εἶναι, ὃ δ' ἂν μὴ τοιοῦτον, μὴ φῶ.[1]

[1] On the ground of this passage, and of debt to other Dialogues, Professor Natorp (p. 38—here and throughout I refer to his *Platos Ideenlehre*) doubts the authenticity of the *Euthyphro*; if genuine, it comes close to the *Meno* in chronological order, he thinks, not to the *Apology* and *Crito*. Dr. Lutoslawski (pp. 199, 200—here and throughout I refer to his *Origin and Growth of Plato's Logic*), regarding the *Euthyphro*, on stylometric grounds, as one of the earliest Dialogues, tries to minimize the importance of the occurrence of ἰδέα and παράδειγμα, which he thinks are not used here in their later technical sense. They seem to me to be used here exactly as they are used in later Dialogues. Dr. Raeder, again (p. 128—here and throughout I refer to his *Platons philosophische Ent-*

Here, then, the problem is to make Piety object of knowledge, to find its εἶδος or ἰδέα which shall serve as παράδειγμα whereby to judge particular cases; but the Dialogue ends without doing more than stating the problem, for the attempted solutions come, admittedly, to nothing. The method which tries to get ὁρισμός out of ἐπακτικοὶ λόγοι is evidently doomed to failure. That seems to be the logical lesson of the *Euthyphro*. Such λόγοι can result, at best, only in 'empirical laws', in general statements of the ὅτι (as Aristotle would say), whereas knowledge, in the true sense, is of the διότι as determining or defining the ὅτι, and of the ὅτι as determined or defined by the διότι. The Socratic method of ἐπακτικοὶ λόγοι is, to use Bacon's language, *inductio per enumerationem simplicem*, not *vera inductio*. That is, the fault of the Socratic method, as put on the stage for us in these Dialogues of Search, is that of taking each concept, Piety, Justice, Temperance, Courage, by itself, instead of viewing it as part of an organic system of knowledge whereby it is determined: in other words, these Dialogues set forth the futility of trying to define any single virtue without having got some theory of the Social Good to which it belongs and contributes. The advance which Plato's Doctrine of Ideas makes on the Socratic method is just this, that the concept in question is no longer made to depend precariously on the few particulars observed, but is determined, shaped all round as it were, by the system which includes it: in the light of that system we come to see it for what it is, and are finally convinced that it 'cannot be otherwise': it has become *independent* of the few particulars the observation of which first suggested it—its *independence* of these particulars is, indeed, the τὸ χωριστὴν εἶναι which Aristotle (without

*wickelung*), puts the *Euthyphro* after the *Protagoras* and *Gorgias*, arguing that the *Euthyphro* is intended to mark a change in Plato's original view according to which (as in the *Protagoras*) ὁσιότης is a fifth cardinal virtue: in the *Euthyphro* ὁσιότης is not a fifth cardinal virtue, but a form of Justice, i. e. Justice to the Gods. *Quot homines tot sententiae.*

## PART I: THE EUTHYPHRO

properly understanding the meaning of the term which he employs) mentions as the mark which distinguishes the Platonic Idea from the Socratic Concept or Definition.

### The Crito.

The *Crito* has Justice for its subject. Crito goes to the prison and urges Socrates to make his escape, saying that all his friends think that he would be doing wrong if he did not make his escape. Socrates argues that the question of right and wrong, just and unjust, is for *experts*, those who know, to determine. It cannot be determined by reference to 'what people think': *Crito* 47 c καὶ δὴ καὶ περὶ τῶν δικαίων καὶ ἀδίκων, καὶ αἰσχρῶν καὶ καλῶν, καὶ ἀγαθῶν καὶ κακῶν, περὶ ὧν νῦν ἐστιν ἡ βουλή, πότερον τῇ τῶν πολλῶν δόξῃ δεῖ ἡμᾶς ἕπεσθαι καὶ φοβεῖσθαι αὐτήν, ἢ τῇ τοῦ ἑνός, εἴ τίς ἐστιν ἐπαΐων, ὃν δεῖ αἰσχύνεσθαι καὶ φοβεῖσθαι μᾶλλον ἢ σύμπαντας τοὺς ἄλλους; Here, again, the thesis 'Virtue is knowledge' is affirmed. But where is knowledge to be found? Not certainly in 'what people think'—only in the expert's judgement which takes account of the Truth Itself—αὐτὴ ἡ ἀλήθεια (48 A). Without pretending to be such an expert, Socrates is convinced that it cannot be right, by running away, to frustrate the laws of the Athenian people under which he has spent his life, and at last has been tried and condemned to death. The 'knowledge' which Socrates brings, at this great crisis, to bear on the question of right and wrong is not the knowledge desiderated by Moral Science—that may be unattainable—it is rather the intuition of the good man, what is often meant by 'Conscience', in following whose dictates, at a great crisis in his life, a man bears witness to the existence of a Good which is beyond, not merely the objects of sense, but the objects of knowledge—ἐπέκεινα τῆς οὐσίας.[1]

The 'Socrates' of the *Crito* represents a mood, the expression of which in the Doctrine of Ideas—especially

[1] *Rep.* vi. 509 B.

where the Ideas are those of moral qualities—it would be blindness to overlook. The Doctrine of Ideas in the Dialogues treating of moral and political subjects is not only a method of Moral Science but a Metaphysic of Morals —even a Theodicy, for, as Professor Natorp finely puts it,[1] 'God will not forsake the righteous' stands by the side of 'Virtue is knowledge' in the *Apology* and the *Crito*.

## The Charmides.

The *Charmides* comes next with Temperance—σωφροσύνη; and after several unsuccessful answers have been given to the question 'What is Temperance?' an answer which seems to have more than the others to say for itself is given by one of the interlocutors—Critias, viz. that Temperance is self-knowledge (*Charm.* 164 D). But this answer involves serious difficulty, and in the end is rejected; for if Temperance is knowledge of self, *scilicet* as temperate, it will be knowledge of Temperance, and so Temperance will differ from other kinds of knowledge which all have objects distinct from themselves (166 C). Further, if Temperance is knowledge of itself, i. e. if it is knowledge of knowledge, it will also be knowledge of the absence of knowledge—ἐπιστήμης ἐπιστήμη καὶ ἀνεπιστημοσύνης (171 C)—surely a useless kind of knowledge, for Temperance will not be 'knowing *what* one knows and *what* one does not know', but only 'knowing *that* one knows and *that* one does not know' (170 D). And even if we grant, for the sake of argument, that the temperate man is one who knows *what* he does know and *what* he does not know, what good will his knowledge do him, and how can we suppose a community of such men—such mere specialists—attaining to true happiness? Each man will do what he knows, but where among them all is the knowledge of the common end to which their separate doings are relative? All would be done with special knowledge, but nothing would be well done for lack of a knowledge which Temperance as thus

[1] p. 9.

defined does not supply—*the knowledge of Good and Evil*: *Charm.* 173 C κατεσκευασμένον δὴ οὕτω τὸ ἀνθρώπινον γένος [i. e. as a mere aggregate of specialists] ὅτι μὲν ἐπιστημόνως ἂν πράττοι καὶ ζῴη, ἕπομαι· ἡ γὰρ σωφροσύνη φυλάττουσα οὐκ ἂν ἐῴη παρεμπίπτουσαν τὴν ἀνεπιστημοσύνην συνεργὸν εἶναι· ὅτι δ' ἐπιστημόνως ἂν πράττοντες εὖ ἂν πράττοιμεν καὶ εὐδαιμονοῖμεν, τοῦτο δὲ οὔπω δυνάμεθα μαθεῖν. . . . The knowledge needed is not the ἐπιστήμη ἐπιστημῶν καὶ ἀνεπιστημοσυνῶν, but the ἐπιστήμη ἀγαθοῦ τε καὶ κακοῦ (174 D). The latter ἐπιστήμη benefits man; the former cannot benefit him, and therefore cannot be identified with Temperance, which certainly is a virtue and benefits man.

So the Dialogue ends without reaching its ostensible object—a satisfactory definition of Temperance; and yet much has been effected: the need of knowledge of the Good has been made plain—it is useless to discuss the virtues separately, apart from the system of the Good to which they belong as members. Knowledge of the Good is the inwardness of Temperance and of each of the special virtues. No definition of Temperance can be right which does not present it as a phase of knowledge of the Good—or, as we shall see in the *Laches*, does not envisage the special virtue as, in a sense, all virtue. If a virtue is defined as 'a kind of knowledge', without reference to the Good, the 'knowledge' so-called can only be the empirical knowledge of the pleasure or pain to be expected from certain actions.[1] All this the *Charmides* brings home to us by its failure to find a satisfactory definition of Temperance. And even the definition put forward and rejected is itself suggestive. Temperance is not simply 'knowledge', it is 'self-knowledge'—*Charm.* 167 A καὶ ἔστιν δὴ τοῦτο τὸ σωφρονεῖν τε καὶ σωφροσύνη καὶ τὸ ἑαυτὸν αὐτὸν γιγνώσκειν, τὸ εἰδέναι ἅ τε οἶδεν καὶ ἃ μὴ οἶδεν—a definition which recognizes, in terms, the function of 'reflection' in Human Nature, as indicating to each man his peculiar work or duty in the social

[1] See Natorp, p. 23.

system. Knowledge of Self, in time, grows into knowledge of the Good.[1]

The outcome of the *Charmides*, then, as making contribution to the Doctrine of Ideas, is that a definition of the Good is shown to be the great desideratum, the necessary ἀρχή of all discussion of matters moral and political.

### The Laches.

The subject of the *Laches* is Courage. After some suggestions have been offered and dismissed, the discussion comes to turn on the definition given (194 E) by Nicias— ἡ τῶν δεινῶν καὶ θαρραλέων ἐπιστήμη ἐστὶν ἀνδρεία. But, it is argued, 'knowledge' which is thus of the future simply as future is not really 'knowledge'. The objects of true knowledge do not lie in the past, present, or future, simply as such, but are 'out of time', always the same independently of the times of their sensible manifestation. If Courage is 'knowledge' it cannot be knowledge of δεινά and θαρραλέα, which are *future* κακά and *future* ἀγαθά: it must be knowledge of *all* ἀγαθά and κακά belonging to warfare (199 A, B)—we entrust the conduct of an army to the general, not to the soothsayer. Indeed, if we press the meaning of 'knowledge' to the full, we must say that Courage, as knowledge, is knowledge of *all good and evil* (199 C)—οὐ μόνον δεινῶν τε καὶ θαρραλέων ἐπιστήμη ἡ ἀνδρεία ἐστίν, ἀλλὰ σχεδόν τι [this is where he generalizes from knowledge of good and evil *in war* to knowledge of good and evil *in all circumstances*] ἡ περὶ πάντων ἀγαθῶν τε καὶ κακῶν καὶ πάντως ἐχόντων. Thus Courage is not *a* virtue, but *all virtue* (199 E)—οὐκ ἄρα, ὦ Νικία, μόριον ἀρετῆς ἂν εἴη τὸ νῦν σοι λεγόμενον, ἀλλὰ σύμπασα ἀρετή—and the man who has Courage, *as knowledge*, has *ipso facto* all the other virtues—καὶ τοῦτον οἴει ἂν σὺ ἐνδεᾶ εἶναι σωφροσύνης ἢ

[1] Cf. Raeder, p. 157, who gets the same conclusion—that knowledge of Self is knowledge of the Good—that the Good is identical with the true Self—out of the *Lysis*.

δικαιοσύνης τε καὶ ὁσιότητος, ᾧ γε μόνῳ προσήκει καὶ περὶ θεοὺς καὶ περὶ ἀνθρώπους ἐξευλαβεῖσθαί τε τὰ δεινὰ καὶ τὰ μή, καὶ τἀγαθὰ πορίζεσθαι, ἐπισταμένῳ ὀρθῶς προσομιλεῖν; Yes; but we started by assuming that Courage is *a* virtue, and in defining it as such we have lost it—it has vanished into Virtue generally (199 E).

The result of the Dialogue is thus, like that of the *Charmides*, to bring it home to the reader that no virtue can be understood simply by itself out of relation to the Good; but to leave him without any clue to the particular way in which the virtue in question must be defined so as to be exhibited in that relation. Yet thus much is made out regarding the particular virtue—Courage or Temperance—that the 'knowledge' involved in it is not the empirical knowledge of the pleasure or pain to be expected from actions—not knowledge of the future empirically derived from mere observation of the past.[1] It is the knowledge of the Good—of the essential and immutable, not of the phenomenal. In the account of ἐπιστήμη as concerned with what things *always* are, given in *Laches* 198 D (μία οὖσα ἐφορᾷ ⟨ἡ ἐπιστήμη⟩ καὶ γιγνόμενα καὶ γεγονότα καὶ γενησόμενα), Plato, Professor Natorp says,[2] has already made a great advance towards—I should prefer to say, expresses himself fully in accordance with—the Doctrine of Ideas as we find it expressed in *Theaet.* 178 C-179 B, and *Rep.* 516 C. The Doctrine set forth is that of the Idea as scientific point of view—point of view, not uncritically assumed after observation of a few particulars, but critically fixed, as the only right point of view, after a survey of the whole system of classes to which the class of particulars observed belongs.

### *The Protagoras.*

'Can Virtue be taught?' is, again, the question of the *Protagoras*. Protagoras maintains that it can be taught, and yet will not admit that it is knowledge. Socrates

---

[1] See Natorp, p. 23.  [2] pp. 22, 23.

maintains that it is knowledge, and yet will not admit that it can be taught. This is the deadlock with which the Dialogue ends. The only escape from it, Socrates urges, is the discovery of the true nature and definition of Virtue—ἀρετή. That is the problem with which the *Protagoras* leaves us—360 E–361 A οὗτοι, ἦν δ' ἐγώ, ἄλλου ἕνεκα ἐρωτῶ πάντα ταῦτα ἢ σκέψασθαι βουλόμενος πῶς ποτ' ἔχει τὰ περὶ τῆς ἀρετῆς καὶ τί ποτ' ἐστὶν αὐτὸ ἡ ἀρετή. οἶδα γὰρ ὅτι, τούτου φανεροῦ γενομένου, μάλιστα ἂν κατάδηλον γένοιτο ἐκεῖνο περὶ οὗ ἐγώ τε καὶ σὺ μακρὸν λόγον ἑκάτερος ἀπετείναμεν, ἐγὼ μὲν λέγων ὡς οὐ διδακτὸν ἀρετή, σὺ δ' ὡς διδακτόν.

'Virtue is knowledge—but it cannot be taught': this is the paradox of the *Protagoras* which the reader may take away with him and digest, if he can, at leisure. 'Virtue is knowledge'—he will say to himself; that is undeniable—'but it cannot be taught': certainly not, if the teaching is that of Protagoras and his like—if the 'knowledge' so-called is something crammed, something taken down from a Sophist's lecture, a mere *datum* empirically received. But there is another kind of 'knowledge' which reflection, stimulated by the proper questions, may discover in the mind itself; a 'knowledge' which is not taken on trust, but is assured by its conformity with the laws of human thought operating in harmony with the nature of things. To bring out the antithesis between the 'lecture' and the 'conversation' as means of imparting or eliciting 'knowledge' is, as Grote says,[1] 'at least one main purpose of Plato in this memorable Dialogue.'

## The Meno.

But we must pass on to the next Dialogue in our list, the *Meno*, to see the suggestion of the *Protagoras* developed in the Doctrine, or Myth, of ἀνάμνησις, and the 'unteachableness' of ἀρετή, which was maintained ironically in the *Apology* and the five succeeding Dialogues of our list, at

[1] *Plato*, ii. 48.

last made the subject of a critical inquiry. And the result of this inquiry is a distinction—'Ἀρετή is unteachable if it is 'knowledge' received from without, but not if it is 'knowledge' recollected from within; and the method of the 'teaching' which arouses 'recollection' is not rhetorical but dialectical.[1] We may say that the doctrine of ἀνάμνησις set forth in the *Meno* (81 A ff.), regarded on its logical side (I defer consideration of its other side till we reach the Second Part of this Essay), makes explicit what is implicit in the *Charmides* and *Laches*—in the *Charmides* with its suggestion of 'self-knowledge' as involving 'knowledge of the Good'; in the *Laches* which contends that the 'knowledge' in which virtue consists—'the knowledge of the Good'—is of that which always is; and, indeed, in the *Euthyphro* and *Crito*, which both turn on the futility of trying to define any single virtue without having apprehended the Good, the End, the System to which 'virtues' belong, and, by belonging to which, are what they really are. The rhetorical method pleases people by taking the 'virtues' separately, and describing them 'popularly' as they appear to the superficial conventional mind. The Good, the System, is left entirely out of account by the rhetorical method. Only reflection, hard thinking, stirred by dialectic, can bring us to apprehend the Good, the System. Stripped of its mythical and poetical embodiment, the doctrine of ἀνάμνησις means that true knowledge is not what one picks up casually from lectures and books and such external sources, but what one has thought out for oneself. Mental activity is the one thing needful, which no degree of receptivity can make up for the lack of. And it is by mental activity, by hard thinking, by connected not desultory thinking, that the Notion or Idea is grasped. That it is the Notion or Idea, not any mere particular of sense, which ἀνάμνησις recovers, or brings into consciousness, is perhaps

---

[1] It is in the *Meno* (75 D), as Professor Natorp points out (p. 37), that the term 'Dialectic' is first applied to the method of question and answer by which alone the Notion or Idea is found.

hardly put plainly enough in the *Meno*; but what the *Meno* allows to go without saying, the *Phaedrus* says distinctly: there it is the Pure Form without sensible qualities, which is 'recollected' on the occasion of a sensible object 'resembling' it being presented. The Idea 'recollected' is not a 'thing', it is a point of view from which things are scientifically regarded. It is a careless, though perhaps natural, misunderstanding which transforms the notions 'recollected', or thought out, into 'things'; and we may agree with Professor Natorp[1] in thinking that the mythical presentation of ἀνάμνησις in the *Meno* (81 A ff.) and in the *Phaedrus* (246 A–257 A) has contributed to the misunderstanding of the Doctrine of Ideas on its methodological side; but I cannot follow him in regarding the Doctrine as having only that side, or in deploring Plato's 'desertion of logic for poetry' in the passages mentioned. The aesthetic side, which Professor Natorp ignores, with its Ideas which are 'Things' for Contemplation, not 'points of view' for Discourse, is capable, I hold, only of the poetical and mythical presentation which he rightly regards as uncalled for where the methodological side of the Doctrine is concerned. Here, however, it is ἀνάμνησις, regarded as belonging not to the aesthetic, but to the methodological side of the Doctrine of Ideas, that we have before us; and, as so regarded, it stands in Plato for what we, in our modern language, speak of as the activity of Human Understanding which, by means of conceptual instruments expressing its own needs, 'makes nature', 'moulds environment'. These conceptual instruments are, indeed, for Plato, 'Eternal and Immutable Ideas', necessary points of view; whereas we moderns regard them rather as working hypotheses, postulates, convenient, not necessary, points of view: but this difference ought not to make us shut our eyes to the importance of the *aperçu* opened up by Plato in his doctrine, or myth, of ἀνάμνησις—that the Ideas (be they

---

[1] p. 36.

absolutely fixed or relatively changeable, that is a matter of detail merely), without which there can be no 'scientific knowledge', are more properly regarded as having a dynamic than as having a static existence—their static existence is what we have 'forgotten', it has no reality for us; the Ideas must be 'recollected', must assume dynamic existence, in order to become real—they are, in fact, ways in which the mind reacts, according to its own peculiar constitution, upon the influences which come to it from without; ways in which it, bit by bit, makes its world, even as the physical organism of elm-tree or rook, in living its own proper life in detail, makes the world in which it lives—every organism its own proper world.

So much for *Meno* 81 A ff., where the doctrine, or myth, of ἀνάμνησις is introduced—a doctrine, or myth to which we shall return when we come to the *Phaedrus* in the Second Part of this Essay. Let us now conclude our review of the *Meno*, as illustrating the methodological side of the Doctrine of Ideas, with reference to two other passages in which that Doctrine appears, viz. 72 A–E, and 97 A ff.

In the former passage the εἶδος ἀρετῆς is contrasted with the σμῆνός τι ἀρετῶν, and the word οὐσία (μελίττης περὶ οὐσίας ὅτι ποτ' ἐστι) is used as equivalent to εἶδος—the εἶδος being described (in the case of the πολλαὶ καὶ παντοδαπαὶ ἀρεταί) as that δι' ὃ εἰσὶν ἀρεταί, εἰς ὃ καλῶς που ἔχει ἀποβλέψαντα τὸν ἀποκρινάμενον τῷ ἐρωτήσαντι ἐκεῖνο δηλῶσαι ὃ τυγχάνει οὖσα ἀρετή. Here in ἀποβλέψαντα the 'paradeigmatic' view of the Idea is indicated; and dialectic is assumed to be the method by which the Idea is reached, 'recollected,' thought out.

The other passage (97 A ff.) deals with the distinction between δόξα and ἐπιστήμη. The distinction is that between empirical knowledge, on the one hand—knowledge of the effect without its cause, of the mere particular without the context which explains it, or, at most, of a 'uniformity of experience', and on the other hand, scientific knowledge which is expressly stated to be knowledge of the causal ground in each case. The former kind of knowledge, δόξα, does not abide with us; the latter, ἐπιστήμη, does, for it is bound by the chain of thinking which connects effect with cause—αἰτίας λογισμῷ (98 A)—and this αἰτίας λογισμός is expressly identified with ἀνάμνησις (98 A). The apprehension of, or the having thought out, the *causation* is the apprehension of, or the having thought out, the *Idea* in each case. Nothing could be clearer than that this is the meaning of the Doctrine of Ideas as set forth in the *Meno*. The Idea is the Law of Nature, or Causal Context, which a scientific explanation of any class of objects, qualities, or events, must set forth. If, as I hold, ἀνάμνησις has another meaning for Plato beside the logical meaning, and, according to that other meaning, is of *Things* perceived in some shadowy way, not of *Laws* clearly conceived and even mathematically formulated, this, it must surely be admitted, has not in any way damaged the presentation of the logical meaning in the *Meno*. If, as Professor Natorp contends,[1] the mythical investiture of ἀνάμνησις in *Meno* 81 A ff. contributed to the Aristotelian misinterpretation of the Idea *in Logic*, to the error of supposing that *in Logic* Plato regarded the Idea as a Thing and not as a Law, I submit that the misinterpretation is inexcusable, for Plato has expressly said that αἰτίας λογισμός and ἀνάμνησις are convertible terms—that the Idea, in Logic, is the Causation or Law, not a Thing.

### The *Euthydemus*.

The *Euthydemus*, which Dr. Lutoslawski places immediately after the *Meno*, Professor Natorp[2] places immediately

[1] p. 36.
[2] p. 116. Dr. Raeder (pp 139 ff.) connects the *Euthydemus* with the attack on Plato made by Isocrates in the *Hel. Encom.* and *Adv. Soph.* Plato, Dr. Raeder thinks, wishes to show that he is not an eristic Socratic like Antisthenes with whom (without naming either) Isocrates had confounded him. The *Euthydemus* addresses itself both to eristics and to rhetors—to Antisthenes and to Isocrates—without naming any one.

## PART I: THE EUTHYDEMUS

after the *Theaetetus* to which, he thinks, it is really an appendix, being directed against the logical atomism of Antisthenes [1] whose view of the soul as a tablet impressed from without is, he supposes, that refuted in the *Theaetetus*. Be this as it may—for Antisthenes is not referred to by name in the *Euthydemus*—the Dialogue illustrates the Dialectical method by means of which 'notions' are thought out, contrasting it as practised by the Sophists Euthydemus and Dionysodorus on the one hand, and by Socrates on the other—Socrates endeavouring to draw out what is in the minds of his respondents, the two Sophists being merely concerned to put misleading questions. The *Euthydemus* is perhaps chiefly remarkable as an *exposé* of fallacies, and, as such, anticipates Aristotle's *Sophistici Elenchi*.

### *The Gorgias.*

Dr. Lutoslawski and Professor Natorp agree in placing the *Gorgias* close after the *Meno*.

In the *Gorgias*, as Professor Natorp observes,[2] the question is the 'notion of morality'—as, indeed, it is in all the Dialogues hitherto examined. Here, as in these Dialogues, it is still said that the 'notion' has not been found; yet it is made out that 'morality', or ἀρετή, is knowledge, and knowledge of the Good. Hitherto, however, there has hardly been any attempt to define the notion of the Good. In the *Gorgias*, Professor Natorp tells us,[3] this notion is defined for the first time: it is determined *negatively*, as 'different from Pleasure' (I agree that the contrast between Good and Pleasure is put very plainly in the *Gorgias*, but submit that it is fully recognized in earlier Dialogues), and *positively*, as 'end' (τέλος—this is its general positive determination) and as 'law', 'order' (εἶδος—this is its special positive determination): the Good is not pleasure, but end—τέλος εἶναι ἁπασῶν τῶν πράξεων τὸ ἀγαθόν, καὶ ἐκείνου ἕνεκεν δεῖν πάντα τἆλλα πράττεσθαι ἀλλ' οὐκ ἐκεῖνο τῶν ἄλλων

---
[1] For Antisthenes, see my *Notes on Nic. Eth.*, i. 75.
[2] p. 42.   [3] p. 42.

(*Gorg.* 499 E)—that which makes a thing orderly—τεταγμένον τε καὶ κεκοσμημένον πρᾶγμα (504 A)—makes it object of τέχνη, 'pleasant things' being objects of ἐμπειρία. The Good is, in short, 'organism which maintains itself,' as Professor Natorp puts it,[1] remarking that we have here the very kernel of the Doctrine of Ideas, and comparing *Philebus* 64 D μέτρου καὶ τῆς συμμέτρου φύσεως μὴ τυχοῦσα ἡτισοῦν καὶ ὁπωσοῦν σύγκρασις πᾶσα ἐξ ἀνάγκης ἀπόλλυσι τά τε κεραννύμενα καὶ πρώτην αὐτήν.

The final determination of the notion of Good as 'order', 'system', 'organism'—κόσμος τις ἄρα ἐγγενόμενος ἐν ἑκάστῳ ὁ ἑκάστου οἰκεῖος ἀγαθὸν παρέχει ἕκαστον τῶν ὄντων (506 E)—stands in close connexion with the notion of τέχνη, 'science,' as distinguished from ἐμπειρία, 'rule of thumb.' The best example of τέχνη is mathematics (see *Gorg.* 451 C, 508 A, and other places), and it is by following method like that of mathematics that the knowledge of the Good—i.e. a connected view of Life—is attained to. 'Rhetoric,' as commonly practised (there is a good as well as a bad 'Rhetoric'—504 D πρὸς ταῦτα αὖ [*sc.* τάξιν καὶ κόσμον ψυχῆς, νόμον, νόμιμον] βλέπων ὁ ῥήτωρ ἐκεῖνος, ὁ τεχνικὸς καὶ ἀγαθός), is the very opposite of the τέχνη which leads to the knowledge of the Good. This false Rhetoric gives, not ἐπιστήμη, but πίστις—454 E δύο εἴδη θῶμεν πειθοῦς, τὸ μὲν πίστιν παρεχόμενον ἄνευ τοῦ εἰδέναι, τὸ δ' ἐπιστήμην. It is in φιλοσοφία (482 A)—nearly equivalent to τέχνη (φιλοσοφία means a scientific point of view steadily maintained; τέχνη, rather the method pursued in detail by the man with the scientific point of view)—it is in φιλοσοφία and τέχνη, not in ῥητορική, that 'morality', the life actuated by knowledge of the Good, has its foundation. The φιλόσοφος, as τεχνικός, looks to (ἀποβλέπει πρός) the εἶδος (503 E). Those who, following the rhetorical method, have failed to get a 'connected view of things', are like the uninitiated in Hades who carry water in leaking vessels—their minds have got no hold of things (493 A, B, C).

[1] pp. 47 ff.

## PART I: THE GORGIAS

The τέχνη by which the φιλόσοφος thinks out the notion of the Good is, of course, Dialectic, which, we may take it, is fully recognized in the *Gorgias* as the special art, or science, concerned with the definition of εἴδη, and of the supreme εἶδος, the Good; but the term διαλεκτική has not been appropriated. That, however, is probably accidental—διαλεκτικώτερον occurs in *Meno* 75 D. From the first, throughout the whole series of his Dialogues, Plato is clear that it is only through the method of question and answer, whether called 'dialectic' or by some other name, that concepts or Ideas can be thought out.

I conclude these remarks on the *Gorgias* as contributing to the Doctrine of Ideas by referring to two opinions advanced by Professor Natorp and by Dr. Lutoslawski respectively.

In the *Gorgias*, according to Professor Natorp,[1] Plato made 'his great discovery of Logic (i.e. connected thinking) as the Power which creates Science and reforms Life'; and the πάθος produced in the poetic sensibility of the man by this discovery caused a reaction—he went off for a while from Logic into Poetry, and wrote the *Phaedrus* (the first Dialogue—Professor Natorp puts it immediately after the *Gorgias*—in which, after the hints of the *Meno* and *Gorgias*, Plato deals definitely with the Idea)—the *Phaedrus*, a work which is responsible for the erroneous interpretations which the Doctrine of Ideas afterwards received. This is the view of Professor Natorp. If Dr. Lutoslawski is right in putting the *Republic* and other Dialogues between the *Gorgias* and the *Phaedrus*, Professor Natorp's view is deprived to a large extent of plausibility; and, in any case, it is hard to see how a great logical discovery could have caused Plato to leave Logic for a while and cultivate Poetry. I think, however, that the 'discovery', viz. that there can be no science and no conduct without 'connected thinking', and consequently without 'dialectic',

[1] p. 51.

was made by Plato many years before he wrote the *Gorgias*, and that, in fact, the very earliest Dialogues were inspired by it, and written to illustrate it. As for Professor Natorp's other point, that the poetical presentation of the Idea, however occasioned, was responsible for misunderstanding of the Idea in Logic—its only legitimate place according to Professor Natorp—I have only to say that the misunderstanding (which has undoubtedly prevailed, largely through the influence of Aristotle) need not have occurred if it had been perceived that the Idea had, for Plato, not only a methodological significance which he most carefully sets forth in the Dialogues which we have hitherto examined and elsewhere, but another and equally important significance as object of aesthetic feeling. In methodology the Idea is 'Law which explains phenomena'[1]; in aesthetics, it is—we shall see later on.

Dr. Lutoslawski's opinion I shall give in his own words:[2] 'Looking back over our survey of Plato's first steps in Logic, we see that he started from ethical problems, agitated by his teacher, and that his first attempts to find a definition of particular virtues and of virtue generally were made with moral purposes.... Among such inquiries on particular virtues Plato became interested in the more general problem of a definition of virtue. This he began to seek, and after some vacillation recognized the identity of virtue and knowledge. But he was still unable to attain certainty of knowledge; only after years of educational practice he found that such certainty is possible, and not to be sought for in the assent of any majority, nor in tradition, nor in idle discussion, but in the inward power of the soul which sees the truth with absolute certainty. To trace the origin of this power, felt by him when he imparted his moral convictions to his pupils, he recurred to the hypothesis of a previous existence of the soul, and deduced also the soul's immortality.

[1] See my *Notes on the Nicomachean Ethics*, vol. i, p. 74.
[2] pp. 216-18.

'We see the influence of his activity as a teacher in the rules for dialectic discussion, consisting in starting from recognized premisses, in dividing and distinguishing notions, in following up the consequences of each hypothesis, and avoiding unjustifiable generalization. By these means Plato reached a degree of certitude not experienced before. ... The new power of philosophy, acquired by logical exercises undertaken with ethical purposes, reacted first on the moral problems from which Plato started. He applied his logical method first to the great questions which had been unsuccessfully discussed in his earlier writings, and he produced a consistent theory of virtue and of the aims of life in the *Gorgias*. But the logical progress achieved will not be limited in its effect to the subject for which it has been devised. We see already in the *Meno*, in the *Euthydemus*, and in the *Gorgias*, that Plato begins to feel an interest in logical method independently of its applications, and this logical interest, once awakened, will lead him to special logical investigations, and to further development of methods in order to acquire and communicate to others an infallible knowledge. ... He obtained a glimpse of a world different from the world in which he lived, and he had the audacity to believe more in the reality of this new world of his thoughts than in all other authorities. Thus he progressed out of the Socratic stage to his own philosophy, and created the theory of ideas, which has been so often identified with Platonism. We cannot agree with Zeller who sees vestiges of this theory of ideas already in the *Meno, Euthydemus*, and *Gorgias*. Here we have only the germ from which the theory of ideas was afterwards developed. This germ is the consciousness of infallible knowledge arrived at when Plato wrote the *Meno*, becoming a special science in the *Euthydemus*, and in the *Gorgias* entrusted with the direction of human life. This consciousness was in the beginning purely personal and based on experience in teaching. Plato enjoyed it as a new sense, a feeling of higher life, and he did not yet undertake to explain it fully. The absolute certainty was reached in his own mind, and referred really only to a few ethical truths; he had imparted it to some of his pupils, and he generalized the faculty of absolute knowledge, postulating such knowledge for all departments of being. The complete theoretical explanation of the possibility of such knowledge was not yet given—scarcely asked for. But the consciousness of absolute knowledge created in the soul of Plato was transmitted from generation to generation, and since his time has never deserted European philosophy.'

There is one point, in this, on the whole, admirable survey, to which I would demur—that the 'Theory of Ideas is not yet expressed' (I quote the marginal summary) in the *Meno, Euthydemus*, and *Gorgias*. The theory, as logical method, seems to me to have been clearly expressed and instructively illustrated in these and other Dialogues of the Socratic Group—for the theory, as logical method, is that of the concept regarded as grasp of the law, or cause, which explains the particulars in each case. Detail is added in later Dialogues, but all that is essential to the Doctrine of Ideas, as logical method, is present, I submit, from the first. Thus Categories of the Understanding, employed in the process by which the law or cause in each case is reached, are afterwards made explicit and enumerated in the lists of the *Theaetetus* and *Sophistes*; but that Plato had such categories in view before he had occasion to draw up any formal list of them is plain from such a passage as that in *Republic* v. 453-4, where the dialectical or critical employment of the categories of 'same' and 'different' (τί εἶδος τὸ τῆς ἑτέρας τε καὶ τῆς αὐτῆς φύσεως καὶ πρὸς τί τεῖνον ὡριζόμεθα, 454 B) is contrasted with the eristic or uncritical employment of them.

## The Cratylus.

The *Cratylus* heads what Dr. Lutoslawski calls the First Platonic Group, but Professor Natorp places the

PART I: THE CRATYLUS

*Phaedrus, Theaetetus*, and *Euthydemus* between the *Gorgias* and *Cratylus*. I shall not attempt to decide which of the two arrangements is the more likely, because I do not think that our view of the Doctrine of Ideas, as set forth in the *Cratylus*, ought to be affected by our view of the chronological place of the Dialogue. The Doctrine of Ideas, as Logic, has been set forth, in all respects that are essential, in the Dialogues of the Socratic Group; no vital modifications, in presumably later Dialogues such as the *Cratylus* and those which follow it in our list, have to be noted—only, for the most part, merely verbal alterations in the statement of it, according as the different subjects of the various Dialogues make such alterations natural. The chronological treatment of the Doctrine of Ideas has, in my opinion, diverted attention from what is constant in it to verbal alterations in the statement of it which are made to appear as essential modifications of its methodological character—modifications which, if they had existed, would, indeed, have left the Doctrine without any methodological character at all.

The relation of appearance to reality, of particulars to the Idea, is discussed in the *Cratylus* à propos of the question whether names are connected with things φύσει, or νόμῳ.[1] In the first part of the Dialogue Socrates seems to maintain the φύσει-view, only to show, in the second part, that it is not tenable.[2] The function of a name is to declare the nature of a thing. The maker of names must always look to that which is the ideal name for each thing —ἀποβλέποντα εἰς τὸ τῇ φύσει ὄνομα ἑκάστῳ—and must be able to impress the form of that name upon letters and syllables—καὶ δυνάμενον αὐτοῦ τὸ εἶδος[3] τιθέναι εἴς τε τὰ γράμ-

[1] See Raeder (pp. 147-8) for the association of the φύσει-view with Antisthenes (represented by Cratylus in this Dialogue), and the νόμῳ-view with Protagoras (represented by Hermogenes).

[2] See Natorp, pp. 119-20.

[3] Dr. Raeder (pp. 153 and 178), wishing to distinguish εἶδος in the *Cratylus* from the 'Platonic Idea' proper, tells us that, as used in 389 b (and presumably in the whole context), it is merely a 'model'. I cannot

μάτα καὶ τὰς συλλαβάς (*Crat.* 390 E). Here we have the Idea of a name. But a name is an instrument, and the Idea, or true nature, of an instrument is always relative to the work which it has to perform. The work which a name has to perform is to declare the nature of a thing; which it does by *resembling* the thing. The Idea, or true nature, of the thing must therefore be known, if it is to be rightly named. The Idea of the name must fit the Idea of the thing, and it is not the maker, but the user, of names who must be accounted the ultimate authority as to whether or no a name has been rightly given—does its work. The user of names is the Dialectician (390 C, D, E). He alone has knowledge of the true nature of the things named, and of the names which he uses. The 'use' of a name, as the Dialectician understands that 'use', is, in fact, the Idea of the name. The 'Idea' here is the 'Final Cause'. We are reminded of *Rep.* x. 601 D πολλὴ ἄρα ἀνάγκη τὸν χρώμενον ἑκάστῳ ἐμπειρότατόν τε εἶναι καὶ ἄγγελον γίγνεσθαι τῷ ποιητῇ κτλ.

From the Idea, or εἶδος, of an instrument, described, in the *Cratylus* and *Republic*, as its use adequately known only by the user, it is an easy step to the Idea, or εἶδος, of a virtue. This, too, is its 'use', the function of the virtue—temperance, or courage—in the Good Life. It is only the 'Idea' of the Good Life itself which carries us beyond 'use' to 'end'. To maintain that, in a 'Later theory of Ideas', there are no 'Ideas' of σκευαστά, or of virtues, is really to exclude from the purview of science the two departments of technic and of morals—for science is always identified by Plato with the discovery of the

see that the terms in which εἶδος is spoken of in the *Cratylus* differ from the terms in which it is described where all admit that it is the 'Platonic Idea' proper. Plato-scholars are very often found involved in a circular argument: 'this Dialogue occupies such and such a chronological place, therefore exhibits such and such a phase of Doctrine; and, exhibiting that phase of Doctrine, occupies that chronological place.'

PART I: THE CRATYLUS 37

'Idea': and, further, to empty the Doctrine of its methodological significance, setting up, instead of methodology, a theory of Eternal Things such as Aristotle erroneously conceived the Doctrine of Ideas to be. No better example of an 'Idea', according to my view, could be given than αὐτὸ ὅ ἐστι κερκίς in the *Cratylus*, or ἡ ἐν τῇ φύσει κλίνη in the Tenth Book of the *Republic*. In each case the Idea is unique, eternal, immutable; but it is a law, a rule, a need to be met in a definite way, not a Thing; and is as fully entitled as *man* or *ox* to admission into the 'world of self-existing Ideas'—'self-existing Ideas' as distinguished from 'notions' or 'concepts' by the critics. So far as methodological doctrine is concerned, the 'self-existing Ideas', assigned to Plato's later teaching (e. g. by Dr. Lutoslawski, p. 224), are simply 'notions', or 'concepts', or 'points of view', some of them of universal application, others restricted to special spheres of inquiry, by the use of which science makes *sensibilia* intelligible.

So much for the major part of the *Cratylus*, which proceeds on the view that there is a natural connexion between names and things. But from 437 E to the end of the Dialogue this view is abandoned—so Professor Natorp seems to put it[1]—or, as I should prefer to say, limited. Although the Dialectician (defined 390 c as ὁ ἐρωτᾶν ἐπιστάμενος καὶ ἀποκρίνεσθαι) fits the right names to things, he is not supreme arbiter of nomenclature. Misleading names are widely current; and it is wise to proceed on the principle that the true nature of things is to be apprehended, not from their names, but from themselves—439 B οὐκ ἐξ ὀνομάτων ἀλλὰ πολὺ μᾶλλον αὐτὰ ἐξ αὐτῶν ⟨τὰ ὄντα⟩ καὶ μαθητέον καὶ ζητητέον, and 437 E οἱ πρῶτοι νομοθέται τὰ πρῶτα ὀνόματα, γιγνώσκοντες τὰ πράγματα οἷς ἐτίθεντο, ἐτίθεντο.[2] The 'things' (τὰ ὄντα, τὰ πράγματα) of these passages are, of course, not particulars, but universals (with the naming of which alone

[1] p. 123.
[2] Cf. the question 'Whether Definitions are of Names or of Things' discussed by J. S. Mill (*Logic*, book i, ch. 8).

the Dialectician is concerned)[1]; and knowledge of these
'things' is reached, we are told, by comparing together
such of them as are akin, and thinking-out others by
themselves—438 E μαθεῖν . . . δι' ἀλλήλων, εἴ πῃ συγγενῆ
ἐστιν, καὶ αὐτὰ δι' αὑτῶν—just the method illustrated in all
the Dialogues which we have hitherto reviewed—the
method of discovering the specific 'law' valid for a given
class of phenomena, by bringing the general 'categories' of
the understanding (same, different, &c.) distinctly to bear
on the phenomena. That there are such ὄντα to be known,
such 'laws', or Ideas, is indisputable, otherwise 'knowledge'
is impossible. 'Knowledge' is possible, therefore must
have objects; the Heraclitean flux is not objectively, only
subjectively, real. It is not in things, but in ourselves who
have made ourselves dizzy with our own aimless gyrations
among them (411 B). There is a permanent Beauty, a
permanent Good, and so forth—440 B εἰ δὲ ἔστι μὲν ἀεὶ τὸ
γιγνῶσκον, ἔστι δὲ τὸ γιγνωσκόμενον, ἔστι δὲ τὸ καλόν, ἔστι δὲ τὸ
ἀγαθόν, ἔστι δὲ ἓν ἕκαστον τῶν ὄντων . . . οὔ μοι φαίνεται ταῦτα
ὅμοια ὄντα ῥοῇ οὐδὲν οὐδὲ φορᾷ. A beautiful face changes,
but Beauty itself is unchangeable. If it were not unchangeable, we could not think it, or give it a name (439 D).
Here, as Professor Natorp puts it,[2] we have, in αὐτό or
εἶδος, simply the 'content of predication', the predicate
'beautiful', to which *a fixed meaning* belongs.

The continuous flux of sense is not, as continuous, object
for discursive thought; it becomes that only in so far as
we translate it into a discrete series of juxtaposed pieces—
photograph, as it were, stretches of its movement into rest;
and having arranged our 'photographs' into sets convenient
for future reference, use them as giving points of view
always to be taken by any one who would 'understand',
and deal successfully with, that movement which, after
all, *as so understood*, is the true reality. Plato's insistence
on the necessity for discursive thought of a system of

[1] See Natorp, p. 122.
[2] p. 125.

'Immutable Ideas' need not surprise any one who is familiar with the trend of modern Psychology, as indicated, for example, in the following passage :—' Les concepts sont en effet extérieurs les uns aux autres, ainsi que des objets dans l'espace. Et ils ont la même stabilité que les objets, sur le modèle desquels ils ont été créés. Ils constituent, réunis, un "monde intelligible" qui ressemble par ses caractères essentiels au monde des solides, mais dont les éléments sont plus légers, plus diaphanes, plus faciles à manier pour l'intelligence que l'image pure et simple des choses concrètes ; ils ne sont plus, en effet, la perception même des choses, mais la représentation de l'acte par lequel l'intelligence se fixe sur elles. Ce ne sont donc plus des images, mais des symboles. Notre logique est l'ensemble des règles qu'il faut suivre dans la manipulation des symboles. Comme ces symboles dérivent de la considération des solides, comme les règles de la composition de ces symboles entre eux ne font guère que traduire les rapports les plus généraux entre solides, notre logique triomphe dans la science qui prend la solidité des corps pour objet, c'est-à-dire dans la géométrie. Logique et géométrie s'engendrent réciproquement l'une l'autre. C'est de l'extension d'une certaine géométrie naturelle, suggérée par les propriétés générales et immédiatement aperçues des solides, que la logique naturelle est sortie. C'est de cette logique naturelle, à son tour, qu'est sortie la géométrie scientifique, qui étend indéfiniment la connaissance des propriétés extérieures des solides. Géométrie et logique sont rigoureusement applicables à la matière. Elles sont là chez elles, elles peuvent marcher là toutes seules. Mais, en dehors de ce domaine, le raisonnement pur a besoin d'être surveillé par le bon sens, qui est tout autre chose.'[1]

## *The Phaedo.*

Reserving the *Symposium*, the next Dialogue on the list, for the Second Part of this Essay, we come to the *Phaedo*,

[1] Bergson, *L'Évolution créatrice*, pp. 174-5.

in which the Doctrine of Ideas, as Scientific Method, is very systematically set forth. Professor Natorp, indeed, goes the length of saying that the *Phaedo* is really consecrated to this Doctrine.[1] The Immortality of the Soul, he thinks, is only ostensibly the subject of the Dialogue; in 'personal immortality' Plato takes little interest, as man of science, and cannot have regarded it as proved by his arguments. What he is really interested in is the 'immortality' which is realized at every moment by one who rises in thought to the Eternal. The *Phaedo* has more to do with Life than with Death—with the Life of the Philosopher which is the Life Eternal—Life in the Eternal, that is, Apprehension of the Ideas: hence Schleiermacher is right when he says that the theme of the *Phaedo* is the 'notion of the Philosopher'; equally right it would be to say that its theme is 'the Idea'.

The 'Idea' is that very Being (αὐτὴ ἡ οὐσία, 78 D) of which we give account in Dialectic (ἧς λόγον δίδομεν τοῦ εἶναι καὶ ἐρωτῶντες καὶ ἀποκρινόμενοι, 75 C), the art (ἡ περὶ τοὺς λόγους τέχνη, 90 B) with which rests the decision whether or no, in any case, we have attained to scientific truth (ἡ τῶν ὄντων ἀλήθειά τε καὶ ἐπιστήμη, 90 D). That which is thus reached is, as Professor Natorp rightly urges,[2] no transcendent Idea (the 'transcendent Idea', in Plato's *Logic*, is, I believe, the figment of Aristotle and those who have perpetuated his misunderstanding), but simply the content of the scientific answer to the question, 'What is the Beautiful, the Good, the Just?' The scientific answer is arrived at by a method (τρόπος τῆς μεθόδου, 97 B) indicated at 93 C, 94 D, and elsewhere, in which Professor Natorp finds the essentials of Aristotle's ἀποδεικτικὸς συλλογισμός—a method which substitutes certainty for probability, which adopts ὑπόθεσις A only after its consequences have been found to be consistent with already established truth; then looks out for ὑπόθεσις B, the best ὑπόθεσις among those immediately

---

[1] pp. 126-7.  [2] p. 131.

## PART I: THE PHAEDO

above A, and deduces A from B; then similarly rises to C, and so on till ἱκανόν τι is reached—a ὑπόθεσις which is an indisputable first principle (101 D). Thus, as Professor Natorp says,[1] the 'Idea' is 'deepened' by being connected, not only with Definition, but with Inference. The 'Idea' has become more than the fixed meaning of the predicate 'good' or 'beautiful'—it is seen to be valid, as 'Law' in a multitude of cases; and it is truer to say that it is developed into these cases than that it is merely applied to them.

Professor Natorp, whose treatment of the *Phaedo* is very informing,[2] distinguishes[3] four connected passages in which the 'Idea' is dealt with in this Dialogue:—

(1) 65–8. There is no *exactness* (ἀκριβές) in the senses. To get at what *is by itself* (αὐτὸ καθ' αὐτό), the mind (ψυχή, διάνοια) must work *by herself*. This means that 'abstractions' are the tools with which exact science works.

The *existence* of these 'abstractions' or 'notions' is maintained (φαμέν τι εἶναι δίκαιον αὐτό . . . καὶ καλόν γέ τι καὶ ἀγαθόν . . . to which are added μέγεθος, ὑγίεια, ἰσχύς—in short, ἁπάντων ἡ οὐσία, ὃ τυγχάνει ἕκαστον ὄν, 65 D), and the faculty which apprehends them is ἡ τοῦ φιλοσόφου ψυχὴ ἣ μάλιστα ἀτιμάζει τὸ σῶμα . . . καὶ ζητεῖ αὐτὴ καθ' αὑτὴν γίγνεσθαι (65 D).

In this first section of the *Phaedo*-presentation of the Doctrine of Ideas, the Moral Ideas are to the front; then comes *magnitude*, but the logical categories are not mentioned. We also notice that the separation of the intelligible from the sensible is very sharply expressed, and that in 67 C, D (and cf. 76 C) the 'dangerous' terms, as Professor Natorp characterizes them,[4] χωρίζειν, χωρισμός, χωρίς, which gave Aristotle his chance, occur. In characterizing these terms

---
[1] p. 132.
[2] In the First Part of this Essay throughout I am, as my frequent references to him indicate, I hope, sufficiently, much indebted to Professor Natorp. In the Second Part I venture to go beyond his assistance.
[3] pp. 132 ff.    [4] p. 137.

as 'dangerous'—*scilicet* for logic—Professor Natorp seems to me to neglect the mythical setting in which they occur; for in describing the χωρισμός of mind from body, and the objects of mind from *sensibilia*, as κάθαρσις (67 c), Plato has evidently Orphic rites in view. We ought not to press χωρισμός so as to make it mean in logic what it means in mythology—the entire separation of mind from body, involving the separate existence, as *Things*, of the abstractions which mind, as such, apprehends. We ought not to do this, and Plato, I submit, warns us against doing so by comparing the mental concentration of the Philosopher on his scientific points of view to the flight of the soul from the body in ecstatic vision or in death—a flight which Plato does not, I take it, expect his readers to understand literally. At any rate, in spite of the recommendation of 'flight from sense', the *Phaedo* lays the foundation of 'a science of *sensibilia*'—of 'natural science': the phenomenal world is presented as a second kind of being, and its position secured by the side of the world of Ideas—79 A θῶμεν οὖν δύο εἴδη τῶν ὄντων, τὸ μὲν ὁρατόν, τὸ δ' ἀειδές.[1]

(2) 72–7. On Learning and Reminiscence. The thought of this second passage, says Professor Natorp,[2] is that one gains knowledge only by recovering it out of one's own consciousness. Here, in the *Phaedo*, that which is recovered is much more definitely limited, he thinks, than it is in the *Meno*, to the pure forms of thought. I hardly think that Professor Natorp is justified in thus distinguishing the *Phaedo* from the *Meno*. Although the logical categories are not in evidence in the *Meno*, as they are in the *Phaedo* (76 A), yet the two Dialogues agree substantially so far as other categories are concerned: in the *Meno* we surely have 'mathematical categories' as well as in the *Phaedo*—the experiment with the slave-boy implies that—and the Ideas of καλόν and ἀγαθόν which appear in the *Phaedo*-list (75 c) are surely those which one endeavouring to get at the εἶδος of ἀρετή—the objective of the *Meno*-inquiry—

[1] See Natorp, p. 138.   [2] p. 138.

must, above all, endeavour to 'recollect'. What it is safe to say is that in the *Phaedo*, as in the *Meno*, it is the *original* of some copy now presented in sense, not a formerly presented copy, that we 'recollect'. We say (*Phaedo*, 74 A), 'There is equality itself (αὐτὸ τὸ ἴσον)'. This 'equality' we 'recollect' on occasion of seeing 'equal things', which are themselves, after all, both 'equal' and 'unequal', or rather, never truly 'equal'. But 'equality' is always the same. And 'equality' we must have had in our minds before we began to use our senses—75 B πρὸ τοῦ ἄρξασθαι ἡμᾶς ὁρᾶν καὶ ἀκούειν καὶ τἆλλα αἰσθάνεσθαι τυχεῖν ἔδει που εἰληφότας ἐπιστήμην αὐτοῦ τοῦ ἴσου ὅτι ἔστιν, εἰ ἐμέλλομεν τὰ ἐκ τῶν αἰσθήσεων ἴσα ἐκεῖσε ἀνοίσειν . . . πρὶν γενέσθαι ἀνάγκη ἡμῖν αὐτὴν εἰληφέναι. Here the *a priori* element in experience is figured as previous knowledge of an *original*.

After enumerating the 'mathematical categories', ἴσον, μεῖζον, ἔλαττον, &c., he goes on to give the 'moral categories' καλόν, ἀγαθόν, δίκαιον, ὅσιον, &c. (75 C), adding (76 A) 'logical categories'—forms of pure thought, ἀνόμοιον, ὅμοιον.

The difference between 'moral categories' and the two other kinds is profound; and that Plato recognized this seems to be proved by a passage in the *Theaetetus* (186 C), where the fundamental predicates are finally distributed under the two heads of οὐσία, Being, and ὠφέλεια, Value. Here Plato seems to me to anticipate the distinction, lately associated with the name of Ritschl, between 'theoretic' and 'value' judgements, and to bring the distinction back to its basis in the *a priori*.

To return to the *Phaedo*: the 'recollected Ideas' described in 72-7 are *a priori* conditions of thought and conduct, ways in which we *must*, or *ought to*, think and act on the occasion of the presentation of objects and opportunities in this world of sense-impressions. These ways of thinking and acting are *ours*—it is *in us*, not in the 'external world', that they are to be looked for. 'Equality' and 'Justice' stand for *rules* which the intellectual and moral nature of man is bound to follow in the exercise of its functions—in this sensible world, it is to be noted, not in a supersensible world. Plato speaks as if these 'rules' were absolutely, rather than relatively, fixed. As it is, they are relative to human nature, being hypotheses thrown out by man himself to help him in his practical task of thinking and using this world in the manner most conducive to the peculiar needs of human nature. We now see, what Plato perhaps did not see, that 'abstractions', so far from being 'eternally true', are not 'true' at all. They always involve partial one-sided views: but, although 'untrue', they are indispensable, because it is only the one-sided view—the thing viewed from our own side—that matters. The distinction between 'true' and 'what matters', to which I may be thought to have committed myself in my last sentence, is a purely academic one. The 'eternal frame and constitution of animals' (to quote Hume's remarkable phrase [1]), as specialized in human nature, is always there; and it is really all the same whether, in speaking of the fundamental judgements, we use the old description, 'eternal truths', or the new one, 'pragmatic postulates'.

(3) 78-84. There are δύο εἴδη τῶν ὄντων (79 A), that which is always the same with itself, and that which varies continually.

The ψυχή seems to fall under the first head. But Professor Natorp[2] would pass over here, as insignificant, the proof of its 'immortality': what is really important in this Section of the Dialogue is the definite recognition of the Sensible as a class of Being by the side of the Intelligible. Dialogues presumably later than the *Phaedo*, such as the *Sophistes* (248 ff., 254 D), and one certainly later, the *Timaeus* (51 and 27), are in favour of recognizing the Sensible as a kind of Being.

The thought of this section of the *Phaedo* (new, Professor Natorp holds—by no means new, I think) is that the

[1] *Enquiry Concerning the Principles of Morals*, Appendix i (end), § 246 (Selby-Bigge).
[2] p. 144.

sensible is mere appearance *till it is determined* intelligibly ; then it has its own proper reality.[1]

The two kinds of Being distinguished in this third Section imply two kinds of Judgement. This brings us to the fourth, and last, Section marked by Professor Natorp as presenting the Doctrine of Ideas, viz.—

(4) 96–107, which deals with pure fundamental judgements, and the founding of empirical judgements upon them.

The first among the pure fundamental judgements is that ' the World is Good '. The Good is the principle of Cosmos (97 E–99 C); it is ' the ought-to-be ', the principle of maintenance, order, balance, which is the ' sufficient reason ' for everything within its borders.[2] Thus (109 A) the central position of the Earth is explained as being involved in the self-maintaining organism of the Cosmos.

The εἴδη are laws, and the Good is the system of these laws.

The μέθεξις of the particular in the Idea means—in logic —simply the relation of particular case to law. What makes a thing ' beautiful ' is the παρουσία of the 'Beautiful ', or κοινωνία with it—ἡ ἐκείνου τοῦ καλοῦ εἴτε παρουσία εἴτε κοινωνία (100 D). The statement ' this thing is beautiful ' is, if true, justified by its conformity with the fundamental judgement which sets forth the notion of the Beautiful.

Such a fundamental judgement is, according to Plato's way of speaking, an ' eternal truth ' ; but no harm is done, I think, by describing it as a ' pragmatic postulate '. We deal with particulars by looking at them in lights suitable to the outlook peculiar to human nature. Spinoza, who makes *pulchritudo,* and the like, relative to human nature, not absolutely existing qualities in things,[3] realized this

[1] See Natorp, p. 145.
[2] We have here the principle implied in the two τύποι περὶ θεολογίας which lie at the foundation of the system of education set forth in the *Republic*—see *Rep.* ii. 379 ff.
[3] *Epist.* lviii (ed. Bruder).

fully; but Plato hardly realized it, nor did Kant, although the doctrine of *a priori* categories common to both philosophers—forms of thought which 'make experience possible'—implies it. The points of view from which, and, it may be added, the shades of feeling through which, we look at things, express our inmost nature.

The εἴδη, or fundamental judgements, are assured by deduction [1]—by the exhibition of their internal interconnexion with one another, as all ultimately dependent on one principle—see 101 D, E: taking an εἶδος, we first deduce consequences from it; if they contradict already ascertained truth, we reject the εἶδος which gives such consequences; if its consequences warrant us in retaining the εἶδος, we then ascend from it to a higher εἶδος from which it can be plainly 'derived'; and so on, till we reach what is called here ἱκανόν τι, i. e. a true ἀρχή [2] (cf. 107 B). The criterion of scientific truth is thus consistency over a large area, what is called σαφήνεια in a similar passage at the end of the Sixth Book of the *Republic*. The object is always to integrate each new 'truth' or 'discovery' with the system of already achieved knowledge.

The form of the empirical judgement (called τὸ ἐν ἡμῖν 102 D, E) is '$x$ is $A$', '$x$ is not-$A$', '$x$ is $B$', '$x$ is not-$B$', $A$ and $B$ being εἴδη defined in fundamental judgements. But there is no contradiction involved in '$x$ is $A$' and '$x$ is not-$A$'; for, in such empirical judgements, the contradictory predicates are either not simultaneous or are applied to what are practically different subjects, viz. to $x$, now, and then, or in this relation, and in that other relation.[3]

The $x$—the subject of the empirical judgement, then, is receptive, in different relations, of contradictory predicates; but these predicates, the εἴδη predicated, are themselves abiding—thus Life, ζωή (105 D), is abiding—although they may change their subjects. The argument for the immor-

[1] See Natorp, p. 153.   [2] See Raeder, p. 225.
[3] See Natorp, p. 155.

tality of the Soul turns on the abiding nature of the εἶδος 'Life', ζωή. Life is always Life, without change: the ψυχή is Life; *ergo*. I may say, in passing, that it is difficult to see how Plato could have regarded this argument as proving 'personal immortality'; why should the changeless predicate 'Life' not cease to be applicable to this or that *particular* ψυχή, as other predicates, themselves equally changeless, cease to be applicable to this or that subject in the sensible world? The argument, at most, proves that the *world-soul* is eternal.

The result of the *Phaedo*, then, is this, that, of the two orders of Being—the sensible and intelligible—we know the former through the latter. The Dialogue lends no countenance to the view that 'knowledge' of the *intelligibilia*, in any conceivable way, is possible except of them as performing their function of making the *sensibilia* intelligible. It is as true of Plato's Ideas as of Kant's Categories, that, without sense, they are empty. The Ideas, so far as Logic, or Methodology, is concerned, are merely the ways in which human understanding performs its function of interpreting the world—this sensible world, not a world beyond.

## The Republic.

The first passage of the *Republic* in which the Ideas are mentioned is iii. 402 c οὐδὲ μουσικοὶ πρότερον ἐσόμεθα ... πρὶν ἂν τὰ τῆς σωφροσύνης εἴδη καὶ ἀνδρείας καὶ ἐλευθεριότητος καὶ μεγαλοπρεπείας καὶ ὅσα τούτων ἀδελφὰ καὶ τὰ τούτων ἐναντία πανταχοῦ περιφερόμενα γνωρίζωμεν καὶ ἐνόντα ἐν οἷς ἔνεστιν αἰσθανώμεθα καὶ αὐτὰ καὶ εἰκόνας αὐτῶν. Here, Adam [1] argues, the εἴδη are not the 'Ideas'. The 'Ideas' he regards as 'transcendent', or 'separate', χωρισταί, and as not coming up in the *Republic* till the 'philosophical', as distinct from the 'musical', education of the guardians is reached.

[1] *The Republic of Plato*, note ad loc.

'Transcendent' Ideas, Adam holds, do not occur in *Rep.* i–iv. I follow Zeller[1] in thinking that the εἴδη here are the 'Ideas'—the language used here (πανταχοῦ περιφερόμενα —cf. πανταχοῦ φανταζόμενα, *Rep.* v. 476 A—ἐνόντα, αὐτά) is the same as that employed in passages where the 'Ideas' are admittedly referred to—and I further hold that the view, maintained by Adam and many scholars, which makes the Ideas 'separate' or 'transcendent' in a sense incompatible with their being 'immanent' as concepts, cannot be maintained on a broad survey of the methodological side of Plato's Doctrine. The εἴδη of the virtues, here in *Rep.* 402 c, as elsewhere, stand for the *meaning* of the virtues in each case; he who knows the εἶδος of Temperance is he who looks at it in the light of its end, the social system to which it belongs and contributes; and it is only he, we are told, who can either produce, or appreciate when produced, its εἰκών in art. This meaning can be formulated; in this sense it is 'separate' from the cases which it covers; and, at the same time, it is 'immanent', ἔνεστι, in each case.

Professor Natorp, who apparently takes the εἴδη of *Rep.* 402 c as 'Ideas', remarks[2] on the connexion of the passage with *Symposium* 210 : the καλὰ σώματα and καλὰ ἐπιτηδεύματα of the *Symposium* answer to γυμναστική and μουσική respectively in the *Republic*; while the καλὰ μαθήματα and αὐτὸ τὸ καλόν (or ἀγαθόν) answer to the scientific and the dialectical parts of the *Republic* curriculum.

The Doctrine of Ideas appears definitely—this is generally admitted—in *Rep.* v. 476 A περὶ δικαίου καὶ ἀδίκου καὶ ἀγαθοῦ καὶ κακοῦ καὶ πάντων τῶν εἰδῶν πέρι ὁ αὐτὸς λόγος, αὐτὸ μὲν ἓν ἕκαστον εἶναι, τῇ δὲ τῶν πράξεων καὶ σωμάτων καὶ ἀλλήλων κοινωνίᾳ πανταχοῦ φανταζόμενα πολλὰ φαίνεσθαι ἕκαστον—the passage extending to 486 in book vi; and in vi. 507 B πολλὰ καλά, ἦν δ' ἐγώ, καὶ πολλὰ ἀγαθὰ καὶ ἕκαστα οὕτως εἶναί φαμέν τε καὶ διορίζομεν τῷ λόγῳ ... καὶ αὐτὸ δὴ καλὸν καὶ

[1] *Plato*, p. 274 (Eng. transl.).
[2] p. 180.

αὐτὸ ἀγαθόν, καὶ οὕτω περὶ πάντων ἃ τότε ὡς πολλὰ ἐτίθεμεν, πάλιν αὖ κατ' ἰδέαν μίαν ἑκάστου ὡς μιᾶς οὔσης τιθέντες, 'ὃ ἔστιν' ἕκαστον προσαγορεύομεν . . . καὶ τὰ μὲν δὴ ὁρᾶσθαί φαμεν, νοεῖσθαι δ' οὔ, τὰς δ' αὖ ἰδέας νοεῖσθαι μέν, ὁρᾶσθαι δ' οὔ.

No care is taken in these passages to avoid the sharp opposition between Idea and Appearance; each Concept, or Idea, is itself one, but appears many in its connexions with particular actions, particular bodies, and other Ideas.[1] The γνωστόν, ἐπιστητόν, νοητόν, or 'object of scientific knowledge' is the εἶδος, which is the one point of view taken by γνῶσις, ἐπιστήμη, νόησις, or 'scientific thought' in all the cases belonging to a group. The one point of view taken is logically distinguished from, 'separated' from, any particular case in which it is taken; but this logical separation does not amount to a real separation. The point of view is not a 'thing' co-ordinate with the things with regard to which it is taken: and this is made abundantly clear to any one who reads *Rep.* vi. vii. 502–18, candidly, and not through Aristotle's eyes—the Idea is the scientific point of view in each case. It is in this passage, describing the Philosophical Part of the Education of the Guardians, that we have the *locus classicus* for the ἰδέα τἀγαθοῦ.

Socrates begins by pointing to what the Good is not: it is not φρόνησις, and it is not ἡδονή. What, then, does Socrates think it is? asks Adeimantus (506 B, C, D). Socrates replies that what he *thinks* is of no consequence—mere opinion is a wretched substitute for scientific knowledge; and scientific knowledge of the Good he does not profess to have ready to impart at present. At this juncture, Glaucon, afraid that Socrates is going to stop short, takes up the conversation, and begs him to go on and discuss the Good in the same way as he discussed the moral virtues, i. e. in an admittedly insufficient way, but yet to discuss it. Socrates agrees to go on; but will not try to define the

---

[1] On ἀλλήλων κοινωνία—the 'Communion of Ideas', see *infra*, pp. 82, 83, 87.

Good itself in its essential nature (506 E)—that is more than can be done at present:—he will point out its Offspring and Image (506 E). Before doing so, he recalls the distinction between the many particulars apprehended by ὄψις, ἀκοή, &c., and the One Form in each case apprehended by νόησις: and then goes on to distinguish the relation between ὄψις and τὰ ὁρώμενα from that between all other faculties of sensation and their respective objects:—ἀκοή and τὸ ἀκουόμενον, for example, need no *tertium quid* to link them together; but ὄψις and τὸ ὁρώμενον are beautifully linked together by φῶς, without the presence of which *tertium quid* eye could not see or coloured object be seen.

And the source of this φῶς is the Sun (508 A), which is not identical with either ὄψις or ὄμμα (508 A), although ὄμμα is of a more sun-like nature than any other organ of sense; and it is the Sun which dispenses to ὄμμα the faculty of ὄψις, by which he himself is seen.

'The Sun, then,' continues Socrates, 'is the Offspring and Image of the Good which I said I should point to in lieu of giving a scientific definition of the Good.' What the Sun is in relation to seeing and things seen in the visible world, that the Good is in relation to Thought or Reason and its objects (τὰ νοούμενα, the Ideas) in the intelligible world (508 B, C). The ἰδέα τἀγαθοῦ is that which sheds ἀλήθεια upon the objects of true knowledge (τοῖς γιγνωσκομένοις, the other Ideas), without the illumination of which they would not be 'known'; just as the Sun sheds φῶς upon the objects of sight, without which they would not be 'seen': and it is the ἰδέα τἀγαθοῦ which, at the same time, gives the knower ἐπιστήμη, the power of knowing the objects on which it sheds ἀλήθεια; just as the Sun gives the seer the power of seeing the objects on which the sunlight is shed. This cause of ἀλήθεια and ἐπιστήμη—though apprehended by ἐπιστήμη (508 E)—transcends them both: they are both ἀγαθοειδῆ (509 A), but not the ἀγαθόν itself; just as φῶς and ὄψις are ἡλιοειδῆ, but not ὁ ἥλιος which

PART I: THE REPUBLIC 51

transcends them both. 'What a marvellous Thing of Beauty the Good must be,' cries Glaucon (509 A), 'if, while producing both Truth and Knowledge, it is itself far more beautiful! you cannot mean that it is Pleasure?' 'Hush! Let us go on with our image,' says Socrates (508 A), 'and add this (509 B): that, as the Sun causes the γένεσις of the things which he also makes visible, but is not himself γένεσις, so the ἰδέα τἀγαθοῦ imparts οὐσία to the objects which it also makes known, but is itself something transcending οὐσία, surpassing it in dignity and power—οὐκ οὐσίας ὄντος τοῦ ἀγαθοῦ, ἀλλ' ἔτι ἐπέκεινα τῆς οὐσίας πρεσβείᾳ καὶ δυνάμει ὑπερέχοντος (509 B).'

This, then, is the *locus classicus* for Plato's ἰδέα τἀγαθοῦ.

The most significant thing, to my mind, in the passage is the refusal of Socrates at 506 D, E—he will not say τί ποτ' ἐστὶν τὸ ἀγαθόν, but will only describe its ἔκγονος. This is not mere literary affectation, or even εἰρωνεία: it indicates a philosophical position—that we must not seek to know the Good as we know 'things' and their 'Laws', the other 'Ideas'. All we can do is to 'throw out' figurative language at it. The position of Socrates towards the Good is just that which Matthew Arnold recommends towards religious truth. 'The language of the Bible,' he says,[1] 'is literary, not scientific language; language *thrown out* at an object of consciousness not fully grasped, which inspired emotion. Evidently, if the object be one not fully to be grasped, and one to inspire emotion, the language of figure and feeling will satisfy us better about it, will cover more of what we seek to express, than the language of literal fact and science; the language of science will be *below* what we feel to be the truth.'

The Good is ἐπέκεινα τῆς οὐσίας: that is, since οὐσία is the object of scientific knowledge, of ἐπιστήμη, the Good is not an object of scientific knowledge, one among other objects. It is rather the fundamental principle, the ἀνυπόθετος ἀρχή (511 B), of οὐσία and ἐπιστήμη, of Being and Knowledge.

[1] *Literature and Dogma*, ch. i, § 4, p. 41 (4th ed.).

It is not 'known' as Laws, the εἴδη subordinate to it, are 'known', in relation to, and as limited by one another. It is unique: not object of the Understanding, but, together with God and Soul, of the Reason, as Kant would say. The Good is that which, in the last resort, makes the existence of parts, and our knowledge of them, possible: it is the Whole Universe over against the Whole Man. As faculties are non-existent without the Man; so the Laws of Nature are insignificant without the Cosmos, or System of the Good. The Cosmos transcends its Laws—τὸ ἀγαθόν is ἐπέκεινα τῆς οὐσίας, transcends the other ἰδέαι which are οὐσίαι, objects of scientific knowledge, Laws of Nature. This is undoubtedly the meaning of the passage before us, so undoubtedly that we need not trouble ourselves about the fact that, in the same context, the Good is placed in the νοητὸς τόπος (509 D), and ἐν τῷ γνωστῷ (517 B), and is said to be τοῦ ὄντος τὸ φανότατον (518 C), τὸ εὐδαιμονέστατον τοῦ ὄντος (526 E). If we wish, on the strength of these statements, to say that the Good is 'known', we must remember that it is not for the Understanding with its Categories, but for the Intuitive Reason, that it is 'known'. And it is worth remembering, too, that in the *Theaetetus* (185 A–186 C) the 'Categories' of the ψυχὴ αὐτή are distinguished under the two heads of οὐσία (Being) and ὠφέλεια (Value), and that Good, with Beauty, falls under the latter.

Although the Good, then, is not co-ordinate with the other ἰδέαι, and is not, like them, οὐσία, object of science, without it, nevertheless, there could be no science. It is the ideal of a single connected System of Natural Laws, the ideal of the 'Reign of Law', without the inspiration of which there could be no scientific interpretation of Nature. And it is as 'ideal' that it is described as *good*; it is not posited as actually realized—at least for Knowledge—as the other εἴδη are; it is *what ought-to-be* rather than *what is*: the *ought-to-be* is beyond the *is*—ἐπέκεινα τῆς οὐσίας. It is that which we always strive to realize, but never do

PART I: THE REPUBLIC 53

realize—*the Good as Ideal*.[1] Even for God, if we may refer in this connexion to the mythology of the *Timaeus*, it is an ideal, not an accomplished result. If the other εἴδη answer to Laws of Nature and Categories of the Understanding, the Good answers to the Ideas of Reason.

The equation, 'φῶς in the sensible world = ἀλήθεια in the intelligible world,' which occurs in the present passage, meets us wherever Plato's influence is felt. Aristotle's comparison of the νοῦς ποιητικός to Light (*de An*. iii. 430 a, 10 ff.) is doubtless suggested by it; and in the Neoplatonic treatment of the ἰδέα τἀγαθοῦ and the νοῦς ποιητικός (which are practically identified) it is always being referred to. Christian theology too, from the Fourth Gospel downwards, has always made much of the text *Dominus illuminatio mea*; and in the *Divina Commedia*, Beatrice, Divine Wisdom, is compared to 'Light intervening between Truth and Intellect'—*Che lume fia tra il vero e l'intelletto*.[2]

Scientific knowledge, then, is like seeing things in clear daylight (508 c)—we see them as they are, in their true positions and aspects and connexions. In the twilight we see them out of their proper connexions; now they seem to be this, now that: the mental condition is that of δόξα, τὸ μεταξύ (478 D).

'It is remarkable,' says Jowett,[3] 'that, although Plato speaks of the Idea of the Good as the first principle of Truth and Being, it is nowhere mentioned in his writings except in this passage. Nor did it retain any hold upon the minds of his disciples in a later generation; it was probably unintelligible to them. Nor does the mention of it in Aristotle appear to have any reference to this or any other passage in his extant writings.'

Although it does not appear under the name of ἡ τοῦ ἀγαθοῦ ἰδέα elsewhere, the thought is not new to Plato; we have it in his earliest pieces—*Laches, Charmides, Gorgias*— where the 'Good' appears as the highest ethical notion,

[1] See Natorp, p. 191.  [2] *Purg*. vi. 45.
[3] *Introduction to the Republic*, p. xcviii (separate edition).

standing above the notions of this and that virtue, and giving them meaning. About its hold on the minds of Plato's 'disciples in a later generation'—although it may not have taken a very important place in the teaching of the Academy after the Master's death, perhaps on account of the discredit into which the Aristotelian criticism brought it—it certainly held a position of paramount importance in the Neoplatonic teaching: the whole doctrine of Plotinus is dominated by it. As for Aristotle's criticism of the ἰδέα τἀγαθοῦ in *E. N.* i. 6, it seems to have been written without reference to this *locus classicus*—certainly a most remarkable fact, for which it is difficult to suggest any explanation. Aristotle knew the *Republic*, and yet writes his criticism of the ἰδέα τἀγαθοῦ as though he were not acquainted with the great passage in the *Republic* specially devoted to it.

We may now look at the account which the *Republic* gives of Dialectic, the method by which the Idea of the Good becomes known to man, that is, becomes clearly explicit in his consciousness; for, after all, the 'knowledge' of it is not one of the data, but the fundamental condition, of experience. This account is given in *Rep.* vi. 510 B–511 C, a passage too long to quote here, which the reader ought to have before him, however, in order to follow the observations which I now offer.

What is said in the passage about the method of geometrical investigations (this is the meaning of the plural τὰς γεωμετρίας, 510 C; see Adam, ad loc.)—that it starts from assumptions, ὑποθέσεις, principles which it takes for granted, and, aiding itself by sensible objects, diagrams, and the like, τελευτᾷ (510 D), comes to conclusions, which follow necessarily from the assumptions, but, of course, have no more than a 'hypothetical' validity, is true, not only of the mathematical sciences, but of all sciences taken apart from Philosophy, the *scientia scientiarum*.[1] The assumptions of the separate sciences only cease to be assumptions when, and so far as, they are seen to be integral parts of the whole

[1] Cf. Jowett's *Introduction to the Republic*, p. xcv (separate edition).

system of knowledge and reality—καίτοι νοητῶν ὄντων μετὰ ἀρχῆς (511 D). When we have formed 'clear and distinct ideas' of them (see 511 E) they cease to be assumptions; just as passions cease to be passions, according to Spinoza,[1] when we have formed clear and distinct ideas of them, have come to view them *sub specie aeternitatis*. A man might regulate his conduct on the 'hypothetical method' of assuming that his passions were given him to be satisfied, and might construct a system of ethics consisting of hedonistic 'conclusions' and of a 'hedonistic calculus', after the model of 'the incontinent man's syllogism',[2] leading, in the most convincing manner, to these conclusions. Opposed to such a 'Method of Ethics' would be that advocated in the earlier Dialogues of Plato—the method which gets at the 'Good', and in the light of it sees 'virtues' and 'duties' as parts of one connected system of life.

As distinguished from the separate sciences, which are 'deductive', which proceed logically from assumptions, taken as principles, to conclusions, Dialectic is, first, 'inductive', goes up to an ultimate principle from, and through, the assumptions of the separate sciences, which it takes as being what they really are, assumptions, not principles (511 B), and uses merely as stepping-stones and suggestions (511 B), ascending till it reaches an ἀνυπόθετος ἀρχή, which is no mere assumption or hypothesis, to be taken up or laid aside as it happens to suit one's convenience, but *must* be accepted as soon as it is grasped—the ultimate principle of the Good, of the connexion of all things in one beautiful System:—at first Dialectic is 'inductive', appears as a process of 'integration', a process by which the empirical generalizations and assumptions of the separate sciences are so modified, so reshaped, that they take their places in a more or less lucidly seen, more or less consistent, Whole. Then comes the second stage of the dialectical process; it becomes 'deductive' (511 B), descends from the conception of the Whole so gained, and, in the light

[1] *Eth.* v. 3.   [2] *E. N.* vii. 3, §§ 9-11.

of it, reviews the parts, the original assumptions, and so completes their reshaping that at last they take their places as εἴδη, as ascertained truths, as 'derivative' laws—νοητὰ μετ' ἀρχῆς (511 D). This process is effected without any employment of sensible images or examples, such as is necessary in the mathematical sciences (510 D): only εἴδη, scientific laws, are in evidence; the 'deductive' part of Dialectic consists entirely in the concatenation of such laws, and does not go beyond them to particulars (511 C); it stops in its descent where the special sciences began, having converted such of their ὑποθέσεις as it retains into εἴδη.

As distinguished from Dialectic, which is the *scientia scientiarum*, Geometry, which may be taken as a good example of a special science, explicates the implications of such 'forms' as τετράγωνον αὐτό (510 D), assisting itself by means of images, diagrams actually drawn, which come pretty near the 'forms' themselves. These 'forms', represented by diagrams, are ὑποθέσεις, are assumed, without inquiry as to the nature of the Space of which they are determinations. It is Dialectic which inquires 'what is Space in the System of Knowledge and Reality?' Dialectic does not employ diagrams, but examines the ground of the 'forms' which, in Geometry, the diagrams represent. The relation in which Dialectic stands to the special sciences (which, as I have said, are all based on assumptions, in so far as they are prosecuted in separation) is that of a *critique*. It examines their principles as elements in the Whole of Knowledge and Reality. Of course, the comprehension of this 'Whole' is an ideal; but in proportion as a science succeeds in explaining its facts and empirical generalizations by wider and wider laws, to that extent it has become 'dialectical' in its method. Thus, while Zoology, before Darwin, acquiesced in a multitude of separate ὑποθέσεις— the various specific types, each one of which was assumed to be ultimate, it now regards them critically as parts of a great Whole, consisting of the Laws of Life, vegetable as well as animal: it is with these Laws, not with particular instances as such, that the philosophical zoologist of the present day, as distinguished from the descriptive zoologist of the past, is properly concerned—it may be said of him as of Plato's Dialectician, αὐτοῖς τοῖς εἴδεσι δι' αὐτῶν τὴν μέθοδον ποιούμενος (510 B) . . . τελευτᾷ εἰς εἴδη (511 c).

Adam[1] distinguishes between the 'Idea of Square' and the 'mathematical square', and says that we have the latter in the τετραγώνου αὐτοῦ of 510 D. The 'mathematical square' —τὸ ἐν διανοίᾳ—seems to me to be just the 'Idea of Square' or 'squareness': for, how does this τετράγωνον αὐτό stand to its diagram? Let Spinoza[2] answer for us: 'Idea vera est diversum quid a suo ideato. Nam aliud est circulus, aliud idea circuli; idea enim circuli non est aliquid habens peripheriam et centrum, uti circulus.' The τετράγωνον αὐτό is not an image, but a concept—*a rule according to which squares are drawn, imperfectly of course*. This rule 'has no sides'; the rule for drawing circles 'has neither centre nor circumference'. It is only the square or circle drawn, more or less imperfectly, according to the rule, that has. The τετράγωνον αὐτό, then, of 510 D, is the rule which the πολλὰ γεγραμμένα follow: and what else is the 'Idea of Square'?

About the intermediate position assigned (511 D) to the objects of διάνοια, i. e. to τὰ μαθηματικά, between αἰσθητά and νοητά, I shall have something to say when we come to the *Philebus*,[3] and need only explain here, in two sentences, the conclusion which I have come to after perusing a good deal of the literature which has accumulated on the subject. The Ideas are set forth in the *Philebus* as the various operations of the First Cause, the Good: these operations can be mathematically expressed in each case: without τὸ ἄπειρον to work upon the operations could not take place at all: without the principle of τὸ πέρας they would

---

[1] *The Rep. of Plato*, note on 510 D, and Appendix I to book vii, vol. ii, p. 159.
[2] *De Intellectus Emendatione*, vi. 33.   [3] See *infra*, pp. 93, 94, 99, 100.

not possess the definiteness which belongs to them as real, and as objects of knowledge. The τὸ πέρας class is, in fact, that of 'the mathematical determinants—τὰ μαθηματικά—which Aristotle speaks of as a mediating element, in Platonic theory, between Ideas and sense-objects'.[1]

At the end of the passage before us (at 511 E) Plato lays down 'Clearness', σαφήνεια, as the test of Truth. His test is that which meets us in the ' clear and distinct ideas must be true' of Descartes and Spinoza, in Kant's ultimate proof of the 'Categories', that 'we cannot think them away', and in Spencer's 'inconceivability of the opposite a test of truth'. 'Qui veram habet ideam,' says Spinoza,[2] 'simul scit se veram habere ideam, nec de rei veritate potest dubitare . . . sicut lux se ipsam et tenebras manifestat, sic veritas norma sui et falsi est.'

J. S. Mill, in his discussion of 'Inconceivability of opposite as a test of Truth',[3] does not seem to me to distinguish properly between this test as evidence, on the one hand, for the truth of a proposition relating to a *datum of* experience (e. g. the blackness of swans), and as evidence, on the other hand, for the effective existence of *conditions necessary to* experience—Categories of the Understanding which we 'cannot think away', and Ideas of Reason, such as that of a Perfect God, whose existence, for Descartes, is given in the 'clear and distinct idea' which we have of him, as it is also, for Berkeley,[4] given in the *notion* which we have of him—a 'notion' to be carefully distinguished from an 'idea' or datum of sense.

The evidence for the ἰδέα τἀγαθοῦ (which covers the three Kantian Ideas of Reason—Soul, World, God) is obviously, according to Plato, its own 'clear intelligibility'. It is a System which we see 'cannot be otherwise'.

A few words may be added about the relation of the Idea of the Good to God, as he appears in the *Timaeus*.

---

[1] R. G. Bury, *Philebus*, p. lxvii.
[2] *Eth.* ii, Prop. 43, and Schol.
[3] *Logic*, book ii, ch. 7.
[4] *Principles*, §§ 89, 137, 142.

## PART I: THE REPUBLIC

Professor Natorp is of opinion [1] that, in the *Republic*, as in the *Gorgias*, the Idea of the Good is simply the principle of maintenance or organization, and that there is no theological reference. The Idea of the Good is simply the highest methodological notion of Dialectic.

Adam, on the other hand,[2] identifies the αὐτὸ ἀγαθόν and God, and, in doing so, has most Plato-scholars on his side.

I cannot agree. In the *Republic* the Idea of the Good is the conception, or rather ideal, in which science culminates; it is not a person, but a principle; whereas the δημιουργός of the *Timaeus* who, because he is good, makes the world, is essentially a person for the religious consciousness, and cannot be identified, as personification, or otherwise, with a scientific principle. The scientific point of view is entirely different from the mythological; but Plato takes the one and then the other at different times, the latter quite as seriously as the former.

It may be mentioned that Zeller [3] affirms the identity of the Idea of the Good and God.

It remains now to notice the Doctrine of Ideas as set forth in *Rep.* x. 596 A ff.

It is set forth there à propos of the discussion of Imitation, μίμησις, in Life and Education. What is μίμησις (595 C)? We have (1) the ἰδέα which no human δημιουργός makes (596 B); (2) the *thing*, which the human δημιουργός makes, copying the ἰδέα (596 B); and (3) the copy which the painter (or poet) executes of the thing, holding up, as it were, the mirror of his art (596 C, D, E) to receive the reflections, not of τὸ ὄν, but of τὸ γιγνόμενον. Thus we have (1) ἡ ἐν τῇ φύσει κλίνη, which is unique (597 C), and made by God, ὁ φυτουργός (597 D); (2) the κλίνη made by the κλινοποιός, ὁ δημιουργός; and (3) the κλίνη 'made' by the ζωγράφος, or other μιμητής—an imitation-κλίνη, which is far removed from the reality (598 A, B, C, D).

---

[1] p. 193.  [2] *Rep. of Plato*, vol. ii, pp. 50, 51.
[3] *Plato*, pp. 279 ff. (Eng. transl.).

The tribe of tragic poets, with Homer at their head, instead of having all wisdom, as is generally supposed, are mere copiers of copies, are 'thrice removed from the truth' (599 A). They do not represent the real nature even of the sensible objects which they copy, but only certain modes in which these objects appear: the painter who represents in his picture the κλίνη as it *appears* from a certain point of view, from the front or the side (598 A), is the type of all μιμηταί, poets and others.

How are we to interpret this attack on artists, coming, as it does, from one who is himself a great artist?

Of course Poetry is μίμησις, ' representation.' It is not simply as μίμησις that Plato condemns it, but as μίμησις, too often, of the wrong object—of the sensible thing, not of the 'Idea'—of the isolated effect, not of the cause—of matters of fact, not of principles. True art, like nature, embodies the 'Idea', and its products are *parallel to* those of nature, not *copies of* them. Between the lines of Plato's criticism of bad art here, as copying the particular, we must read the doctrine that true art copies, or in some way sets forth, the 'Idea'.

The ἡ ἐν τῇ φύσει κλίνη, the Idea, made by God, which the carpenter copies, is that need in human life which it is possible to meet by making κλῖναι. That need is part of the constitution of Human Nature and of the Universe, is not made by man. The Idea as need, or use, we have had already in the *Cratylus*, 389 A ff.

The ἡ ἐν τῇ φύσει κλίνη is not a thing co-ordinate with these κλῖναι, but the *rule* in accordance with which, and the *final cause* for the sake of which, they are made. If it were a *thing*—this is the τρίτος ἄνθρωπος argument—there might be *two of it* (597 C); and these two would require a higher εἶδος to unify them. Here, it seems to me, we have, in Plato, the same distinction—between the ideal, which is unique, and the many concrete things, which imperfectly represent it—which Spinoza wishes to impress,

PART I: THE REPUBLIC 61

when he argues that there can be only *one* Universe, *one* Substance, *one* God.[1]

Stallbaum, on *Rep.* 597 D, notes that in *Timaeus* 52 A the ἰδέαι are described as ἀγέννητοι, whereas in the *Republic* they are said to be made by God. But these two statements are not really inconsistent. The *Timaeus* presents the Ideas as elements in the Eternal Nature of God, integral parts of his σοφία; while the *Republic* lays stress on the point that the Divine Nature is *causa sui*. The ἰδέαι, we are to understand, are not *arbitrary* products of God's *Will*: they are in accordance with his eternal *Wisdom*. 'Though the will of God,' says Cudworth,[2] 'be the supreme efficient cause of all things, and can produce into being, or existence, all things, and can reduce into nothing what it pleaseth, yet it is not the formal cause of anything besides itself, as the schoolmen have determined in these words—Deum ipsum non posse supplere locum causae formalis. . . . It is impossible anything should be by will only, that is, without a nature or entity, or that the nature and essence of anything should be arbitrary.'

Three points are to be noted in the Doctrine of Ideas as we have now seen it set forth in the Tenth Book of the *Republic*.

1. The paradeigmatic view of the Idea, which Professor Jackson regards as characteristic of the 'later' doctrine, is taken.[3]

2. We have Ideas of σκευαστά. That Plato, as we know him from his Dialogues, ever abandoned this position, or that he did not hold it seriously, is a perfectly gratuitous assumption.[4] Whatever admits of *scientific explanation* has its 'Idea'.

[1] *Eth.* i. 14, and cf. *Timaeus* 31 A, B.
[2] *Concerning Eternal and Immutable Morality*, book i, ch. 2, vol. iii, p. 531 (ed. Mosheim and Harrison).
[3] Cf. *Rep.* vi. 484 c, where the Idea is called παράδειγμα—the paradeigmatic view is more in keeping with the doctrine of *Rep.* vi, vii, as Adam remarks (*Rep.* vol. ii, p. 173, Append. iii to Book vii), than the μέθεξις-view.
[4] On the subject of Ideas of artefacta see M. Robin's *Théorie Platonicienne*

3. The error of conceiving the Idea as a *thing* is prominently in Plato's mind here, and refuted by the 'third man' argument, just as in the *Parmenides*.

## The Phaedrus.

Professor Natorp's order is: *Apology, Crito, Protagoras, Laches, Charmides, Meno, Gorgias, Phaedrus, Theaetetus, Euthydemus, Cratylus, Phaedo, Symposium, Republic*. In pursuance of this view of the chronological order, he speaks of the *Phaedrus*[1] as the first Dialogue in which, after the hints of the *Meno* and *Gorgias*, Plato deals definitely with the Idea; and further, he expresses the opinion that the presentation of the Idea given in the *Phaedrus* is responsible for the erroneous interpretations which afterwards prevailed. What is new, Professor Natorp thinks,[2] in the *Phaedrus* is the doctrine of the pure concept, free from all sensible admixture, the object of pure reason. The logical meaning of the passage (247 c), in the *Phaedrus* Myth, where the Idea is presented, and of following passages, is, he thinks, that the concept is

*des Idées et des Nombres d'après Aristote*, pp. 174 ff. It is likely enough that some of Plato's disciples denied Ideas to σκευαστά—see *Met*. A. 991 b 6 οἷον οἰκία καὶ δακτύλιος ὧν οὔ φαμεν εἴδη—where φαμέν seems to imply that this was the doctrine of disciples of Plato, among whom Aristotle reckoned himself: while *Met*. Λ. 1070 a 18 διὸ δὴ οὐ κακῶς ὁ Πλάτων ἔφη ὅτι εἴδη ἐστὶν ὁπόσα φύσει, was not written by Aristotle (see Rose, *De Arist. lib. ord. et auct*. p. 242), and seems, with its ἔφη, to refer to oral teaching which may well have been erroneously attributed to Plato himself by a writer who was not a contemporary. The reasonableness of denying Ideas to artefacta, very clearly set forth by M. Robin (op. cit. pp. 179 ff.), is more apparent from the stand-point of the Aristotelian than from that of the Platonic εἶδος: there is an Idea of Man, M. Robin urges, which manifests itself in the *function* which men perform; but there is no Idea of the statue of a man, for a statue cannot perform the function of a man. True, we reply; and Plato, according to the doctrine which he lays down in the Tenth Book of the *Republic*, would agree with you: such a mere 'imitation' is entirely divorced from union with an 'Idea': but not so an artefactum, like κλίνη or κερκίς, which does not 'imitate' a mere particular, but embodies a principle, meets a standing need, has a use. Such an artefactum admits of scientific explanation.

[1] p. 51.      [2] pp. 70, 71.

## PART I: THE PHAEDRUS

not a mere *instrument* for the treatment of impressions, but a *creation* of pure thought, and, as such, the only object of true science. This is why Dialectic in the *Phaedrus* first appears as an independent science, no longer as a method immanent in other sciences, mathematical or moral: διαλεκτική, he argues, is so precisely determined in the *Phaedrus*, that no Dialogues which assume the term as understood can come before the *Phaedrus*; so with Ueberweg, he places after it the *Euthydemus, Cratylus, Symposium, Phaedo,* and *Republic*, which all assume the technical meaning of the term.[1]

The abstraction of the concept, which we have in the *Phaedrus*, is that from which Aristotle's objection to the Ideas starts.[2] Plato, according to Aristotle, makes the Pure Forms separate *Things*. This is false, for Plato's Ideas, Professor Natorp contends, are, from first to last, not Things, but Methods, Pure Suppositions of Thought; and not external, though supersensible, objects. The Idea is the Pattern, the Original; the empirical is the derivative. It is in the *Phaedrus* (see 250 A, B, 251 A, 253 B) that the notion of Pattern and Copy comes out in full force; and it was on this terminology that Aristotle seized: although Plato, in the *Parmenides*, shows that he himself saw how it might be misunderstood: Aristotle, however, had no sense of the metaphorical, and took all literally.

It is the mixture of 'psychological' with logical considerations, Professor Natorp further tells us,[3] that spoils the Doctrine of Ideas as set forth in the *Phaedrus*: to apprehend the Idea, the soul must be freed from the senses and body: the Idea thus seems to be externalized as something, somewhere, if not in Space, yet in Overspace adjacent to Space. The *Phaedrus* does not guard against the

---

[1] Natorp, pp. 63, 64.      [2] Natorp, pp. 73, 74.
[3] pp. 84-6. For 'psychological' he might have written 'mythological'. It is the mythology of the *Phaedrus* presentation of the Ideas which is Professor Natorp's stumbling-block.

'danger', as he calls it, of 'Transcendence': the 'transcendental' becomes 'transcendent'. The Law of Unity is, indeed, conceived, not purely, however, as Law for our knowledge of objects in experience; but also as an object to be known in itself beyond experience, as something which 'is' for itself. In the *Theaetetus, Phaedo, Symposium*, and *Republic*, however, we are assured,[1] Plato steers away from the dangerous 'transcendent' of the *Phaedrus*, and finally reaches the safe waters of the 'transcendental' in the *Parmenides*. By the time that the *Phaedo* is reached the sharp Eleatic[2] separation of the Intelligible and Eternal from the Sensible and Temporal characteristic of the *Phaedrus* is already abolished, the distinction is recognized as that between two kinds of judgement, and the movement of Becoming is explained as the movement of predicates in the judgement occasioned by change in relations or point of view.[3]

To prove that the Doctrine of Ideas is set forth distinctly for the first time in the *Phaedrus*, and that the Dialogues mentioned are later, Professor Natorp[4] points to the following passage: *Phaedrus*, 247 C τὸν δὲ ὑπερουράνιον τόπον [afterwards, 248 B, called τὸ τῆς ἀληθείας πεδίον] οὔτε τις ὕμνησέ πω τῶν τῇδε ποιητὴς οὔτε ποθ' ὑμνήσει κατ' ἀξίαν. ἔχει δὲ ὧδε—τολμητέον γὰρ οὖν τό γε ἀληθὲς εἰπεῖν, ἄλλως τε καὶ περὶ ἀληθείας λέγοντα—ἡ γὰρ ἀχρώματός τε καὶ ἀσχημάτιστος καὶ ἀναφὴς οὐσία ὄντως οὖσα, ψυχῆς κυβερνήτῃ μόνῳ θεατὴ νῷ. The Soul visiting this Place καθορᾷ μὲν αὐτὴν δικαιοσύνην, καθορᾷ δὲ σωφροσύνην, καθορᾷ δὲ ἐπιστήμην.

I have referred particularly to Professor Natorp's view of the *Phaedrus*, as contributing to the Doctrine of Ideas, not because I agree with it. It errs, in my judgement,

[1] Natorp, p. 86.
[2] The chariots of the *Phaedrus* Myth come from the Poem of Parmenides.
[3] Natorp, p. 87.
[4] p. 61. Dr. Raeder (p. 278, cf. p. 214), on the other hand, assures us that all evidence, linguistic, philosophical, and historical, makes it plain that the *Phaedrus* is subsequent to the *Republic* and the *Panegyricus* of Isocrates (B. c. 380).

## PART I: THE PHAEDRUS

in making the *Phaedrus* the first Dialogue in which the Doctrine is definitely dealt with, even if we take the Dialogues in Professor Natorp's own order. The Doctrine is dealt with definitely, if not yet quite adequately, in the group to which the *Laches* and *Charmides* belong. It also errs in regarding the Plato of the *Phaedrus* as a logician spoilt by his poetic imagination. I refer to Professor Natorp's view because, mistaken though it is, it is a view which could hardly have been adopted by so competent a critic as he is, unless the Idea, as presented in the *Phaedrus*, were really something different from the Idea as elsewhere presented. Whatever place in the chronological order we give to the *Phaedrus*, the Idea of that Dialogue (and of the *Symposium*) differs, I maintain, from the Idea as elsewhere presented. It is not the 'logical concept', or 'scientific point of view', or 'law of nature', of other Dialogues, but a Real Presence for ecstatic experience; and I shall therefore postpone all discussion of it till we come, in the Second Part of this Essay, to the psychology of that experience, concluding the present notice of the *Phaedrus* by simply mentioning that the Doctrine of Ideas, as Logic, also finds a place in the Dialogue, in 237 c—οὐκ ἴσασι τὴν οὐσίαν ἑκάστου—and 270, 271, where scientific method is described, and contrasted with the τυφλοῦ πορεία of empiricism.

### The Theaetetus.

The *Theaetetus* follows the *Phaedrus* immediately in Professor Natorp's list as well as in Dr. Lutoslawski's, while Dr. Horn[1] places it after the *Parmenides*.

The question of the *Theaetetus* is 'What is Knowledge?' or 'How is Knowledge possible?'—a pressing question for those who maintain that 'Virtue is Knowledge'.

The answer, in substance, is this: The senses are merely the occasional causes of 'Knowledge', ἐπιστήμη. 'Know-

---

[1] *Platonstudien*, ii. 278-9; cf. pp. 388 and 341.

ledge,' ἐπιστήμη, is what the 'mind itself', αὐτὴ δι' αὑτῆς ἡ ψυχή (185 D), works out. 'Knowledge' is possible in that the ψυχὴ αὐτή, as 'unity of apperception', brings its fundamental notions, or 'categories', to bear on the data of sense. The fundamental notions, or 'categories', called κοινά, are given (185 A–186 C) as Being and Not-Being (οὐσία καὶ τὸ μὴ εἶναι), Similarity and Dissimilarity (ὁμοιότης καὶ ἀνομοιότης), Identity and Difference (τὸ ταὐτόν τε καὶ τὸ ἕτερον), Unity and Number (τὸ ἓν καὶ τὸν ἄλλον ἀριθμόν), Odd and Even (περιττὸν καὶ ἄρτιον), Beauty and Deformity (καλὸν καὶ αἰσχρόν), Good and Evil (ἀγαθὸν καὶ κακόν).

These κοινά, then, are apprehended, not by any sense-organ, but by the 'mind itself'—they are 'pure notions': ὅτι μοι, says Theaetetus (185 D), δοκεῖ τὴν ἀρχὴν οὐδ' εἶναι τοιοῦτον οὐδὲν τούτοις οὐδὲν ὄργανον ἴδιον εἶναι ὥσπερ ἐκείνοις, ἀλλ' αὐτὴ δι' αὑτῆς ἡ ψυχὴ τὰ κοινά μοι φαίνεται περὶ πάντων ἐπισκοπεῖν—and the list contains moral and aesthetic 'categories' along with mathematical and logical 'categories', under two heads, however—the mathematical and logical, under the head of Being (οὐσία), and the moral and aesthetic, under that of Value (ὠφέλεια): for this is how we ought, I take it, to understand 186 C [1] οὐκοῦν τὰ μὲν εὐθὺς γενομένοις πάρεστι φύσει αἰσθάνεσθαι ἀνθρώποις τε καὶ θηρίοις, ὅσα διὰ τοῦ σώματος παθήματα ἐπὶ τὴν ψυχὴν τείνει, τὰ δὲ περὶ τούτων ἀναλογίσματα πρός τε οὐσίαν καὶ ὠφέλειαν μόγις καὶ ἐν χρόνῳ διὰ πολλῶν πραγμάτων καὶ παιδείας παραγίγνεται οἷς ἂν καὶ παραγίγνηται; We have here the distinction between 'theoretic' and 'value' judgements recognized, and the *a priori* nature of the latter, as well as of the former, affirmed [2]—I say 'judgements', for, when 'the mind by itself' employs these categories of οὐσία and of ὠφέλεια, it *judges*, κρίνει [3]: and I say *a priori*, because they are what

---

[1] Professor Natorp (see p. 110) seems to understand the passage in this way.

[2] Similarly in the *Phaedo*, 97 E ff., 'The world is good' is an *a priori* value-judgement.

[3] See Natorp, pp. 110–11, on 189 ff., for the use of δοξάζειν = κρίνειν, and for the employment of the terms διάνοια, διανοεῖσθαι, and λόγος, as in-

## PART I: THE THEAETETUS

the structure of the mind itself, as distinguished from the impress of the sensible world, makes them.

With the 'critical' position (in the Kantian sense of 'critical') thus set forth in the first part of the *Theaetetus* up to 186 E, the 'dogmatic' position is contrasted, according to which objects are not constructed by the activity of mental categories, but are simply given, and impress themselves on the *tabula rasa* of the mind, 'knowledge' being thus merely ὀρθὴ δόξα or δόξα μετὰ λόγου: and, from 187 A to the end of the Dialogue, this latter position is examined, and reduced to absurdity—this is, in substance, how Professor Natorp,[1] admirably I think, summarizes the *Theaetetus*.

The dogmatic, or uncritical, position is first presented in the form which Antisthenes—so Professor Natorp thinks—gave it and handed on to the Stoics—the Soul is a tablet impressed from without, 191 C θὲς δή μοι λόγου ἕνεκα ἐν ταῖς ψυχαῖς ἡμῶν ἐνὸν κήρινον ἐκμαγεῖον κτλ. For the 'tablet' the 'bird-cage', περιστερεών, is substituted at 197 D. But it is to be noted that the 'bird-cage' is part of the *reductio ad absurdum* of the dogmatic position. We get 'ideas' (='impressions') from without, and cage them till required—and thus cage, not only 'truths', but also 'errors'. Surely a 'Knowledge' is needed to distinguish between these; and another 'Knowledge' to certify that this has distinguished correctly; and so on *ad infinitum* (200 B). The dogmatic position, with its *tabula rasa*, or bird-cage, evidently cannot explain 'how Knowledge is possible'.

It is the Categories set forth in the first part of the *Theaetetus* as the forms which make knowledge possible, which, together with other forms, are rejected by Professor Jackson from the list of 'Ideas', left by him with only

dicating that the mind, in operating through its 'categories' on the world of sense, 'judges': and see Lutoslawski, pp. 375-6, for δόξα, in 189 ff. and 187 A, as meaning, not 'opinion', but 'judgement'.

[1] pp. 112-14.

'natural kinds' remaining in it. The rejection of forms which make Knowledge possible from the list of 'Ideas' seems to me to be unreasonable; but there is an important distinction between these forms and the other 'Ideas', which, although it does not justify the rejection, is worth very careful attention, and there can be no doubt that Professor Jackson has done good service in bringing it into prominence. The other 'Ideas'—of courage, of justice, of ox, of bed—are 'explanations' of particulars belonging to special departments of Knowledge, and it is our business to seek for them, and *find* them: but the 'Ideas' or 'Categories' of Substance, Same and Different, Like and Unlike, Motion and Rest, are not confined to special departments, nor are they to be sought for and found: we *have* them, implicitly at least, from the first, and *employ* them in our methodical search for the other 'Ideas', for 'explanations' in the special departments. It is by the employment of its *general* Ideas (κοινά) of Substance, Same and Different, Like and Unlike, Motion and Rest, that human understanding finds, after difficult special inquiries, the *special* Ideas— the Idea of courage, the Idea of ox, the Idea of bed. The place, in special inquiries, of mathematical, as distinguished from these logical 'Ideas' or Categories, I shall have something to say about when we come to the *Philebus*.

## The Parmenides.

The first part of the *Parmenides*, to 135 A, is a criticism of the Doctrine of Ideas. The 'young Socrates' maintains the Doctrine, and 'Parmenides' criticizes. Who is the 'young Socrates', and whose version of the Doctrine of Ideas is it that he maintains?

It is chronologically possible that the real Socrates may have met Parmenides: but the point is, what is the rôle of the 'Socrates' of this Dialogue?

Dr. Raeder[1] thinks that the fact that, in the *Parmenides*,

[1] p. 299.

'Socrates' plays only an inferior part shows that Plato had now come to have doubts about the correctness of the views which he had hitherto put into the mouth of 'Socrates'. To this it may be replied that, if 'Parmenides' is to speak at all, it must be in the leading rôle; and chronological conditions make it necessary, or natural, to introduce 'Socrates' as a very young man.

Who, then, is this very young man? Is he a Pupil of the Academy who misunderstands the Doctrine of Ideas as taught by Plato? I think it impossible to suppose that the Doctrine which the young 'Socrates' defends is the Doctrine of Ideas as held by Plato himself when he wrote the *Parmenides*: for the criticism is obviously intended to overthrow the Doctrine in the form in which its defender holds it. Nor can the inference from the first part of the *Parmenides* be that Plato has now entirely abandoned the Doctrine of Ideas. Aristotle, as Professor Natorp acutely remarks,[1] would have mentioned that, and would not have written, as he did, against an abandoned Doctrine. And to argue that the *Parmenides* is spurious because it gives the *coup de grâce* to a Doctrine which Plato continued to hold, proves too much: for then, he did not write the *Sophistes*, *Politicus*, and *Philebus*. It is true that the great critical weapon of the *Parmenides*, the τρίτος ἄνθρωπος, is used by Aristotle in *Met.* A. 9. 990 b 17, without acknowledgement to the *Parmenides*: but this does not prove, as Ueberweg thinks[2] it does, that the *Parmenides* is later than the *Metaphysics*; for the τρίτος ἄνθρωπος was common property. It was not an invention of Plato's, which Aristotle can be accused of appropriating without acknowledgement. It was a Megaric argument, according to Alexander on *Met.* A. 9, due to Polyxenus, a pupil of Bryson.[3] The Eleatics were closely connected with the

---
[1] p. 226.
[2] *Untersuchungen über die Echtheit und Zeitfolge platonischer Schriften*, pp. 176 ff.
[3] See Natorp, p. 231; Raeder, pp. 305-6.

Megarics; and the Eleatic Parmenides is very naturally represented by Plato as making use of it.

If, then, we assume the genuineness of the *Parmenides*, and, at the same time, find it impossible to suppose that Plato, who to the end of his life adhered to the Doctrine of Ideas, held it, when he wrote the *Parmenides*, and continued to hold it, in the form defended by the 'young Socrates'—what position do we take up? If we do not accept the conclusion that the Doctrine of the 'young Socrates' is Plato's consistent Doctrine as misunderstood by pupils or others, we must accept, as alternative conclusion, the view that it is an earlier Doctrine of Ideas, once held by Plato himself, but now superseded, or in course of being superseded, by a better, that the criticism of the *Parmenides* deals with. Which of these alternatives is the more likely? Is the 'young Socrates' a pupil who misunderstands Plato's true teaching, or is he Plato himself at an earlier period of his development?

Mr. R. G. Bury,[1] in the course of an instructive criticism of Professor Jackson's views, remarks that 'there is a strong *a priori* improbability in conceiving' that Plato, in the *Parmenides*, should publicly criticize and overthrow his own 'earlier doctrine'. The 'young Socrates' of the *Parmenides*, therefore, he concludes, is not equivalent to the Plato of the *Republic* and *Phaedo*, as distinguished from the Plato of the later period: the 'young Socrates', indeed, 'labours with an imperfect and fractional Idealism owing to his lack of acquaintance with logical method and the insufficiency of his philosophic training,' but is yet 'in fundamental agreement' with 'Parmenides', by whom the 'mature Plato himself' is symbolized—a Plato to be taken simply, not as having had an earlier, to be distinguished from a later, Doctrine; while the ἀπορίαι brought against the 'young Socrates' by 'Parmenides'

---

[1] 'The Later Platonism,' in *Journal of Philology*, vol. xxiii, no. 46 (1895), pp. 174-5.

were first evolved by the Megarics, and then adopted by Aristotle. Here I think that Mr. Bury goes too far when he speaks of 'Parmenides' (whom I regard, with Mr. Bury, as standing for Plato) and the 'young Socrates' as being 'in fundamental agreement'. Plato obviously regards the τρίτος ἄνθρωπος as a good argument—it is employed by 'Socrates' in the Tenth Book of the *Republic* (597 c), and appears in the *Timaeus* (31 A, B): it is an argument which is obviously intended to be fatal to the Doctrine, defended by the 'young Socrates', of Ideas as 'separate substances', Things, which, as Things, must be regarded as co-ordinate with the things—the particulars—which they are brought in to explain. Although, then, the Doctrine demolished in the first part of the *Parmenides* cannot be a Doctrine still held by Plato, I cannot follow Mr. Bury in finding it hard to conceive it as a Doctrine which he once held and taught, and now wishes to supersede by a better.[1] I do not feel any difficulty in supposing that a man of Plato's candour should publicly criticize and overthrow his own earlier Doctrine. But is the Doctrine here overthrown his own earlier Doctrine? I agree with Mr. Bury that it is not, although my reasons for thinking that it is not are, I fancy, somewhat different from his. In the *Republic*, at any rate, the Doctrine of Ideas is carefully stated in such a form as not to be exposed to the τρίτος ἄνθρωπος refutation; and examination, such as that which Professor Natorp has made, of the Doctrine as set forth in the *Phaedo* shows that neither there have we Ideas absolutely 'separate' from particulars, thing-like Ideas, mere doubles of particulars, but rather principles in accordance with which particulars are explained. I take it, then, that the Doctrine of Ideas defended unsuccessfully by the 'young Socrates' against 'Parmenides' is not, and never was, Plato's own. I agree

[1] This is Dr. Horn's view, *Platonstudien*, ii. 167. He thinks that the *young* 'Socrates' is put up to defend the Doctrine of Ideas in the undeveloped, almost embryonic, form in which it first arose in Plato's mind.

with Zeller, against Dr. Raeder,[1] that, in the first part of the *Parmenides*, Plato simply sets forth objections which he does not regard as really touching the Doctrine as rightly understood. The Doctrine defended unsuccessfully by the 'young Socrates' is that which makes Ideas *Things*, while, as Professor Natorp rightly says,[2] 'Zeno' and 'Parmenides' represent the true Platonic view. This erroneous version of the Doctrine maintained by the 'young Socrates' is exactly the version which Aristotle sets before himself for criticism in the *Metaphysics*; and if we could suppose that Plato had his young pupil Aristotle in his mind when he invented the part of the 'young Socrates' in the *Parmenides*, we should find ourselves assisting at a very entertaining comedy. We should have Aristotle defending unsuccessfully his own erroneous view of the Platonic Doctrine of Ideas! There is some difficulty, however, in supposing that Aristotle, at least as a critic of his master's teaching, could have risen above Plato's horizon at the time when the *Parmenides* was written. Aristotle came to the Academy at the age of seventeen,[3] and the *Parmenides* must have been written soon after, otherwise Plato's lifetime would not have sufficed for the composition of the works which we have good reason for placing after the *Parmenides*.[4] The 'young Socrates', with his separate thing-like Ideas in which sensible things participate in some incomprehensible manner, is, at any rate, some one, most likely a pupil of the Academy, who took up the Doctrine of Ideas exactly as Aristotle took it up. And, as Professor Natorp remarks,[5] it is easy to understand how 'young *Socrates*' should play the part of a pupil of the Platonic School. These young pupils all aped Socrates. And the meeting of the old Parmenides and the youthful Socrates being chronologically possible, the *mise en scène* and cast of the Dialogue give Plato the opportunity at once of setting forth his own debt and

[1] p. 308.     [2] p. 219.
[3] See Stahr, *Aristotelia*, i. 40; but cf. Grote, *Aristotle*, i. 4, 5.
[4] See Lutoslawski, p. 401.     [5] p. 220.

## PART I: THE PARMENIDES

relation to the Eleatics, and of 'scoring off' his own pupils. '"Socrates" and "Aristotle" in the *Parmenides*,' says Professor Natorp,[1] 'represent the young Academy, and the whole Dialogue is *eine academische Seminarstunde* with the Eleatic Professors. The Doctrine of Ideas is discussed by all—by "Parmenides", "Zeno", "Socrates", "Aristotle", in the terminology of the three central pieces, the *Phaedo*, *Symposium*, and *Republic*, and Plato gives the Eleatics full credit for having originated the Doctrine.'

Let me now give a rapid sketch of the discussion which occupies the first part of the *Parmenides* down to 135 A, interpolating remarks as I go along. I am especially indebted to Professor Natorp for guidance through the intricacies of this part of the *Parmenides*, and indeed of the whole Dialogue. His interpretation of the Doctrine of Ideas as a contribution to Methodology is nowhere in his great work, not even in his examination of the *Phaedo*, more brilliantly and more convincingly carried out than it is in his examination of the *Parmenides*, and I have been glad to follow him closely. I have also derived much advantage from the study of Professor A. E. Taylor's papers on the *Parmenides*.[2] These papers were written some years before the appearance of Professor Natorp's work, when the author was a very young man. From the first they seemed to me to be illuminating in no ordinary degree, and my original impression is only deepened now that they can be placed by the side of Professor Natorp's work, the general conclusion of which they anticipated. Professor Taylor, like Professor Natorp, brushes aside much learned dust with which expositors have obscured the meaning of the *Parmenides*, and brings psychological canons and common sense to bear. How close his interpretation is to Professor Natorp's may be gathered from the following sentences: 'Plato conceived the relation between

[1] p. 223.
[2] 'On the Interpretation of Plato's *Parmenides*,' in *Mind*, July, 1896, October, 1896, and January, 1897, and, 'On the First Part of Plato's *Parmenides*', in *Mind*, January, 1903.

an Idea and the corresponding particular to be in principle
the same as that between what we should now call the
general equation to a curve, and such a special instance of
the curve in question as can be got by giving a numerical
value to the coefficients of the equation, and proceeding to
trace the line thus determined.' 'The Idea of the circle, as
defined by its equation in the general form, is not itself
properly speaking a curve.... Such an equation, like the
ideal number, is at once many, as synthesizing an indefinite
plurality of positions, and one, as synthesizing them in
accord with a definite law.' 'The "ideal" world simply
means the real world, in so far as it becomes an object for
knowledge.' Plato asserts that 'τὸ ἕν, the supreme reality,
can be the object not only of full and adequate knowledge,
but even of opinion and sense-perception (see 155 D)....
Taken in connexion with the attack on the absolute separation of γένεσις and οὐσία in the *Sophistes* 248 ff. and *Theaetetus* 155 E, and the conception of γεγενημένη οὐσία in the
*Philebus*, it forms perhaps the most decided repudiation
possible to Plato of the doctrine frequently ascribed to him
by persons whose knowledge of his system is derived from
a superficial reading of the *Republic*, that the world of
knowledge and the world of perception are two different
worlds, and not the same world more or less adequately
apprehended.'

The discussion which occupies the first part of the *Parmenides* down to 135 A is, briefly, as follows [1]:—

'Zeno' begins by showing that multiplicity or movement
is mere *appearance*; there *is* only Unity or Rest. Here
the 'young Socrates' sets forth a theory of unchangeable
eternal Ideas in which phenomena participate. The Idea
is an indivisible unity, comprehensible by thought alone, in
which the Other (τἆλλα) participates. A phenomenon can,
indeed, participate in contradictory Ideas—a thing can be
both 'equal' and 'not equal'—so 'Zeno's' argument that

[1] Cf. Natorp, pp. 224 ff.

there is only Unity or Rest, because there *cannot* be Movement with its contradictions, is met; and yet all contradiction is excluded from the world of Ideas, for each Idea is αὐτὸ καθ' αὑτό—the Ideas are not 'mixed' (129 D, E). This is Plato's Doctrine of Ideas as understood by Aristotle and the public. This is the τὸ χωρίζειν criticized by Aristotle; but it is not Plato's real Doctrine as set forth, e.g. in *Phaedo* 74 A, 100 C, where, as Professor Natorp puts it, the καθ' αὑτό of the Idea means only that it is a *definite* notion or point of view. It would seem that pupils of the Academy, as pupils are apt to do, took their teachers' phrases—χωρίς, αὐτὰ καθ' αὑτά, μετέχειν, κτλ.—too literally; and Aristotle formulated their misunderstanding, making the Ideas, not Methods, but 'a second order of Things behind, or beside, or above, the things of sense, related to the latter as the latter are to one another. . . . It is only one who has no better notion of the meaning of Ideas than this Aristotelian one who can wonder why Plato should attack "*his own* theory" so unmercifully in the *Parmenides*, even with the same arguments with which Aristotle afterwards attacked it'.[1]

To return to our sketch: 'the young Socrates' is obliged by 'Parmenides' to admit that there are 'Ideas' wherever there are objects of scientific inquiry (see *Parm.* 130), and this is doubtless the true Platonic doctrine.

Five classes of Ideas are given: (1) *Logical Ideas*, the Ideas, notions, or categories of Similarity and Dissimilarity, of Unity and Multiplicity, of Rest and Motion; (2) *Ethical Ideas*, the Ideas or notions of the Beautiful, the Good, the Just; (3) Ideas or notions of *Biological Kinds*, of man, of horse; (4) Ideas or notions of *the Elements*, of fire, air, water, earth; and (5) Ideas or notions of *Material Combinations*—as Professor Natorp calls them [2]—Ideas or notions of hair, mud, dirt. The 'young Socrates' does not like to admit the fifth class of 'Ideas'. He would rather keep to more dignified abstractions: he feels that the 'Idea of Dirt' can

---

[1] Natorp, p. 226.  [2] p. 227.

hardly be a χωριστόν in the sense in which he had understood the term. But 'Parmenides' urges that nothing is too common or mean not to have its 'Idea', i. e. not to be worthy of the notice of the scientific man. This passage (130), in which 'Parmenides' exhibits the extent of the field of the 'Ideas', is the best evidence that we could have against the view of Professor Jackson, a view which rests on the literal interpretation of Platonic terms, and takes no sufficient account of the methodological significance of the Doctrine of Ideas. Professor Natorp, who has done so much for the recognition of that significance, has an instructive passage [1] on the theme, 'The Ideas extend over the whole ground of science,' which I will here give in substance. He specifies, in order, the Dialogues in which the extension is gradually made, his contention, of course, being that the 'Ideas' are not 'substances apart', but 'points of view' taken by science—in short, 'notions.' In the early Dialogues *ethical*, and occasionally *mathematical*, notions are noticed: then, from the *Theaetetus* onward,[2] attention is paid to *logical* and *mathematical* (not distinguished from *logical*) notions: then, in the *Phaedo*, to *physical* notions—hot, cold, and to *elements*—fire, air, &c., as well as to *biological* notions—life, health, disease, strength: in the *Cratylus* we find that 'logical being' is not denied to notions of *human action*, and with these notions we have *technical* notions, κερκίς in the *Cratylus*, and κλίνη in the *Republic*, the method which employs these notions being teleological: lastly, mud and dirt come in, involving a *law of chemical combination*.

The extension, then, of the 'Idea' to all departments of scientific inquiry is shown by 'Parmenides' to be absolutely necessary; and can be misunderstood only by those who regard the 'Idea' as a mere double of the sensible object.

The particular, says the 'young Socrates', 'participates in' the Idea (μετέχει, 130 B, μεταλαμβάνει, 130 E). But how,

[1] pp. 228-9.
[2] See pp. 62 and 65, *supra*, for place assigned by Professor Natorp to the *Theaetetus*.

asks 'Parmenides' (131 A ff.), can the indivisible Idea be broken up among particulars? This is exactly Aristotle's objection to the Doctrine of Ideas. Aristotle did not see that μέθεξις is really *predication*: he failed to recognize the great contribution to methodology made by Plato in the *Phaedo*, where the deductive establishment of the predications, or propositions, of science is set forth as the aim—a given proposition (or case of μέθεξις) is carried back to another proposition which explains it, and that to another higher, and so on till ἱκανόν τι is reached: a process described also in the Sixth Book of the *Republic*, where the progress of scientific knowledge appears as a continuous process of integrating Ideas, or Laws, till, after many up- and downward movements of συναγωγή and διαίρεσις have been effected, a self-consistent system, an ἀρχὴ ἀνυπόθετος, is thought out with convincing clearness. It would be difficult, I think, to give a truer general account of the course followed by the advance of the interconnected natural sciences of the present day than that given by Plato in the *Phaedo* and Sixth Book of the *Republic*, and ignored by Aristotle in his criticism of the Doctrine of Ideas. The difficulty about μέθεξις involving the breaking up of the 'Idea', the 'young Socrates' cannot meet. The τρίτος ἄνθρωπος is unanswerable: μέγεθος αὐτό (132 A ff.) being, on his view, a *thing* co-ordinate with the particular μεγάλα which 'participate' in it, must be included, together with them, in a higher μέγεθος αὐτό, and so on indefinitely. But although 'Socrates' cannot meet the difficulty about μέθεξις involving the breaking up of the indivisible 'Idea', 'Parmenides' puts him on the right track, as Professor Natorp says,[1] for meeting it, by suggesting (merely by a turn of expression in the course of his destructive criticism—ἐὰν ὡσαύτως τῇ ψυχῇ ἐπὶ πάντα ἴδῃς, οὐχ ἕν τι . . . φανεῖται; 132 A) that the unity of the 'Idea' comes from, amounts to, the unity of Consciousness, the unity which is effected for us when we

[1] p. 230.

regard many things from one fixed point of view, or ἰδέα—
the point of view, I would say, which, in given circumstances, expresses the peremptory need of Human Nature in these circumstances—the point of view which expresses the *individuality* of the thinker, or agent, as that individuality realizes itself in these circumstances—realizes itself *fully* in these circumstances, each 'idea' being thus, as it were, the light cast on the given subject-matter by the whole self-conscious mind. And 'this unity of Consciousness is not a *thing* to which the notions of whole and parts can be applied'.[1] 'Distinguons donc,' says M. Bergson,[2] 'deux formes de la multiplicité, deux appréciations bien différentes de la durée, deux aspects de la vie consciente. Au-dessous de la durée homogène, symbole extensif de la durée vraie, une psychologie attentive démêle une durée dont les moments hétérogènes se pénètrent; au-dessous de la multiplicité numérique des états conscients, une multiplicité qualitative; au-dessous du moi aux états bien définis, un moi où succession implique fusion et organisation. Mais nous nous contentons le plus souvent du premier, c'est-à-dire de l'ombre du moi projetée dans l'espace homogène. La conscience, tourmentée d'un insatiable désir de distinguer, substitue le symbole à la réalité, on n'aperçoit la réalité qu'à travers le symbole. Comme le moi ainsi réfracté, et par là même subdivisé, se prête infiniment mieux aux exigences de la vie sociale en général et du langage en particulier, elle le préfère, et perd peu à peu de vue le moi fondamental.'[3]

'Socrates' adopts (132 B) the suggestion of 'Parmenides' so far as to speak of the εἶδος as a νόημα existent only ἐν ψυχαῖς. But, urges 'Parmenides', it must be the νόημα, or notion, of *something existing*. 'Socrates' agrees, and then falls back into the old track: the something existing which, in order to escape 'subjective idealism', we must posit as corresponding to the νόημα, he still figures as a *Thing*—this time, as a Thing which the particulars 'resemble': for

[1] Natorp, p. 230.  [2] *Les Données immédiates de la Conscience*, p. 97 (6th ed.).
[3] Cf. M. Bergson's *L'Évolution créatrice*, pp. 4 ff.

μέθεξις he substitutes παράδειγμα (132 D). But here again the Thing-like Idea is co-ordinate with the particulars: e. g. μέγεθος αὐτό is only another item in the list of τὰ μεγάλα which 'resemble' it, and the τρίτος ἄνθρωπος again applies (133 A).

So much for the insuperable difficulty involved in the μέθεξις-παράδειγμα-view. The 'chasm', as Jowett[1] calls it, is that between particulars and Ideas of the same name, and it cannot be bridged by us so long as the Ideas are regarded as Things. But there is a deeper and wider chasm between the Ideas 'in us' and the Ideas 'absolutely'—between 'possible experience' and 'Things in themselves', to use Kantian language. How can the World of Experience be brought into touch with the World of Ideas (133 B, C)? Surely the Ideas 'absolutely'—καθ' αὐτάς—will be unknowable by human faculties. Pure knowledge is related only to pure objects and empirical knowledge to empirical objects. But we have only the latter knowledge—ἐν ἡμῖν, παρ' ἡμῖν ἔχομεν (133 D, 134 B)—we have no knowledge of the pure objects, the absolute Ideas: they are καθ' αὐτάς, by themselves, not 'with us': they are not *given*, for, if they were, they would be empirical, not pure[2]: and even, if we had them, we could not know the empirical objects through them. It is meaningless to speak of the εἴδη in us as ὁμοιώματα of the εἴδη αὐτὰ καθ' αὐτά. The two worlds are entirely separate. This is the *impasse* into which those who stand up for the Ideas as 'separate substances' are brought in the first part of the *Parmenides* ending at 135 A.

The second part, from 135 B to the end of the Dialogue, whether or not we regard it, with Dr. Raeder,[3] as Plato's 'answer to the Eleatics and Megarics', at any rate shows up the misunderstanding which brought Academicians like the 'young Socrates' into the *impasse* of two entirely separate worlds. The notion of a cut-off world of thing-

---

[1] *The Dialogues of Plato*: Introduction to the *Parmenides*, vol. iii, p. 237 (ed. 1871).
[2] See Natorp, p. 234.     [3] p. 315.

like Ideas is unmeaning—the Idea can be affirmed to exist only in so far as it can be shown to be the ground of the possibility of experience—it is not to be 'separated' from experience—its true function, wherein its true reality consists, is that of making experience possible.[1] I incline to the view which Professor Natorp seems to favour,[2] that the second part of the Dialogue, though it is still 'Parmenides' who makes the points, is directed against Eleatics as well as against Academicians. Plato is, indeed, anxious to exhibit his debt to the Eleatics, but, at the same time, he is their critic in so far as, with their abstract One, they, like the 'young Socrates' with his 'Idea', set up an unknown and unknowable Thing-in-itself. We may take it, I think, that 'Parmenides', throughout the whole Dialogue, is Plato, first criticizing his own pupils, and then his Eleatic masters; and the connexion between the two parts of the Dialogue is, as Jowett puts it,[3] that 'from the Platonic ideas we naturally proceed to the Eleatic one or being which is the foundation of them.'

The inquiry about the One, with which the second part of the *Parmenides* is concerned, is conducted thus :—

1. What results, if the One *is*—
   (*a*) for the One itself,
   (*b*) for the not-One, or Other?
2. What results, if the One *is not*—
   (*c*) for the One itself,
   (*d*) for the not-One, or Other?

Each of these four questions is answered in two contradictory ways, so we get right answers, which amount in substance to this: That an absolute separation of the One and the Other involves the destruction of both—of the One, because, as abstracted and taken by itself, it can have no predicates, not even the predicate of existence; of the Other, because the Other, as Many, must have 'ones' as

---

[1] See Natorp, pp. 234-5.      [2] p. 235.
[3] *Dialogues of Plato*: Introduction to the *Parmenides*, vol. iii, p. 254.

parts, i. e. cannot exist unless it can participate in the One : whereas, if we assume the concretely existent, as distinguished from the abstract, One, we assume that which no longer eludes our grasp—we assume Unity beside which, or rather within which, Multiplicity naturally takes its place. 'The nett result,' says Professor Taylor,[1] 'of the long and complicated reasoning of 142 B-155 E is this: that if we once start with the conviction that the ultimate reality must at least be real we are driven so to conceive of its unity as to permit the recognition of all the diversity of the actual world as falling somehow within it. Every affirmation and every negation that can significantly be made about anything in the world will come in the end to be a partial statement of the nature of the single and ultimate reality. Judgements which assert the world's unity or its diversity, which attach to it spatial, temporal, qualitative, and quantitative relations of the most various kinds, will all have their own truth, while none will be the whole truth. This last qualification is added advisedly; it seems to me to be the main if not the only function of the negative side of the successive contradictions of the argument to remind us that every assertion we can make about the real on the strength of our experience is, though true, only a part of the truth. And I hope I am not reading modern notions into Plato when I say that I find the underlying idea of the whole in the conception of a reality which, while it can only be real because it realizes itself in the details of experience, is never fully realized in any of them.'

There is some difference of opinion as to what the One discussed in the second part of the *Parmenides* exactly stands for. Is it (*a*) the whole System of Ideas, 'The Good,' of the *Republic*, the Other, or Many, opposed to it, being the separate Ideas contained in the System? Or (*b*) does it represent any of these separate Ideas, the Other, or

---

[1] 'On the Interp. of Plato's *Parmenides*': *Mind*, October, 1896, p. 505.

Many, being the sensible particulars corresponding to that Idea? Or (c) is it the pure notion of Unity, the Other, or Many, being the pure notions other than Unity, viz. Plurality, Being and Not-Being, Identity and Difference, Similarity and Dissimilarity, Motion and Rest? Professor Taylor, who seems to have only questions (a) and (b) before him, decides in favour of the former[1]; while Professor Natorp[2] answers (c) in the affirmative. I am in favour of a composite answer. I think that the immediate subject of discussion is the pure notion of Unity together with the other pure notions mentioned with which it is shown to have κοινωνία (I use here, for convenience, the term which becomes technical in the *Sophistes*), this pure notion of Unity being exemplified both in any single Idea— erroneously conceived by 'Socrates' as absolutely 'separate'—and in the whole System of Ideas, conceived erroneously as an abstract One by the Eleatics, conceived by Plato himself as an organic Whole, or Good. The relation of any single Idea to the sensible particulars corresponding to it, or of the whole world of Ideas to the sensible world, is not, I take it, directly before us in the second part of the *Parmenides*, as it was in the first part; but it is indirectly before us, for the real object of the *Parmenides*, as a contribution to methodology, is to show that the Ideas are related to their respective sensible particulars in such a way that scientific knowledge of the sensible world is possible: and this object is held to be furthered if it can be shown that within the world of Ideas itself, and more especially within that part of it which comprises the pure logical notions— Unity and Plurality, Being and Not-Being, Identity and Difference, Similarity and Dissimilarity, Motion and Rest, there is κοινωνία: this κοινωνία is insisted on because it is necessary to that other κοινωνία, on the possibility of which 'Natural Science' depends, between the world of Ideas and the world of sensible particulars. The Eleatic atmosphere of the *Parmenides* doubtless accounts for the

[1] *Mind*, October, 1896, pp. 483-4.   [2] p. 237.

prominence given to the notion of Unity in the discussion; but the real subject of the second part of the Dialogue is general—the κοινωνία εἰδῶν, the interconnexions between certain pure logical notions, or εἴδη, among which Unity has a place. These notions—Unity Plurality, Being Not-Being, Identity Difference, Similarity Dissimilarity, Rest Motion—it is shown, cannot be treated as absolutely separate; they must be treated as only relatively separate; and, Unity being taken as an instance, it is asked, How can Unity, posited absolutely, have Being? How can we say, 'The One *is*'? Of the absolute One we can only say that 'it is *One*', not that 'it *is*', or that 'it is *identical*', or that 'it is *different*', or that 'it *rests*', or that 'it *moves*'. This is the *reductio ad absurdum* of the absolutely isolated One incapable of receiving added determinations—of the One, in short, which is not also Many. We must therefore posit the One which is One, not absolutely, but relatively; we must posit the One which is a ὅλον (142 D)—an Organism. The blank One cannot explain experience.[1]

The outcome, then, of the *Parmenides* is that the Intelligible cannot be severed from the Sensible, that the 'Ideas', whether general logical forms of thought, or special concepts—for 'Ideas' are of these two kinds—are meaningless abstractions unless they are regarded as *functions* necessarily related to 'the Other', the sensible world. In order to make out this—the real conclusion of the argument contained in the *Parmenides*—it is shown, in the second part of the Dialogue, that, even within the intelligible world itself, the 'One' is related to the 'Other', to an intelligible 'Other': the κοινωνία within the intelligible world is a guarantee that there is also a κοινωνία between that world and the sensible world. 'Parmenides,' representing Plato himself, tries to get the 'young Socrates' and the Eleatic standers-up for the Absolute One to

---

[1] See Horn, *Platonstudien*, ii, pp. 128-9 and 155.

see this. Professor Taylor seems to me to put the connexion between the two parts of the *Parmenides* admirably: 'As soon as we realize what Plato is constantly trying to make us understand, that the "ideal" world simply means the real world in so far as it becomes an object for knowledge, we should have no difficulty in seeing that the problem how one "Idea" can be present to many "things" and the problem how one "Idea" can, while preserving its unity, enter into relations with many other "Ideas", are only two ways of raising the same question. For a thing, in the only sense in which a thing is knowable, is nothing more or less than a certain System of Universals, or, in Platonic phraseology, Ideas.'[1]

## *The Sophistes.*

The *Sophistes* undoubtedly marks a new start in the history of Plato's development. Stylometric tests place it with his five latest works. The language is technical and new-fangled, with inverted order and careful avoidance of the hiatus. Thus, according to statistics given by Dr. Raeder,[2] the hiatus *is not avoided* in the following percentages of cases in the following Dialogues: in the *Lysis*, 45.97 per cent.; in the *Cratylus*, 31.18 per cent.; in the *Menexenus*, 28.19 per cent.; in the *Phaedrus*, 23.90 per cent.; while in the *Laws* the percentage of non-avoidance has fallen to 4.70, and in the *Critias, Sophistes,* and *Politicus*, to under 1.00.

Although the *Sophistes* may have been written at some interval after the *Parmenides*, it undoubtedly takes up and develops the results reached in that Dialogue. Dr. Horn,[3] who places the *Theaetetus*, as well as the *Sophistes*, after the *Parmenides*, regards the *Theaetetus* as taking up again the first part of the *Parmenides*, while the *Sophistes* takes up the second part. If there is any weight, however, and I think

[1] *Mind*, October, 1896, p. 484.   [2] p. 41, and cf. Lutoslawski, 437.
[3] *Platonstudien*, ii, pp. 278-9; cf. 341.

there is great weight, to be attached to the stylometric evidence marshalled by Campbell and those who have followed his lead, the *Sophistes* does not come before the *Republic*, as Dr. Horn argues.[1] Dr. Horn's placing it before the *Republic* is one of the most curious, among the many curious, results of that love, which he shares with so many scholars, of rending the unity of a great genius, of making Plato not only change his mind weakly from Dialogue to Dialogue, but come out unexpectedly with entirely new thoughts of immense import. These minute inquiries, detecting alterations, small and great, in Plato's mind, ignore, among many other considerations, the dominant consideration that he was a great dramatist. Such and such thoughts did, or did not, occur to such and such dramatis personae—that is why they are present in, or absent from, such and such pieces. Subject-matter is thus a much less safe ground for chronological arrangement of the Platonic Dialogues than stylometric considerations are; and even they are perhaps less conclusive than they would be in the case of a non-dramatic writer.

The chief results reached in the *Parmenides* were: the fundamental conditions of pure thought, the categories or notions of Unity and Plurality, Rest and Motion, Being and Not-Being, combine with one another; and Plurality, Motion, Not-Being or Appearance, the attributes of the world of sense, involve the Unity, Being, and Rest characteristic of the intelligible world. The reality of the intelligible $A$ is constituted by the fact that it performs its function of making the $x$ of the sensible world intelligible in the formula $x$ is $A$.[2]

The *Sophistes* is one of a trilogy *Sophistes, Politicus,* and ⟨*Philosophus*⟩. The ostensible object of the *Sophistes* is to find the definition of the 'Sophist'. He is 'one who makes images which have only an apparent resemblance to reality'. The shell of the Dialogue, as Dr. Raeder

[1] op. cit. ii. 338 ff.   [2] See Natorp, pp. 273-5.

calls it,[1] is concerned with the discovery of this definition; but the kernel is concerned with the questions, How to distinguish between *apparent* and *real* resemblance, and (236 E–237 A) How it is possible to say, or mean, what is *false*: if it is possible, then we must assume the Being of Not-Being. Unless we have found the nature of Not-Being, we cannot declare the nature of the Sophist. The problem of the nature of Not-Being is solved, on the lines sketched in the *Parmenides*, by showing that thought involves a system of categories, or pure notions, which do not stand each one isolated by itself, but combine with one another in certain ways. This is the doctrine of the κοινωνία εἰδῶν, which, as I remarked in the section on the *Parmenides*, is held to guarantee the further κοινωνία between the world of Ideas and the sensible world, without which there could be no natural science.

Just as there is an art to tell what sounds or notes go with what, so there must be an art to tell what εἴδη, γένη, or ἰδέαι combine with what. This art, or science, is Dialectic (253 A–E): τὸ κατὰ γένη διαιρεῖσθαι καὶ μήτε ταὐτὸν εἶδος ἕτερον ἡγήσασθαι μήτε ἕτερον ὂν ταὐτὸν μῶν οὐ τῆς διαλεκτικῆς φήσομεν ἐπιστήμης εἶναι; (253 D). It is with those which are strictly fundamental among the γένη, εἴδη, or ἰδέαι dealt with by the Dialectician that the *Sophistes* is specially concerned— μὴ περὶ πάντων τῶν εἰδῶν ἀλλὰ τῶν μεγίστων λεγομένων (254 C). The judgement, ὁ λόγος, rests on the conjunction, συμπλοκή, of notions generally (259 E). 'The fundamental kinds of judgement rest on the fundamental kinds of conjunction which run through all conjunctions and make them possible —those between the Logical Categories.'[2] These Categories, or fundamental notions, are given (250 ff.) as five:—

1. τὸ ὄν.
2. στάσις.
3. κίνησις.
4. ταὐτόν.
5. θάτερον.

[1] p. 323.  [2] See Natorp, p. 287.

## PART I: THE SOPHISTES

Here 2 and 3 do not combine with each other; but both do with 1; while 1, 2, and 3 are, each of them, *identical* with itself, i. e. combine with 4, and *different* from the others, i. e. combine with 5; yet 4 and 5 are not merely equivalent to 1, 2, and 3 (254 D). Again, 2 and 3, 4 and 5, are ἐναντία; but 1 has no ἐναντίον, because τὸ μὴ ὄν is only ἕτερον from, not ἐναντίον to, τὸ ὄν (257 B). The absolute μὴ ὄν, indeed, cannot be defined—it is unthinkable; but τὸ μὴ ὄν, as ἕτερον, has its οὐσία as well as τὸ ὄν—'even a negatively determined reality has many predicates'.[1] Moreover, since (263 B) τὸ μὴ ὄν is ἕτερον, false affirmation is possible, and the ostensible purpose of the Dialogue—to show that the Sophist is one who passes off the false as true, is effected. But its real purpose is to show that the absolute separation of Form from Matter, of the Ideas from *sensibilia*, is fatal to Knowledge. Motion and Difference are real. True reality (τὸ παντελῶς ὄν, 248 E) must either have motion in it, or be beyond knowledge; for knowledge involves ποιεῖν and πάσχειν, both of which are denied to the Ideas by 'their friends', the Separatists (248 c).[2]

This doctrine, that the Real contains Motion, means that the Real is Force. The Ideas, *qua* real, are expressions of Force—of the Force inherent only in ψυχή. The Ideas,

[1] Taylor, *Mind*, January, 1897, pp. 21-2.

[2] The τῶν εἰδῶν φίλοι of 248, about whose identity there has been so much difference of opinion, seem to me to be plainly the 'separatists', those who made the Ideas immutable Things—that is, not Megarics, not Plato himself at any period of his career, but his muddle-headed pupils. Dr. Raeder (p. 328) thinks that they are neither Megarics (for the *objections* urged against the Ideas come from them), nor Platonic pupils, but Plato himself in the *Theaet.*, *Phaedo*, *Symp.*, where the Ideas are sharply separated. Professor Taylor (*Mind*, January, 1897, p. 36) makes them 'the historical Megarians'. Grote (*Plato*, ii, 458-60) makes them equivalent to Plato in *Rep.*, *Tim.*, *Phaedo*, *Phaedrus*, *Cratylus*, &c. Dr. Horn (*Platonstudien*, ii, 320) thinks that the reference is quite general to those who believe in separate Ideas. Professor Gomperz (*Greek Thinkers*, iii, 172, Eng. transl.) says, 'By these "friends of the Ideas" Plato meant none other than himself and his adherents—a stroke of humour not intelligible or credible to all Platonic students.' Professor Natorp (p. 284) holds that they are the scholars of the Academy who misunderstood the Doctrine in the sense of making the Ideas Things. This seems to me to be right.

apart from the ψυχή, are not real. The ψυχή alone is real and source of motion (248 E ff.). This is undoubtedly Plato's doctrine in the *Sophistes*,[1] but I do not think, with Dr. Lutoslawski,[2] that it is a new doctrine. Plato always held it. We have it, for example, in the αὐτὴ δι' αὐτῆς ἡ ψυχή of *Theaet.* 185 D,[3] and, indeed, in the doctrine of ἀνάμνησις, mental activity, set forth in the *Meno*. Nor can I follow Dr. Lutoslawski's κλῖμαξ of the development of the Doctrine of Ideas in Plato's mind.[4] The Ideas, he tells us, were (1) immanent, (2) transcendent, (3) models of things, and (4) notions (still, however, *fixed* notions) inherent in a Soul. The Ideas, I take it, were all these from the beginning; although, in the *Sophistes*, their character of being forms of Force, i. e. not quasi-material substances at rest somewhere, but modes of spiritual activity, is dwelt on with more than ordinary insistence. The Idea as δύναμις, set forth in *Soph.* 247 E, is undoubtedly an *aperçu* of the first importance; and Dr. Horn[5] does not exaggerate when he tells us that it is one of the greatest achievements of the genius of Plato. In the *Sophistes*, he tells us, Plato reaches the highest point of his philosophy with the identification of Being (*Sein*) and Force (*Kraft*). But, as I have said, this identification, so prominent in the *Sophistes*, is not new. To ignore it is to make the Ideas *Things*—a misunderstanding which Plato, as I read him, was alive to from an early period in his career, and, if one may judge from the methodology of his earliest pieces, could never have been himself guilty of. Dr. Horn, therefore, seems to me to put in quite a misleading way the difference between the teaching of the *Sophistes* and that of the *Republic* (which, on his view of the chronology of these Dialogues, would be a falling away from the high point reached by the teaching of the *Sophistes*), when he says[6] that, while in the *Sophistes* (as in the *Parmenides*) ὄν and γιγνόμενον are the same thing

---

[1] See Zeller, *Plato*, pp. 261 ff. (Eng .transl.).    [2] pp. 424 ff.
[3] See p. 66, *supra*.    [4] pp. 424 ff. ; cf. pp. 447 ff.
[5] *Platonstudien*, ii, 343, and 319 ff    [6] ii, p. 332.

PART I: THE SOPHISTES 89

viewed from different points of view, in the *Republic* they are sharply opposed. I would put the 'difference' rather in this way—the γιγνόμενον of the *Republic* is the world as not yet sufficiently explained; while in the *Sophistes* it is impressed upon us that explanation consists not in the assignment of a fixed ὄν which shall supervene *ab extra*, and somehow make the γιγνόμενον intelligible, but in the assignment of an ὄν which already contains a γιγνόμενον in itself, is, in fact, a γιγνόμενον which is ὄν, or an ὄν which is γιγνόμενον. The world, it is impressed upon us, is to be explained by the assignment of dynamical, not statical, principles. The 'sharp opposition' between ὄν and γιγνόμενον is not in the *Republic*, but in the minds of those who take certain passages, in that and other Dialogues, *au pied de la lettre*, out of the context of Plato's methodological system. It is against the literal interpretation of these people that the *Sophistes* enters a protest.

### The Politicus.

The *Politicus*, which is the second piece in the trilogy, *Sophistes, Politicus, ⟨Philosophus⟩*, contributes to the Doctrine of Ideas by its insistence on the recognition of τὸ μέτριον—' a definite standard '—as characteristic of the true Statesman (*Pol.* 283–4). There are two kinds of 'measurement', μετρητική, the 'Eleatic stranger' tells the 'younger Socrates', answering to two essentially distinct kinds of quantity: (1) 'mathematical' measurement, where the quantities, the cases of 'great' and 'small', are measured in relation to one another, where 'objects partake of "great" and "small" in relation to one another'; and (2) that kind of measurement (perhaps the adjective 'teleological' expresses its nature most exactly) where 'great' and 'small' are referred not to one another, but to a definite standard, 283 D, E διέλωμεν τοίνυν τὴν μετρητικὴν δύο μέρη ... τῇδε, τὸ μὲν κατὰ τὴν πρὸς ἄλληλα μεγέθους καὶ σμικρότητος κοινωνίαν, τὸ δὲ κατὰ τὴν τῆς γενέσεως ἀναγκαίαν οὐσίαν ... διττὰς ἄρα ταύτας οὐσίας καὶ κρίσεις τοῦ μεγάλου καὶ τοῦ σμικροῦ θετέον, ἀλλ' οὐχ ὡς ἔφαμεν ἄρτι πρὸς ἄλληλα μόνον δεῖν, ἀλλ' ὥσπερ νῦν εἴρηται μᾶλλον τὴν μὲν πρὸς ἄλληλα λεκτέον, τὴν δ' αὖ πρὸς τὸ μέτριον. This second kind of measurement (which I have ventured to call ' teleological ') is that employed by the true Statesman, being that necessitated by the ' essential nature of Becoming '—τὸ δὲ κατὰ τὴν τῆς γενέσεως ἀναγκαίαν οὐσίαν [1]— that relative to ' the production of the *right* quantity ', πρὸς τὴν τοῦ μετρίου γένεσιν (284 D). If any thing ' real ' (having οὐσία) is to arise (γίγνεσθαι), the ' *right* quantity' (*right* in relation to some end qualitatively characterized) must be hit off. The indefinite must be definitely individualized. If reference were not possible to a definite standard or law, Art would be impossible (284 A, B). The μέτριον of the *Politicus*, described generally as the οὐσία which γένεσις aims at, and specially as the end of the true Statesman's endeavour, evidently bears very close comparison with the ἀγαθόν of the *Republic*, the ideal of the true Statesman's Dialectic ; and it is in accordance with the view maintained in the *Sophistes* that this end, or ideal, is presented not as something ' separate ' from the world of sense and motion, but as that which has its *esse* in *fieri*, exists to be realized in the world of sense and motion. Motion has its own real being. The Philosopher-statesman must keep his eye on τὴν τῆς γενέσεως ἀναγκαίαν οὐσίαν.

Comparing the manner in which the Ideal of the Good is conceived in the *Politicus* with that in which it is conceived in the *Republic*, I am inclined to agree with Dr. Raeder [2] that it is conceived in the *Politicus* as more remote ; I do not mean, however, as more of a logical abstraction, but as *an Ideal which is to regulate conduct*, rather than as *a Constitutive Principle, or scheme to be actually embodied in legislation*. For, although Plato, in the works of his old age, the *Politicus* and *Laws*, puts the Ideal further off than

[1] Cf. the γένεσις εἰς οὐσίαν of *Philebus* 26 D, and see Natorp, pp. 308-9, and Raeder, p. 349.

[2] p. 345.

## PART I: THE POLITICUS

he does in the *Republic*, and consequently gives more attention to the actual with its details, it would be a grave error to suppose that he, even sometimes in his old age, lost sight of the vision of his earlier years. It is always with him—the memory of the Golden Age of Cronos handed down to this Iron Age of Zeus. Much that he may have thought practicable when he wrote the *Republic*, he renounced as impracticable when he came to write the *Politicus* and the *Laws*; but that practice must be *regulated*, even at its most workaday level, by ideal theory—that was his firm faith to the end. Dr. Raeder,[1] relying partly on *Epist*. iii. 315 D, and other letters of Plato, thinks that the change apparent in the *Politicus* is due to Plato's recognition of the fact that the younger Dionysius was a Tyrant who could not be made into an Ideal Ruler or Philosopher King. Plato came to despair of the realization of the Ideal State, and devoted his attention to the realization of the best possible State. If Dionysius could not be made into a True King, he might perhaps be made into an Imitator of the True King.

The terms used in the *Politicus* to express the Statesman's end, τὸ μέτριον, τὸ πρέπον, τὸ δέον, τὸ μέσον (as distinguished from τὰ ἔσχατα), and especially ὁ καιρός (284 E), point plainly to the more workaday view of life which now bulks largely in Plato's mind. Contemplation of the Good, as One great System, will still, indeed, be the chief characteristic of what we may call the inner, spiritual, life of the Statesman; but his outer, workaday, life will be concerned more and more with the practicable forms in which *good may be done*, as the occasion requires or permits. In the *Politicus*, as in the *Philebus*, we are concerned with the specific and individual forms which the Good takes, all of them, as οὐσίαι admitting of more or less exact quantitative expression, being objects of science, rather than with the Good itself which, as the *Republic* teaches, is ἐπέκεινα τῆς οὐσίας, transcends science.

[1] pp. 350-1.

## The Philebus.

The subject of the *Philebus* is 'the Good', or, more accurately, 'the relation of Pleasure and of Knowledge respectively to the Good.' Whether we agree or not with those who, like Dr. Raeder,[1] tell us that the answer to the question 'What is the Good?' given 'allegorically' in the *Republic*, is given 'scientifically' in the *Philebus*, is a matter of secondary importance; what is of primary importance is to note that, in the *Philebus*, as in the *Republic*, Pleasure and the Good are distinguished sharply. Pleasure, indeed, gets its due in the rational life, but is shown conclusively not to be the Good. The *ethical* position is the same in both Dialogues. But in his earlier period Plato would have discussed the main subject of the *Philebus*, the Good, as a purely ethical one[2]; now the *Parmenides* is behind him, and logical *Prolegomena to Ethics* are bound to bulk largely. The logical element in the *Philebus* comes in, in connexion with the discussion of the ethical problem of the Good, in this way: The Good involves φρόνησις and ἡδονή; but there are many εἴδη of each—various species of knowledge, various species of pleasure, some of which may be good, some not good. These εἴδη of each, lying between unity and infinity, Dialectic must be able to separate and even to enumerate (*Philebus*, 14 c–19 b—the passage ending with εἴδη γάρ μοι δοκεῖ νῦν ἐρωτᾶν ἡδονῆς ἡμᾶς Σωκράτης εἴτ' ἔστιν εἴτε μή, καὶ ὁπόσ' ἐστὶ καὶ ὁποῖα· τῆς τε αὖ φρονήσεως πέρι κατὰ ταὐτὰ ὡσαύτως [3]). Thus we are led to the general logical problem of predication or judgement—we have to inquire how One can be Many, and Many One, how Different can be the Same, and the Same Different. This, as Professor Natorp reminds us,[4] does not mean, in the *Philebus*, how can the same *thing* have, at the same time, many attributes; but how can notional unities (ἑνάδες, μονάδες), that is, Ideas, be at once Ones and Manys. It is the difficulty of the One-

---

[1] p. 356.  [2] See Natorp, pp. 296-7.
[3] On this passage see Raeder, pp. 360-1.  [4] p. 297.

and-Many, not in the sensible, but in the notional region, that is raised in the *Philebus*.

All predication involves the One-and-Many, πέρας and ἄπειρον, but Dialectic differs from Eristic in going through the steps between Unity and Multiplicity, not leaping at once from Unity to Multiplicity, i. e. in not applying ultimate principles immediately to particulars, but always seeking for proximate principles of explanation : *Phil.* 17 A οἱ δὲ νῦν τῶν ἀνθρώπων σοφοὶ ἓν μέν, ὅπως ἂν τύχωσι, καὶ πολλὰ θᾶττον καὶ βραδύτερον ποιοῦσι τοῦ δέοντος, μετὰ δὲ τὸ ἓν ἄπειρα εὐθύς, τὰ δὲ μέσα αὐτοὺς ἐκφεύγει· οἷς διακεχώρισται τό τε διαλεκτικῶς πάλιν καὶ τὸ ἐριστικῶς ἡμᾶς ποιεῖσθαι πρὸς ἀλλήλους τοὺς λόγους. Here we seem to have an exact parallel to Bacon's insistence on the method which gradually evolves *media axiomata* to take their places in order between particulars and the *axiomata maxime generalia*.

The possibility of the Dialectic which deals with the One-and-Many depends (as we have seen in the *Sophistes*) on the κοινωνία εἰδῶν, on the fact that the categories, or fundamental notions, are severally unities, and yet can combine with one another. The unity of the notion, or Idea, is, as Professor Natorp puts it,[1] nothing but the *unity of determination*. That is, I would explain, the unity of the Idea—so far as its methodological significance is involved—consists in its being a single point of view from which the phenomena are regarded, a single point of view taken of that which otherwise is undetermined. The undetermined, τὸ ἄπειρον, is the necessary correlate of the εἶδος, or determining point of view. Understanding this, we find it easy to dispose of the difficulty about the unity of the Idea being broken up among the particulars: ' the Idea of the circle,' as Professor Taylor says, ' i. e. the circle as defined by its equation in the general form, is not itself properly speaking a curve.'

The μέσα, or τὰ μεταξύ, which Dialectic, thus rendered

[1] p. 300.

possible, fills in between the highest universal, the Good, and particulars, are successive determinations or specifications of that universal in each case of investigation—what Aristotle calls οἰκεῖοι λόγοι.[1] The method of this Dialectic is what Professor Natorp calls [2] the 'concrete-logical'—it is the method of empirical search for Laws of Nature; and the procedure by which it fills in the μέσα, the *media axiomata*, requires numeration and measurement. Science, Plato sees, depends on quantitative data; and when Aristotle speaks of the εἴδη as ἀριθμοί, he is probably expressing this *aperçu* of Plato's. 'The ideal number,' says Professor Taylor,[3] acknowledging indebtedness to M. Milhaud's *Les Philosophes-Géomètres de la Grèce*, 'is a quantitative law by which a unique quality is determined. . . . The ideal number is, in fact, precisely what we know now as the equation to a curve or surface': and Mr. R. G. Bury says,[4] 'The way to attain true knowledge of the sensible world is by mathematical science; to *know* objects in space, to get at their *Ideas*, we must *measure* them and weigh them': and again,[5] 'The *Philebus* aims at establishing a mathematico-scientific method which will apply to all branches of knowledge—to ethics and aesthetics amongst others. *Qua* sciences, their objects must be mathematically determinable.'

The ethical problem of the *Philebus*, in the working out of which all this methodology is introduced, is, it will be remembered, the relation of Pleasure and of Knowledge respectively to the Good. The relation is made clear by inspection of the related objects as they occupy their respective places in a list of ὄντα which is given and explained on pp. 23 c–31 A. These ὄντα, or Principles of Being,[6] are four:—

1. τὸ ἄπειρον ($= x$).
2. τὸ πέρας ($= A$).

---

[1] *Phys.* Θ. 264 a 7, and elsewhere.  [2] p. 301.
[3] *Mind*, Jan. 1903, p. 17, article 'On the First Part of Plato's *Parmenides*'.
[4] *Philebus*, p. 195.   [5] op. cit. p. 200.   [6] See Natorp, p. 304.

# PART I: THE PHILEBUS

3. τὸ μικτόν (= $x$ is $A$).
4. ἡ αἰτία (= cause of $x$ being $A$).

The *first* is all that admits of degrees, such as Temperature. Here we have comparative predicates—'warmer', 'colder', 'more', 'less'.

The *second* is such as 'Equal', 'Double', and comprises all numerical relations.

When τὸ πέρας is rightly applied to τὸ ἄπειρον, real conditions, beautiful and harmonious, arise: this is the *third*—τὸ μικτόν, ἡ γεγενημένη οὐσία (27 B)—in which the Good and Beautiful are realized, Organism which maintains itself against extremes, i.e. the specific type, the τί ἦν εἶναι, I take it, or οὐσία ἄνευ ὕλης, in Aristotelian language, not any concrete embodiment of that type.

The *fourth* is Reason, νοῦς καὶ φρόνησις (as distinguished from Chance, 28 D), described as the creative principle of the universe, τὸ δημιουργοῦν (27 B), and as participated in by man (29 C). It is this 'Universal Reason' which causes, directly, or through the agency of human Reason, that limitation of the unlimited, or indefinite, which is the μικτόν, always a definite ποσόν or μέτριον in each case; but Reason is not itself a part of the μικτόν. This is the inference which we must draw from the fact that the list distinguishes the μικτόν and the αἰτία; and it may be allowable to refer to Aristotle's doctrine [1] of the νοῦς ποιητικός as ἀμιγής for a parallel in corroboration of this inference. The Doctrine thus set forth is that it is only on the basis of mathematically exact determination of $x$ by the appropriate $A$ that empirical science is possible. Plato is convinced that the qualities instanced on p. 25 A, B, warmth, musical tone, can be scientifically determined only by numeration and measurement, i.e. by being treated as quantities, or changing magnitudes.[2] In the phrase (26 D) γένεσις εἰς οὐσίαν Plato, for the first time, so Professor Natorp thinks,[3] gives quite a positive sense to Becoming. Becoming is the

---

[1] *de An.* iii. 430 a 18.   [2] See Natorp, p. 306.   [3] pp. 308-9.

coming into actuality of the determined Being—determined according to the measure of *a* Law of Determination—not *the* general Law of the Determination of the undetermined, but always a special Law of necessarily mathematical form, which establishes for the given Being—or *natura*, as Bacon would say—a 'How-much', a relative 'How-much', a measure-relation.[1]

Professor Natorp asks[2] what the difference is between 3, the self-maintaining organism, the result of the conjunction of πέρας and ἄπειρον, and 4, the αἰτία, the cause of that conjunction. Is the latter a substantive thing? No; for substantive things[3] are due to the conjunction of πέρας and ἄπειρον. What, then, is the difference between the result of this conjunction, the given organism, as Professor Natorp calls it, or organic type, as I should prefer to call it, and the cause of the conjunction? It is the difference, I take it, between a special law of nature, the οἰκεῖος λόγος, as Aristotle would say, of the given organic type—the inquiry after the special law being conducted φυσικῶς as distinguished from λογικῶς—and the whole Universe of Being and Becoming in which special laws inhere. The αἰτία of the *Philebus* is the Idea of Good conceived as Law of Laws. In passing from 3 to 4 we pass, as Professor Natorp puts it,[4] from λόγοι to λόγος αὐτός. Similarly, in *Republic* 517 c, the Idea of the Good is presented as the cause (αἰτία) of all Being and Becoming. In the *Phaedo* (97 A ff.), on the other hand, there is some hesitation about the place of the Good in science. It seems to be held that, although explanation of Being and Becoming by means of the Good, or Ought-to-be (the final cause) is the best explanation, yet there is another kind of explanation with which we must be satisfied—for, indeed, it is the only kind available—explanation by means of the Idea (formal cause) in which the phenomenon to be

[1] See Natorp, pp. 308-9.    [2] p. 312.
[3] The contents of the μικτόν-class are 'substantive', but not, I take it, 'concrete'; they are οὐσίαι, but, as Aristotle would say, ἄνευ ὕλης, specific types or laws, not concrete embodiments of the specific types or laws.
[4] pp. 314-15.

explained 'participates'.[1] This latter kind of explanation is often merely empirical, being equivalent to explanation by means of a proximate law which has not been affiliated to ever higher laws. When, however, the proximate law has been so affiliated, and, at last, is seen to be deducible from ἱκανόν τι (*Phaedo* 101 D), the explanation is, indeed, *scientific*; but, as Plato insists on contrasting it with that by means of the Good, we must suppose that he regards it as lacking something—it is 'mechanical', not 'teleological'. In the *Republic* and *Philebus* he seems to see his way, as he does not in the *Phaedo*, to making a scientific use of teleology. Explanation by means of the Good, or final cause, is no longer contrasted, as an unattainable ideal, with that by means of 'participation' in the Idea, or formal cause; the conception of the Good, as cause of all Being and Becoming, is made to dominate the investigation of all cases of causation.[2]

The Good, thus placed, in the *Philebus*, in the position of First Cause, is described (64 B) as κόσμος ἀσώματος, and is the union of, or presents itself under, three forms, or ἰδέαι—κάλλος, συμμετρία, ἀλήθεια : 65 A εἰ μὴ μιᾷ δυνάμεθα ἰδέᾳ τὸ ἀγαθὸν θηρεῦσαι,[3] σὺν τρισὶ λαβόντες, κάλλει καὶ συμμετρίᾳ καὶ ἀληθείᾳ, λέγωμεν κτλ.—συμμετρία being the ultimate ground of which κάλλος and ἀλήθεια are expressions.

We return now to the ethical question with which the *Philebus* is concerned :—What is the relation of Pleasure

[1] See Natorp, p. 312.

[2] 'Plotinus criticizes, in an extremely important and interesting book, the various systems of Categories abroad in his day (*Enn.* vi. 1-3). He then suggests a system of his own, which consists of the five ideas assumed by Plato in the *Sophist*, together with a final and supreme principle which he calls indifferently Unity, the Good, the Cause of all things, and which, according to him, transcends all existence—i. e. is ἐπέκεινα τῆς οὐσίας. As this phrase occurs only once in Plato (*Rep.* vi. 509 c), it is natural to infer that Plotinus saw in this passage the expression of Plato's mind as to the ultimate cause and principle of the universe.'—Dr. T. B. Strong, *Platonism*, pp. 107-8.

[3] Professor Natorp (p. 330) thinks that the reference here is to the *Republic*.

and of Knowledge respectively to the Good? And the answer is—the three constituents of the Good—Beauty, Measure, and Truth, are more closely allied to Knowledge, φρόνησις, than to Pleasure, ἡδονή. Ἡδονή belongs to the γένος of the ἄπειρον; and φρόνησις, not, indeed, to that of the πέρας, or to that of the μικτόν, but to that of the αἰτία (see 28 D). Accordingly, values are arranged (65 A–67 A) in the order of worth as follows:—

1. Right measure—μέτρον καὶ τὸ μέτριον καὶ καίριον.
2. Proportion and Beauty—τὸ σύμμετρον καὶ καλὸν καὶ τὸ τέλειον καὶ ἱκανόν.
3. Reason—νοῦς, φρόνησις, involving Truth—ἀλήθεια.
[1, 2, 3, all together constitute the Good.]
4. The Sciences, Arts, and Right Opinions—ἐπιστῆμαι, τέχναι, ὀρθαὶ δόξαι.
5. The Pure Pleasures—ἄλυποι, καθαραί, τῆς ψυχῆς αὐτῆς.
[The other Pleasures are not reckoned (66 C).] [1]

The position of the Idea of the Good, then, in the *Philebus* is clear: but, it may be asked, where are the other Ideas in the System of the Dialogue? In which of the four classes of ὄντα distinguished in 23 C–27 C? Plato-scholars have assigned them to all these classes, except, of course, to that of the ἄπειρον as such.[2] Thus Susemihl assigns them to the class of the πέρας, Zeller to that of the αἰτία, and Professor Jackson (at least in *Journal of Philology*, x, pp. 253 ff., 1882) to that of the μικτόν within which they stand, as fixed types, παραδείγματα, by the side of more or less divergent particulars. According to

---

[1] Grote is interesting on this table of values (*Plato*, ii. 617) which he characterizes as follows:—
 1. Unchangeable Ideas, here considered objectively, apart from any percipient Subject affected by them.
 2. Successive manifestations of 1, but considered not only objectively, but subjectively, as affecting, and appreciated by, some percipient.
 3. Rational Mind: here the Subject is brought in by itself apart from the Object.
 4. Here we have intellectual manifestations of the Subject.
 5. Feelings of the Subject to which worth can be ascribed.
[2] See Raeder, pp. 370-1, and Bury, *Philebus*, pp. lxiv ff., for various views.

PART I: THE PHILEBUS 99

Dr. Raeder, who discusses the subject on the pages referred to in the last footnote, the Ideas are Parts of the ἄπειρον separated off by the action of the πέρας brought to bear by Reason, divine and human: and he gives it as his opinion that Professor Jackson's view, which puts the Ideas in the class of the μικτόν, comes nearest to the truth of all the views advanced by Plato-scholars; his own view, if I understand it rightly, being that the μικτόν is an element within the world of Ideas, rather than the class which contains the Ideas. Mr. Bury, on the other hand, in the passage referred to in the last footnote, objects entirely to Professor Jackson's view, on the ground that the Ideas, being absolute independent principles, cannot be placed in the μικτόν, which of all the four classes, he argues, possesses in the least degree the character of a principle. I cannot follow this objection: for surely, as Mr. Bury himself rightly says,[1] the core of the *Philebus*-doctrine of Ideas is the coexistence of Plurality, τὸ ἄπειρον, with Unity in the Ideas. In the *Philebus*, as Dr. Raeder remarks,[2] the Ideas are no longer described as being 'participated in' by things in the manner maintained by the 'young Socrates' of the *Parmenides*; nor are they absolute unities; but each Idea is regarded as having in itself Unity and Plurality, Limitation and the absence of Limitation. This view of the Ideas (which places them, I submit, definitely in the class of the μικτόν) comes nearest, Dr. Raeder points out, to that described by Aristotle, in *Met.* A. 6. 987 b 20 ff., as Platonic—the view of the Ideas as produced by the ἓν operating on the ἀόριστος δυάς, or μέγα καὶ μικρόν. The Ideas, we may say, are specific realizations, in the μικτόν class, of the Force which proceeds from the First Cause, the αἰτία. The Ideas are the various operations of the First Cause—operations which can be mathematically expressed in each case. Without τὸ ἄπειρον to work upon these operations could not take place at all: without the principle of τὸ πέρας they would not have that definiteness

[1] *Philebus*, p. lxx.      [2] p. 372.

which makes them real and objects of knowledge. The
τὸ πέρας class is, in fact, that of 'the mathematical determinants, τὰ μαθηματικά, which Aristotle speaks of as a mediating element, in Platonic theory, between Ideas and sense-objects'.[1] The one Force (αἰτία) operates in various mathematical or mechanical schemata (τὸ πέρας): the realizations of this Force in these schemata are the Ideas (τὸ μικτόν), the one Force variously schematized. If the Good is the Universe, the Ideas are its Laws. The Universe, as finished Whole, is ἐπέκεινα τῆς οὐσίας, a regulative Ideal, and is therefore rightly set forth imaginatively, as in the Sixth Book of the *Republic*, not in scientific terms; but the Ideas, the Laws of the Universe, are severally objects of science, being so many distinct οὐσίαι mathematically determinable. There is, therefore, no contradiction between the teaching of the *Republic* and that of the *Philebus*, as if the former taught that the Good is not to be determined scientifically, while the latter treated it as object of science. It is the Universal Good that the Sixth Book of the *Republic* is solely concerned with, while the *Philebus* deals chiefly with the specific forms taken by the Universal Good. And let me add, these specific forms of the Good, these Ideas, these Laws of the Universe, are Forces; and, as Forces, modes of the activity of ψυχή—World-Soul and Human Soul—the only possessor of Force. That is, the Ideas are agencies which 'make nature', 'mould environment', to meet the needs of *Life*. They express the inmost nature of that which lives—of God, and then of Man so far as he is the image of God. The 'Pragmatism' made popular by Professor W. James and his disciples is not a new gospel. It is already in Plato's *aperçu* of Idea as Force exerted by ψυχή. The 'Intellectualism' which 'Pragmatism,' in our day, opposes, was represented, in Plato's time, not by Plato, but by the εἰδῶν φίλοι, the stiff standers-up for the Thing-like separate Idea whom he combated.[2]

[1] R. G. Bury, *Philebus*, p. lxvii; cf. Taylor, *Mind*, Jan. 1903, p. 17, and see *Met.* K. 1059b 6 τὰ μαθηματικὰ μὲν μεταξύ τε τῶν εἰδῶν τιθέασι καὶ τῶν αἰσθητῶν.

[2] On the 'Intellectualism' of Plato, see Dr. F. C. S. Schiller's article 'Plato and his Predecessors', *Quarterly Review*, Jan. 1906.

## *The Timaeus.*

The *Timaeus* and *Critias*, like the *Sophistes* and *Politicus*, are two parts of a projected trilogy. In the *Timaeus* we have the Creation of the World and of Man; and in the *Critias* (resting on the *Republic*) we have the life and action of Man as citizen of the καλλίπολις, or Ideal State; while in the projected *Hermocrates*, the Best Possible State, under existing conditions, was to have been discussed. The *Hermocrates* was never written; but its subject was taken up in the *Laws*, which thus, as Dr. Raeder remarks,[1] stand to the *Timaeus* and *Republic-Critias* as the *Epinomis*, in lieu of the unwritten *Philosophus*, stands to the *Sophistes* and *Politicus*.

There are two questions to be answered concerning the *Timaeus* regarded as a contribution to the Doctrine of Ideas:—(1) What is the relation of God in the *Timaeus* to the Idea of the Good? and (2) What is the relation of that God to the other Ideas?

In answer to the first question it is easy, but perhaps not sufficient, to say that the God of the *Timaeus* is the personification of the Good of the Sixth Book of the *Republic*:— He created the World because he is good (*Tim.* 27 D–30 B). He is simply the Good figured as a Person. This amounts, I think, to the identification of the God of the *Timaeus* with the Good of the Sixth Book of the *Republic*, and seems to be the view of Adam.[2] Dr. Raeder,[3] objecting to the identification, speaks of the God of the *Timaeus* as 'developed out of' the Idea of the Good, thus differing diametrically from Professor Natorp, who says[4] that, while Plato often personifies the Idea of the Good or Universe of Natural Laws, he is not led away by his metaphors to think of a substantial God existing somewhere: 'it is not the Idea of the Good that becomes God,' he says, 'but God that becomes the Idea of the Good' for Plato.

---

[1] pp. 378-9.  [2] *The Republic of Plato*, vol. ii, pp. 50, 51.
[3] p. 381.  [4] p. 315.

I think that it is misleading to speak of the God of the *Timaeus* as 'developed out of' the Idea of the Good. God and the Good belong to different regions of Plato's thought. As man of science Plato sets up the conception of the Good, the Universe of Natural Laws; as inspired by religious feeling he speaks of God. The two attitudes, the scientific and the religious, are not necessarily antagonistic, they are only different. While, therefore, it is allowable to say that the God of the *Timaeus* is a personification of the Good, of 'the Law of Laws, the Principle of Law Universal, which evolves itself, and thereby produces the concrete world according to the pattern of the Ideas, that is, in accordance with special Laws of Nature',[1] we must be careful not to suppose that the result of the 'personification' is a mere allegory, or illustration of scientific doctrine. It is an allegory, and much more. It is the fusion of the highest scientific conception with the deepest religious conviction. It is as true, or as untrue, to say that the Good is 'developed out of' God, as to say that God is 'developed out of' the Good. The religious conviction of the existence of a Personal God—discontinuous and ecstatic, I think, rather than continuous and habitual, in Plato's mind—and the scientific conception of the Reign of Natural Law interpenetrate each other. While Discourse moves on, tracing out the articulation of the Whole, Contemplation rests, filled with the vision of its vast contour.

As for the second question—the relation of the God of the *Timaeus* to the other Ideas:—the Ideas in the *Timaeus* are independent of God, being the 'patterns', $\pi\alpha\rho\alpha\delta\epsilon\iota\gamma\mu\alpha\tau\alpha$, according to which he creates sensible things (28 A, B). In the *Republic* (x. 597 B), where also God is substituted for the Good, God is the creator of Being, of the Ideas; whereas, in the *Timaeus*, he is the Creator only of Becoming, of sensible things, according to the pattern of the independent Ideas. It is tempting to reconcile the difference

[1] Natorp, pp. 340-1.

## PART I: THE TIMAEUS

between the *Republic* and *Timaeus*, by saying, with Dr. Lutoslawski[1] and others, that the Ideas in the *Timaeus* are the 'thoughts of God', and, as such, are at once caused by him, and yet different from him; but there is nothing in the *Timaeus* quite to warrant this interpretation, although there is nothing distinctly against it, and it is a view of the relation of the Ideas to God which afterwards prevailed in the Platonic School.

The Ideas, then, in the *Timaeus*, are the 'patterns', according to which God, figured for the imagination as an artificer, 'makes' sensible things; and the absolute separation of these Ideas from sensible things is maintained—παρουσία and μέθεξις seem to be absolutely excluded—52 A ὁμολογητέον ἓν μὲν εἶναι τὸ κατὰ ταὐτὰ εἶδος ἔχον, ἀγέννητον καὶ ἀνώλεθρον, οὔτε εἰς ἑαυτὸ εἰσδεχόμενον ἄλλο ἄλλοθεν οὔτε αὐτὸ εἰς ἄλλο ποι ἰόν, ἀόρατον δὲ καὶ ἄλλως ἀναίσθητον, τοῦτο ὃ δὴ νόησις εἴληχεν ἐπισκοπεῖν. Because the *Timaeus* seems to ignore the criticism of the Doctrine of Ideas in the *Parmenides, Sophistes*, and *Philebus*, and reverts to the position of the *Phaedo* and *Republic*, where the Ideas, he thinks, are absolutely separate from particulars, M. Tocco,[2] referred to by Dr. Raeder, puts it earlier than the *Parmenides*, &c. Against M. Tocco Dr. Raeder argues,[3] I think soundly, that the Doctrine of Ideas in the *Timaeus* does avoid the criticism of the *Parmenides*, because it makes the two elements of Unity and Plurality appear in the Ideas as well as in particulars; and finite Souls can apprehend the Ideas, because these Souls, as well as the World-Soul with which they are consubstantial, contain the same two elements, ἡ ταὐτοῦ φύσις and ἡ θατέρου φύσις (35 A, and elsewhere), as are found in the Ideas themselves. The indissoluble connexion between Unity and Plurality is, Dr. Raeder holds,[4] an axiom with Plato since the *Parmenides*: there is no

---

[1] p. 477.
[2] *Ricerche platoniche*, p. 148 and in *Studi italiani di filologia classica*, ii. 405 ff.
[3] pp. 392-3.     [4] p. 382.

longer the view of the World of Ideas as Unity standing over against that of Particulars as Plurality. The World of Ideas, in the *Timaeus*, indeed stands 'separate' from the World of Particulars, but *both* worlds contain the elements of Unity and Plurality, Limitation and the Unlimited, both contain a Formal and a Material element. We may say, he thinks,[1] that the element of Identity and Indivisibility makes the *essential* nature of the Ideas, and that of Difference and Divisibility the *essential* nature of sensible particulars; yet, in both, both elements are found. Dr. Raeder, in fact, thinks [2] that the *Timaeus* is a reconstruction of the Doctrine of Ideas after the criticism of the *Parmenides* and similar Dialogues. Be this as it may, the 'eternal patterns' of the *Timaeus*, stripped of their mythological vestments, are, as Professor Natorp says,[3] 'merely the predicates of scientific judgements.'

Up to 48 E the *Timaeus* assumes only two γένη—Ideas, and sensible particulars. But now a third γένος is added— that of an original Matter, or Substrate, which mediates between Idea and sensible particular. This original Matter, or Substrate, called ὑποδοχή (49 A), and identified with pure space, χώρα (52 A),[4] is, as it were, the Mother, while the Idea is the Father, of whom sensible things are the progeny (50 D). Between Idea and original Matter or Substrate there is a certain resemblance: neither can be perceived by the senses, and the latter, like the former, is eternal and unchangeable. Is this original Matter, this Substrate, this pure Space, an *intelligibile*, then, equally with the Idea ? No: it is not apprehended by intellect, but reached by 'sham reasoning, independently of sense': it is, that is to say, a pure abstraction, and indeed hardly realizable as object of consciousness—52 A, B τρίτον δὲ αὖ γένος ὂν τὸ τῆς χώρας ἀεί, φθορὰν οὐ προσδεχόμενον, ἕδραν δὲ παρέχον ὅσα ἔχει γένεσιν πᾶσιν, αὐτὸ δὲ μετ' ἀναισθησίας ἁπτὸν λογισμῷ τινι νόθῳ, μόγις πιστόν· πρὸς ὃ δὴ καὶ ὀνειροπολοῦμεν

---

[1] p. 385.  [2] p. 394.  [3] p. 351.
[4] See Mr. Archer-Hind's note, *Timaeus*, p. 182.

βλέποντες καί φαμεν ἀναγκαῖον εἶναί που τὸ ὂν ἅπαν ἔν τινι τόπῳ καὶ κατέχον χώραν τινά, τὸ δὲ μήτ' ἐν γῇ μήτε που κατ' οὐρανὸν οὐδὲν εἶναι. It does not itself 'become'; but it is the place where 'becoming' occurs.[1] It is, as Professor Natorp explains,[2] nothing but pure geometrical Space, regarded, however, as foundation of, or principle rendering possible, the sensible world:[3] this is made clear by the derivation of the 'four elements', which are shaped out of unqualified Space 'according to forms and numbers'—εἴδεσι καὶ ἀριθμοῖς (53 B)—i.e. according to geometrical and arithmetical conditions. 'In the *Timaeus*', concludes Professor Natorp,[4] 'Plato comes nearest, with his doctrine of χώρα as Substrate, to recognizing the Being of the Sensible World. Space is a fixed abiding system of positions, in relation to which the change of predicates can be viewed as something definite, and "Hold on Being" attained to. And yet, while Space is assumed as fundamental, Plato's procedure is through and through *logical*, relying on nothing but the laws which condition judgement, the conditions underlying the definite relations of the predicates of Thinking to the $x$ of Experience. "Idea as Law," and "Law in indissoluble correlation with the problematic[5] objects of Experience"—that is the key to the understanding of the *Timaeus*, a work which, since Aristotle, has been misunderstood in the most obstinate manner.'

[1] See, along with Archer-Hind, *Timaeus*, ad loc., Natorp, pp. 353 ff., and Raeder, p. 388.
[2] p. 355.
[3] A suggestive parallel to Plato's doctrine of the ὑποδοχή is found in M. Bergson's doctrine of succession in Time and juxtaposition in Space as symbolizing 'Pure Duration'; see his *Les Données immédiates de la Conscience*, and *L'Évolution créatrice*.
[4] pp. 357-8.
[5] 'Problematic,' because the attitude is critical, not dogmatic. Criticism accentuates the point that the object is only an $x$, always a *problem*, never a *datum*—a problem to be solved in relation to the Laws of Thought. See Natorp, p. 367.

*The Laws.*

The *Laws* do not contribute anything fresh to the Doctrine of Ideas; but the Doctrine is distinctly affirmed in them; and it is interesting to note that, in this, his latest work, as in his earliest works, it is on the 'one Idea of *Virtue*' that Plato dwells (xii. 965 c–966 a). There is no trace, in the *Laws*, of a 'later doctrine' in which only Ideas of 'natural kinds' are retained.

This concludes my detailed review of the Dialogues as contributing to the Doctrine of Ideas on its methodological side. Before summing up, however, the results of the review, I must devote a few pages to Aristotle's criticism.

# ARISTOTLE'S CRITICISM OF THE DOCTRINE OF IDEAS

THE view of the meaning and value of the Doctrine of Ideas as contribution to methodology which I have taken, in independent agreement with Professor Natorp, is diametrically opposed to that taken by Aristotle and generally accepted since his time as correct.

The reason for the prevailing misunderstanding of the Doctrine doubtless, as Professor Natorp says,[1] lies, deeper than mere deference to the authority of Aristotle, in the inability of dogmatism to understand the critical position. For criticism the object is only an $x$, always a *problem*, never a *datum*, a problem to be solved in relation to the Forms of Thought. In the Aristotelian Doctrine of Categories, which so often comes up where Aristotle is engaged in criticizing the Doctrine of Ideas, the assumption always is that Things, *as Things*, are given. 'Substance' is always assumed by Aristotle as given once for all.[2] But, in truth, it is not given; it is built up to suit our needs. Object is what *we* posit as one and identical: object, as 'Substance', is what we set up as identical meeting-point of our statements—always with relative, never with absolute, claim to this position.[3]

Professor Natorp's discussion of Aristotle's attitude to Plato is so informing, and takes the line which I have so long[4] regarded as the only correct one, that I offer no apology for allowing his order and manner of statement to guide me to a considerable extent in the following sketch: where I do not agree with Professor Natorp, I shall say so;

---

[1] pp. 366-7.   [2] See Natorp, pp. 380-2.   [3] See Natorp, p. 388.
[4] See my *Notes on the Nic. Ethics* (1892), vol. i, pp. 71 ff.

but, as I agree substantially with his interpretation of the Doctrine of Ideas on its methodological side, so do I agree substantially with his estimate of Aristotle's criticism of the Doctrine on that side—substantially, for the other side of the Doctrine, as expressing aesthetic experience, Professor Natorp does not consider at all; and this omission seems to me to make itself felt sometimes to the disadvantage of his treatment of the methodological side, just as Aristotle's like omission injures, though much more seriously, his criticism of that side of the Doctrine for which alone, like Professor Natorp, he has an eye.

Two passages in *Met.* Z indicate the basis—his own Doctrine of οὐσία, or Substance—on which Aristotle's criticism of the Idea rests. Substance is treated in two ways in Z : (1) in chapters 4–6 and 10–14 it is treated logically, as Content of Definition, Principle of Scientific Explanation, Form, τί ἦν εἶναι; (2) in chapters 7–9 it is treated as a Dynamic Principle, a Principle of Actual Production, operating in the region of the physical sciences.

Aristotle's criticism of the Doctrine of Ideas, in *Met.* A. 6, 9, in Z. 13, 14, and in M. 4, 5, 9, 10, accordingly falls under two heads [1] corresponding to his double treatment of Substance : (1) it deals with the relation of the Universal to the Particular, with the *Idea as Form*, or Principle of Scientific Explanation—a logical inquiry; (2) it deals with the *Idea as Source of Motion*, or Principle of Actual Production—a question of physics rather than of logic.

How, then, in the first place, does the Idea compare with Aristotle's own Form as a Principle of Scientific Explanation —how does it satisfy the conditions which a Principle of Scientific Explanation must satisfy ? Aristotle's answer is that it does not satisfy these conditions. It is merely a double of the thing to be explained, not an explanation of it (*Met.* B. 2, 997 b ff., and elsewhere). We have seen, throughout our review of the Dialogues, how mistaken this criticism

---

[1] See Natorp, p. 400, and cf. Zeller, *Aristotle*, vol. i, p. 326 (Eng. transl.).

## PART I: ARISTOTLE'S CRITICISM

is. The Idea is not itself Thing, but explanation of things. If Plato had got his Idea by hypostatizing the predicate (e. g. 'good' or 'small') viewed out of relation to the subject, Aristotle might have had some ground for his objection to the Doctrine. But Plato is always bringing the predicate into relation with the subject, and regards the Idea as 'known' only in so far as found applicable to the explanation of Experience.[1] It is, indeed, a sufficient reply to Aristotle's criticism of the Idea as Form to ask, 'Are the scientific laws which explain phenomena merely doubles of these phenomena?' The Ideas have the Reality of 'Validity', as distinguished, by Lotze, from the Reality of 'Existence';[2] and one is fain to believe that Aristotle had a glimpse of this: his δύναμις-explanation (*Met.* M. 10), which I shall have to refer to immediately, is, rightly understood, equivalent, I would submit, to Lotze's 'Validity'-explanation; and the same may be said of what I have always regarded as the most valuable *aperçu* in Professor Jackson's discussions of the Doctrine of Ideas, his view that 'the existence of the Ideas is only hypothetical'.[3]

The best measure we can have, I think, of Aristotle's want of success as a critic of Plato is to be found in the fact that, partly in consequence of his efforts to meet difficulties belonging to his own doctrine of Substance as Form, and partly in consequence of his initial misunderstanding of Plato's Doctrine of Ideas, he comes out naïvely, in the end, with a Doctrine which differs only in phraseology from

[1] See Natorp, p. 403.
[2] See Lotze, *Logic*, pp. 440 ff. (Eng. transl., 1st ed.). Professor Natorp (pp. 195–6) enters an objection, which I cannot regard as a serious one, against Lotze's view; and Adam (*Republic*, vol. ii, p. 170) says, 'nor indeed can I believe that any scholar who is capable of understanding Greek could read books v–vii of the *Republic* and still agree with Lotze.' Literal translation of Plato's Greek may seem to be against Lotze's view; but psychological interpretation, I feel sure, will eventually establish it.
[3] *Journal of Philology*, vol. xiii, pp. 26 ff. Von Hartmann's view (*Phil. des Unbew.* p. 805, 2nd ed.) is the same: 'die Ewigkeit der Ideen ist nicht als ewige, wenn auch nur ideale, *Existenz*, sondern nur als ewige Präformation oder Möglichkeit zu verstehen'—just the view of Leibniz too: see *Monadologie*, § 44.

Plato's rightly understood. Let me now offer some observations to substantiate this statement, premising that, in doing so, I shall have to part company from Professor Natorp on an important matter of Aristotelian interpretation.

In *Met*. B. 4–6 certain ἀπορίαι are started, raising the question—Are scientific principles Universals or Particulars? If they are Universals, they are not Substances; if they are Particulars, there can be no scientific knowledge of them: *Met*. B. 6. 1003 a 5 ff. ταύτας τε οὖν τὰς ἀπορίας ἀναγκαῖον ἀπορῆσαι περὶ τῶν ἀρχῶν, καὶ πότερον καθόλου εἰσὶν ἢ ὡς λέγομεν τὰ καθ' ἕκαστα. εἰ μὲν γὰρ καθόλου, οὐκ ἔσονται οὐσίαι· οὐθὲν γὰρ τῶν κοινῶν τόδε τι σημαίνει, ἀλλὰ τοιόνδε, ἡ δ' οὐσία τόδε τι ... εἰ δὲ μὴ καθόλου ἀλλὰ ὡς τὰ καθ' ἕκαστα, οὐκ ἔσονται ἐπιστηταί. The solution comes in M. 10—the δύναμις of knowledge is always universal and indefinite, and has an object corresponding; but actual knowledge is always definite and has a definite object—1087 a 15 ἡ γὰρ ἐπιστήμη, ὥσπερ καὶ τὸ ἐπίστασθαι, διττόν, ὧν τὸ μὲν δυνάμει τὸ δὲ ἐνεργείᾳ. ἡ μὲν οὖν δύναμις ὡς ὕλη καθόλου οὖσα καὶ ἀόριστος τοῦ καθόλου καὶ ἀορίστου ἐστίν, ἡ δὲ ἐνέργεια ὡρισμένη καὶ ὡρισμένον τόδε τι οὖσα τοῦδέ τινος. But this is only an apparent solution, Professor Natorp tells us[1]: there is still a hiatus between knowledge and its object—knowledge is universal, its object is particular; for Aristotle cannot conceive anything not substance—that is, anything not *concrete* substance—as prior to substance; he cannot conceive the logical *prius* of the concrete as not itself concrete. It is here, at the words 'anything not *concrete* substance as prior to substance', that I am obliged to part company from Professor Natorp. Surely he forgets Aristotle's οὐσία ἄνευ ὕλης (*Met*. Z. 7. 1032 b 14). Let me, then, leave Professor Natorp for a while, in order to show that although Aristotle misunderstands and misstates Plato's Doctrine of Ideas grossly, yet what he opposes to that Doctrine, as misunderstood and misstated by himself, is a Doctrine of *Laws*, not of concrete,

[1] p. 402.

## PART I: ARISTOTLE'S CRITICISM

or quasi-concrete, *Things*—a Doctrine practically identical with Plato's Doctrine rightly understood.

Aristotle, we must always bear in mind, is, after all, the greatest of the Platonists, although the most persistently hostile critic of Plato and his School. 'Aristotle's whole system,' says Zeller,[1] 'cannot truly be understood until we treat it as a development and evolution of that of Plato, and as the completion of that very Philosophy of Ideas which Socrates founded and Plato carried on.'

The line taken by Aristotle in his criticism of Platonic doctrine is determined by two influences—by his logical formalism, and by his interest in the facts of natural history. He was at once a great logician, and a great naturalist—especially, it is important to note, in the field of biology, for his work in that of inorganic nature is nearly always carried on according to the methods of the mere logician rather than of the naturalist.

As logician, he starts from Platonic premises; as naturalist, he is always tempted to traverse Platonic premises.

The premises which he has in common with Plato are: that the Form, or Idea, is the Real; and that true knowledge is concerned with that, not with particulars of sense. 'As Socrates and Plato always began,' says Zeller,[2] 'by asking for the "idea" of each thing they dealt with, and set this kind of cognition as the basis of all other knowledge, so also does Aristotle delight to begin with an inquiry into the "idea" of whatever his subject for the time being may be.'

As naturalist, on the other hand, he speaks as though particular objects alone were fully real; and universals—said, nevertheless, to be the true objects of scientific knowledge—were only real in a secondary way.

Thus we seem to have a contradiction in the Aristotelian teaching—the contradiction, in fact, or hiatus, which Professor Natorp, in the passage referred to above, finds so

---

[1] *Aristotle*, i. 162 (Eng. transl.).    [2] *Aristotle*, i. 171 (Eng. transl.).

serious: If the Form, or Idea, is the object of true knowledge, it is universal; and if it is universal it cannot be fully real, truly 'substantial', for Substance, or οὐσία, is individual or particular, not universal.

Professor Natorp, it is to be noted, has Zeller to back him in thinking that this 'contradiction' remains, to the end, in the Aristotelian Philosophy. 'The true essence,' says Zeller,[1] ' of things is to be found (Aristotle holds) in their concept, and this is always universal ... but this universal (he holds) has no existence apart from the individual, which he therefore declares to be substance. He cannot explain how these two positions may coexist in one philosophy'; and again,[2] he says that Aristotle is involved 'in the contradiction of maintaining that the essence and substance of things is the form, which at the same time is a universal, and yet that the source of individuality and therefore also of substantiality must be the matter'. This 'contradiction' Zeller regards as one 'which threatens to shake the very foundations of the system'.[3] 'Hard as Aristotle tries to bring form and matter together, still to the last they always remain *two* principles, of which we can neither deduce one from the other nor both from a third.... In this way Aristotle is at once the perfection and the ending of the Idealism of Socrates and Plato.'[4] 'The Aristotelian doctrine may be described as alike the completion and the confutation of the Platonic.'[5]

I venture here to differ from Zeller. My view is that Aristotle's doctrine of Form as the true object of scientific knowledge is not inconsistent with itself; and further, that, in this doctrine, Aristotle unwittingly develops and makes explicit Plato's Doctrine of Ideas, as Plato himself meant it —namely, that the ἰδέα, the object of true knowledge, is not a 'universal substance', but an 'individual substance' —not, however, a concrete individual, but an *abstract individual*, unique, not to be co-ordinated with the indi-

---

[1] *Aristotle*, i. 377.  [2] *Aristotle*, ii. 342-3.  [3] *Aristotle*, i. 374.
[4] *Aristotle*, i. 180.  [5] *Aristotle*, ii. 338.

viduals of sense—a *Law of Nature*, which we come to see 'cannot be otherwise', the Universe, or Good, being what it is, as distinguished from an 'empirical law', or 'universal of sense', which is a uniformity perceived, by itself, out of the context of the Good. Science, in other words, is concerned with the *cause why* an indefinite number of particulars are qualified, and behave, in a certain way. We first come to know empirically *that* they are qualified, and behave, in this way, and we make a general statement to the effect—speak καθόλου about them. But we have yet to discover *why* they are all qualified, and behave, in this way, and cannot be qualified and behave otherwise. This *why* is 'individual essence'—the οὐσία, or 'substance', which science aims at knowing, and makes the first principle of its explanations.

'Individual essence', then, so understood, is what Plato means by 'Idea'; while Aristotle, describing the 'Idea' as χωριστὸν εἶδος, and κεχωρισμένη οὐσία, misses Plato's meaning, and accuses him, notwithstanding the *Parmenides* and *Rep.* x. 597 c, and much other evidence, of making it a Thing co-ordinate with the things which it is brought in to explain. But, indeed, χωριστὸν εἶδος, or κεχωρισμένη οὐσία, may be taken to express—and I do not think that it expresses badly—the meaning conveyed by οὐσία ἄνευ ὕλης, Aristotle's definition of his own τί ἦν εἶναι (*Met.* Z. 7. 1032 b 14). Aristotle's quarrel with the Doctrine of Ideas is that it makes these χωριστὰ εἴδη, these separate and abstracted οὐσίαι, the objects of scientific knowledge, and therefore καθόλου, which they cannot be (*Met.* M. 10. 1087 a 10 ff.); yet he himself maintains that science has always to do with οὐσία—that is, with οὐσία **ἄνευ ὕλης**. When he says, therefore, that science has to do with τὰ καθόλου, he means—so I would interpret him—that its propositions are 'universal and necessary', relating, as they do, to phenomena viewed, not as mere separate particulars, but as effects of laws, i. e. effects of the causal agency of οὐσίαι ἄνευ ὕλης, κεχωρισμέναι οὐσίαι, χωριστὰ εἴδη, each one of which is, indeed, one, unique, individual. For Aristotle (as for Plato) there are thus two kinds of οὐσία, or 'individual essence'—the concrete (Καλλίας), and the abstract (αὐτοάνθρωπος, τὸ ἀνθρώπῳ εἶναι). The former is marked off by its own peculiar matter; the latter is Idea, Form, Law, the true object of science; not itself a 'universal', or mere 'common quality', but the one individual cause why certain things have the common quality, the one individual cause of many similar effects, which, as similar, can be summarily described in a 'universal, or general, proposition'—καθόλου. *The many effects resemble one another, and can be described* καθόλου; *but their common cause is one and individual.* The progress of science may be expressed in the following formula: 1. Callias, Socrates, Crito, &c.; 2. ἄνθρωπος; 3. τὸ ἀνθρώπῳ εἶναι, or 1. marble, snow, foam, &c.; 2. white; 3. whiteness, i. e. the scientific account (if possible, mathematically expressed) of why things are seen 'white'.

Form, then, or the Idea, as Cause is the 'real' or 'essential' to be sought for by science in all its inquiries. But Form must not be taken apart from Matter. This was how Aristotle, as naturalist, corrected the Platonic tendency as he regarded it. Platonism, he thought, tended to acquiesce in bare statements of 'natural laws', and neglected the work of following out their manifestations in the phenomena. 'There is nothing,' says Zeller,[1] 'in the Platonic system which is so distasteful to Aristotle as that dualism between idea and phenomenon which expressed itself sharply in the doctrine of the absolute existence of the ideas, and of the non-reality of matter. His opposition to this dualism is the key-note of his whole reconstruction of the Platonic metaphysics, and of the fundamental ideas peculiar to his own system. And yet earnest and thorough as are his efforts to overcome it, he has not, after all, succeeded in doing so.' That is, according to Zeller, Aristotle fails to trace Form and Matter back to a common

[1] *Aristotle*, ii. 342.

source. Here Zeller seems to me to exaggerate the 'dualism' in Plato which Aristotle is said to strive earnestly, though unsuccessfully, to overcome. Plato was really with Aristotle in deprecating the dualism, in maintaining the necessity of a concrete view of the world. What is the apprehension of the ἰδέα τἀγαθοῦ (criticized by Aristotle in such puerile fashion) but a concrete view of the world as a whole, every part of which exists and is known only in virtue of belonging to the whole? This concrete view is the goal of all education. It can be taken only by those who have mastered the details, as well as the methods, of the special sciences; and when a man thinks that he has attained to it he must beware, for if he acquiesces in the ἰδέα τἀγαθοῦ as it first presents itself to him, it soon becomes a mere abstraction for him. He must always busy himself with the content of it; he must re-examine, in the light of it, the steps by which he has reached it; having pieced together the mere particulars of sense-experience into groups, and these groups into a fairly consistent whole, he must return again with the conception of this whole in his mind, to these particulars and these groups—now no longer *mere* particulars, and possibly *arbitrary* groups, but members of one system—and try to give them still further articulation. This double process of συναγωγή and διαίρεσις he is to carry on, backward and forward, till he attains to that σαφήνεια which amounts to the certitude of truth, to the conviction that this or that 'cannot be otherwise' as member of the clearly perceived System of the Good, or Kingdom of Ideas.

No better general account of the procedure of science, as we now understand it, could be given than Plato's account of the Dialectical Method at the end of the Sixth Book of the *Republic*. But, although Plato himself is as opposed as Aristotle is to the habit of acquiescing in abstract theory—in theory which cannot be, or is not, verified by application to particular cases—the Platonic School doubtless showed a leaning towards abstract theory, and neglected 'natural history'. Against this tendency of the School the Aristotelians protested, perhaps too much. Zeller points out [1] that Aristotle's immediate successors 'brought the purely naturalistic view of the world more and more into prominence, to the neglect of the spiritual side of things'.

Aristotle's first main objection, then, to the Platonic Doctrine of Ideas is that it fails as a theory of Scientific Explanation.

His second main objection is that it gives no account of Change. How can a thing act, he seems to ask, where it is not? But that Plato regarded the Ideas as *in* things, as principles operative within—very like Aristotle's own φύσις [2]—is proved, to any candid reader, not only by the frequent occurrence of such terms as παρεῖναι, ἐνεῖναι, ἐγγίγνεσθαι,[3] but by the whole drift of his Dialogues, more especially of such dialogues as the *Parmenides, Sophistes*, and *Philebus*. The difficulty raised in *De Gen. et Corr.* B. 9. 335 b 9–24 may be taken as a good example of Aristotle's failure to appreciate all that these above-mentioned Dialogues contend for. If the Ideas are eternal, and Matter, τὸ μεθεκτικόν, is also eternal (as the *Timaeus* teaches), why, he asks, are concrete things produced only now and then, not always? Why does the Idea of Health not always keep us healthy, without the intervention of the Doctor? To this puerile question, the best answer is another question: Why do 'natural laws' not always operate? The 'validity' of the law and the actual occurrence of instances of it are two entirely different things.

The development of the Doctrine of Ideas into a Theory of Ideal Numbers, of which little trace is found in Plato's works, although it appeared in his later oral teaching, and was carried out by his School till it resulted in a return to Pythagoreanism, attracted Aristotle most. The germ of

---

[1] *Aristotle*, ii. 347.
[2] I find the similarity between Plato's παρουσία and Aristotle's φύσις noted in M. Robin's *Théorie Platonicienne des Idées et des Nombres d'après Aristote* (1908), p. 116.
[3] See Natorp, p. 409.

this development, however, as Professor Natorp (after Zeller) points out,[1] is in the *Philebus* (best proof of its late date) 16 D ff. τὸν ἅπαντα ἀριθμὸν μεταξὺ τοῦ ἑνὸς καὶ τοῦ ἀπείρου. The meaning of this passage in the *Philebus*, as we have seen,[2] is that between the One, or most general Law of all, and phenomena we must interpolate more and more special laws, *media axiomata*, and find for these mathematical expressions; there can be no exact science otherwise.

It is in *Met*. M. 4. 1078 b 9 ff. that Aristotle distinguishes between the original Doctrine of Ideas and its development into a Doctrine of Ideal Numbers; but *Philebus* 16 D ff. shows that this was quite a natural development. It is as *numbers* (i. e. special laws mathematically expressed) that the Ideas are applied to, appear in, particulars.[3] *Philebus* 16 D ff. stands behind Aristotle's statement in *Met*. A. 6. 987 b 21 that 'out of the great-and-small, by participation in the One, come the Ideas as Numbers', ἐξ ἐκείνων (τοῦ μεγάλου καὶ τοῦ μικροῦ) κατὰ μέθεξιν τοῦ ἑνὸς τὰ εἴδη εἶναι τοὺς ἀριθμούς.[4]

In the εἰδητικοὶ ἀριθμοί, however, we must note, with Bonitz[5] and Professor Natorp,[6] that the notion of Number is extended. The εἰδητικοὶ ἀριθμοί differ *qualitatively*, and the πρότερον καὶ ὕστερον which obtains between them is logical—that of condition and conditioned. Professor Natorp suggests[7] that if we think of algebraic letters, we shall come near to Plato's thought here. To bring the logical relations in which Qualities stand to each other into mathematical form is Plato's thought here—a great thought, as Professor Natorp justly says. That the Doctrine of 'the Idea as Number'—the Idea, so regarded, being a Law

---

[1] pp. 413-14.　　　　　　　　[2] pp. 93-4, *supra*.
[3] See Natorp, pp. 414-15.
[4] 'The circle as defined by its equation, like the ideal number, is at once many, as synthesizing an indefinite plurality of positions, and one, as synthesizing them in accord with a definite law.'—A. E. Taylor, *Mind*, Jan. 1903, p. 19.
[5] *Met*. p. 540.　　　　[6] pp. 419-20.　　　　[7] p. 420.

mathematically expressed—is a *natural development* of the teaching of the *Philebus*—this discovery, due to Zeller, and worked out by M. Milhaud,[1] Professor Taylor, Mr. R. G. Bury, and Professor Natorp, 'lays the ghost,' to use Zeller's words, ' of an " Esoteric Platonism".'[2]

[1] *Les Philosophes géomètres de la Grèce.*
[2] M. Robin (*La Théorie Platonicienne des Idées et des Nombres d'après Aristote*, p. 591) summarizes his elaborate examination of the εἰδητικοὶ ἀριθμοί as follows : ' Les Idées sont des relations organisées ou déterminées selon des types plus simples, qui sont les Nombres idéaux ; de même les choses sensibles sont des relations déterminées et organisées selon des types, moins simples sans doute que les précédents, mais simples pourtant, qui sont les Idées. Les choses sensibles imitent l'organisation des Idées, comme les Idées imitent celle des Nombres idéaux.' This, too, seems to mean that the Ideas, as Numbers, are laws for which quantitative expression has been found. Professor Jackson's view (*Journal of Philology*, vol. x, pp. 287 ff.), according to which, in the 'later theory of Ideas', the numbers, which are the formal causes of particulars, are *not* the ideas, the ideas being mere types or models, from which the particulars caused by the numbers more or less diverge, is, it may be noted, criticized by M. Robin, pp. 303 ff., and rejected chiefly on the ground of its inconsistency with the testimony of Aristotle.

# SUMMARY OF FIRST PART

Let me now close this First Part by summing up the results of our examination of the Doctrine of Ideas as Contribution to Methodology.

What does the Doctrine of Ideas, on its methodological side, stand for in Plato's mind?

When Plato speaks of εἴδη he is generally thinking of *what the scientific man tries to discover* by his inquiries; but *the native categories which human understanding must employ* in any process of scientific discovery he also calls εἴδη, even characterizing them as τὰ μέγιστα τῶν εἰδῶν.[1]

First, then, we have the εἶδος as that which the scientific man tries, in each special inquiry, to discover. This is the *Law* which explains the facts—the Law, the Cause, the Use, the Context, the Right Point of View; for it is advisable to find different expressions for different cases.

The facts with which the earlier Dialogues are concerned are moral and social. The approved courses taken by men, in certain circumstances, are marked by such adjectives as *courageous, temperate, just,* and the dispositions corresponding are named *Courage, Temperance, Justice*. Now, it is obvious that particular courses or dispositions popularly called by any one of these names differ considerably; and the thoughtful man asks, How shall I know which of them are, and which of them are not, rightly entitled to the name? I want to know what Courage *is*, what Temperance *is*, what Justice *is*. This amounts to wanting to know what is the right point of view from which to regard the qualities called by the names of 'Courage', 'Temperance', 'Justice'. How, then, are we to regard them? Surely, in the light of the

[1] *Soph.* 254 c.

System to which they belong; for thoughtful consideration is distinguished from thoughtlessness just by this, that it does not take things separately, but in their connexions: it is feeling, as distinguished from thought, which takes things separately. The 'right point of view', then, from which to look at Courage or Temperance, is that point from which it is seen in its proper place in the Social System. It must be viewed as a special exhibition of ἀρετή, that is, as a way of behaving required by Human Nature as such— by man as living up to his Type in the World in which he finds himself. To determine Type and World is, indeed, a complex problem, which cannot be solved by repeating current names, and allowing oneself to follow the lead of the feelings associated with these names: it is a problem which can be solved only by *reflection*. It is only ἀρετή— consciousness of the Social System, and of his own membership of it, so clear in a man that it *obliges* him to serve that System—it is only ἀρετή which can 'know' ἀρετή— πονηρία μὲν γὰρ ἀρετήν τε καὶ αὐτὴν οὔποτ' ἂν γνοίη, ἀρετὴ δὲ φύσεως παιδευομένης χρόνῳ ἅμα αὐτῆς τε καὶ πονηρίας ἐπιστήμην λήψεται (*Rep.* iii. 409 D, E). This, it may be said in passing, is what is meant by the Socratic 'Virtue is Knowledge'.

The εἶδος, then, of Courage or of Temperance is the whole setting of the quality so named—its *context*. To fill in context is the problem of science; and if we say that the discovery of the εἶδος, or ἰδέα, the *inventio formae*, in any inquiry, is 'the adequate filling in of context round about the object of inquiry', we are using the phrase which perhaps covers the ground better than any other: the εἶδος is the *causal context*. Thus the εἶδος of Courage is stated when the virtue so-called is defined in relation to the part which it plays in the Social System—when its 'final cause', or 'use', is set forth—when the standing need which it meets, and the particular manner in which it meets that need, have been fully explained. Here we have what the discovery of the εἶδος means where a *quality* is to be explained—what Bacon calls a *simplex natura*;

and the explanation of the Blackness of the blackbird would serve the purpose of illustration as well as the Courage of the citizen. Both are acquired qualities, to be explained scientifically by the filling in of the context round about them—by the process of setting forth the influences under which each quality has supervened, some of these influences being specially connected with the organism, others specially with its environment. But sometimes what is to be scientifically explained is, not a quality, but a *thing*, e.g. κλίνη: yet here, again, the εἶδος is the function, or use, of the thing in a system. Put any σκευαστόν in its place in the Life of Man, and you have explained why it exists, shaped exactly as it is shaped—you have found its εἶδος. When we are told that Plato expurgated his list, and ended by dropping 'Ideas' of moral and other qualities, of σκευαστά, of μαθηματικά, and even declined to recognize the logical categories as 'Ideas', retaining only 'Ideas' of 'natural kinds', we are told, it seems to me, that he gave up the possibility of scientifically explaining such qualities and things. Why he should do so, while he retained the 'Ideas' of Man and of Ox, I cannot understand. If such qualities and things as Courage and Bed do not come up for scientific explanation, or are not given as instances of objects requiring scientific explanation, in later Dialogues, that surely does not mean that Plato has come to regard them as incapable of such explanation; for it must be remembered that he has not discarded the term εἶδος to mark the object aimed at by scientific explanation; and if there are no 'Ideas', i.e. no εἴδη strictly so called of such qualities and things, there is no scientific explanation of them—this seems to me to follow necessarily. I cannot believe that, as Plato advanced in maturity of thought, he rejected the moral virtues, and their opposite vices, and retained only the members of 'natural kinds', as capable of scientific explanation. The remark in *Met.* Λ. 1070 a 18 οὐ κακῶς ὁ Πλάτων ἔφη ὅτι εἴδη ἐστὶν ὁπόσα φύσει, to which we are referred, has no warrant in Plato's Dialogues; and it is more reasonable to suppose that it records the opinion of pupils of the Academy than to conclude that Plato himself in his oral teaching committed himself to a view so out of harmony with the Doctrine of Ideas as set forth in his Dialogues. The modifications in the Doctrine of Ideas for which the testimony of Aristotle is quoted by the advocates of a 'Later Theory' seem to me to be such as may best be accounted for by the influence of Aristotle himself—and hence are to be regarded as modifications in the Doctrine, made by disciples of the Academy, Aristotle's contemporaries and juniors, rather than by Plato himself. These modifications, notably the limitation of 'separate Ideas' to 'natural kinds', seem to me to reflect the Aristotelian doctrines of τί ἦν εἶναι and φύσις; wherever, as, for instance, in the case of artefacta, the presence of neither τί ἦν εἶναι nor φύσις could be plausibly maintained, the scholars of the Academy, in deference to the authority of Aristotle, were willing to give up the assumption of 'separate Ideas': see Met. A. 991 b 6, where οὔ φαμεν seems to indicate an understanding come to between the Platonists and Aristotle.[1] As for Plato himself—his view, from first to last, is that, wherever there is scientific explanation of the facts, there is the 'separate Idea'.

Εἴδη, then, in their first sense, as Scientific Explanations, or Laws to be discovered, may be tabulated as follows:—

1. There are εἴδη—

(a) Of all *Qualities* by which man, and natural and artificially produced objects, are characterized and put in various relations to one another—εἴδη of Goodness and the various Virtues in which Goodness appears, of Beauty and Utility and the various Colours and Shapes, natural and artificially produced, in which Beauty and Utility are presented; as well as εἴδη of Vice and Deformity, in themselves, and in their various manifestations; also εἴδη of such Qualities as are marked by the adjectives, hot, cold, hard, soft, healthy, unhealthy, and the like.

(b) Of all *Quantities*, or Amounts, measurable in Objects themselves or in their Qualities, by which the Objects, with

[1] The name of Xenocrates naturally occurs to one in this connexion.

PART I: SUMMARY    123

their Qualities, are put in various relations to one another.

2. There are εἴδη of the *Objects*, possessing these Qualities and presenting these Quantities, and standing to one another in the relations determined by the Qualities which they possess and the Quantities presented in themselves and their Qualities—εἴδη of the members of 'natural kinds', whether biological (man, ox) or belonging to the inorganic world (fire, air), and also of σκευαστά (bed, knife, house).

Passing now from these εἴδη, which are Explanations, or Laws to be discovered by science, we come to the εἴδη which have not to be discovered, but are in our possession to start with—the native Categories of the mind which are employed in the process of discovering the εἴδη tabulated above. These native Categories, apprehended by 'the mind itself', are given, in lists found in the *Parmenides, Theaetetus, Sophistes*, and elsewhere, as Unity, Plurality, Identity, Difference, Similarity, Dissimilarity, Rest, Motion, all involving Being, to which Not-Being (resolved into the Other) is opposed.[1] It is by taking notice of Unity, Plurality, Identity, Difference, Similarity, Dissimilarity, Rest, Motion, in the data of sense, whether Objects, Qualities, or Quantities, that we explain them, discover the special εἶδος, or Law, governing the data belonging to each group—it being always assumed that the data of sense are *real*, are manifestations of Being, or οὐσία. It is in much the same way as that suggested by Plato here that modern science employs its Methods of Agreement, Difference, Concomitant Variations, to explain the data of sense, to discover the Laws of Nature governing them.

I would lay great stress on the point that the εἴδη now under consideration are not special explanations, but general principles of explanation. Thus when I have found the

[1] Cause, or Causation, properly belongs to this list, but does not appear in it, as given in the Dialogues mentioned, although it is involved in the ἐπιστήμη of the *Phaedrus* list, and is taken account of in the αἰτίας λογισμός of the *Meno*.

εἶδος of Courage, I have found the explanation of that Quality; but it is never my object to *find* the εἶδος of Identity or Difference as such—it is itself a Category already involved in my understanding, a Category which I *use* in the process of discovering, say, the εἶδος of Courage. Hence in treating of these general εἴδη, Plato practically confines himself to their κοινωνία with *one another*, and does not trouble with the question of their κοινωνία with *sensibilia*, or even with that of their κοινωνία with the special εἴδη : that is, he is concerned with the theory of the ultimate Categories themselves, as Categories, while elsewhere he is concerned with the theory of the explanation (by means of the employment of these Categories) of *sensibilia*, with the theory of how *sensibilia* may be viewed, in each special case of inquiry, in the proper scientific light, may be placed in their causal context, may have their respective special εἴδη determined—determined, finally, in relation to as large as possible a field of the whole world of εἴδη.

Science, then, involves the conscious use of, the careful reference to, the general εἴδη of Unity, Plurality, Identity, Difference, Similarity, Dissimilarity, Motion, Rest, under Being as their head, throughout the process of searching for the special εἶδος in each case—throughout the process of filling in the context, finding the fitting explanation of this or that, Courage, Whiteness, Bed, or Ox. In one sentence —the Doctrine of Ideas, as worked out in the Platonic Dialogues (which it is a great mistake to regard as a series in which each piece was intended by Plato to *supersede* its predecessor) is the method of discovering special εἴδη, or Laws of Nature, discovered always by means of the application, to the phenomena presented, of certain general εἴδη, Categories, or Schemata, in which Human Understanding, by its very structure, must envisage experience, envisaging it, however, in a *scientific* way, only when these Schemata are consciously realized, made clearly explicit, as they are in what we now speak of as Method of Difference, Method of Agreement, Method of Concomitant Variations—formal realizations of his 'Categories' of Identity, Difference, Similarity, Dissimilarity, &c., which Plato is evidently feeling his way to, and Aristotle actually reached in the τόποι of *Topics* ii. 10 and 11, especially in the τόποι—ἐκ τοῦ ὁμοίως ὑπάρχειν (cf. Method of Agreement), ἐκ τοῦ μᾶλλον καὶ ἧττον (= Method of Concomitant Variations), and ἐκ τῆς προσθέσεως (= Method of Difference).

Professor Jackson has done service in calling our attention to the fact that there are two classes of εἴδη, the special and the general, which must be carefully distinguished; but disservice, in leaving the former class with 'natural kinds' as its sole occupants, to the neglect of many other equally important objects of scientific explanation, fully recognized as such in the Platonic Dialogues; and in so withdrawing attention from the point—which Plato-scholars seem to have so much difficulty in seizing—that the Doctrine of Ideas, on one of its sides, is simply the method of scientific explanation, of interpreting the world —this sensible world, not another world beyond.

Let me close this First Part with some words about 'separate', 'immanent', and 'paradeigmatic'. 'Immanent' causes a difficulty (which 'paradeigmatic' might seem to remove) only if we attach a wrong meaning to 'separate'. 'Separate' does not mean 'separate' as one *Thing* is from another Thing, as one *Person* is from another Person. It means 'abstract'; and when the εἶδος is said to be 'separate' from the particular, the meaning is that, on the one hand, you have the particular Thing, or Event, or Quality, or Quantity, here and now presented to sense—a concrete phenomenon requiring explanation; and, on the other hand, the Law which explains it—not concrete, like the phenomenon here and now, but abstract—an *explanation*, in short, not a *phenomenon to be explained*—an explanation which *always* holds good. Here the 'immanence' (παρεῖναι, ἐνεῖναι) of the 'separate' εἶδος in the particular, or the 'participation' (μέθεξις) of the particular in the essence of the εἶδος, is nothing but the *truth* of the explanation, the *applicability* of the explanation to the thing explained. When we realize that this is the relation between Idea and Particular, we see that the view, according to which Plato ended by recognizing only the members of 'natural kinds' as having 'Ideas', must be rejected. We see that wherever there is scientific explanation—and there is scientific explanation not only of the members of natural kinds, but also of σκευαστά, and of qualities and quantities —of their absence as well as of their presence—and of the various relations in which their presence and absence place the things or persons manifesting them or deprived of them to other things or persons—wherever there is scientific explanation, there is the εἶδος to be discovered.

There is no difficulty, then, in the 'immanence' of a 'separate' εἶδος in the phenomena which needs to be removed by the substitution of μίμησις for μέθεξις or παρουσία. In the chief passage, indeed, in which μίμησις is employed to mark the relation between Idea and Particular (*Rep.* x. 596 ff.) the term is obviously preferred because the subject of discussion is Poetry, which Plato insists on regarding as mere 'imitation'. So far as the Doctrine of Ideas itself is concerned Plato might have employed, in this passage, μέθεξις, or παρουσία, or ἐνεῖναι, just as appropriately as μίμησις. And I think that both terms, 'immanence' and 'imitation', help to give complete expression to the relation between Idea and Particular which Plato tries to make clear. 'What is the Law (εἶδος) "involved in" (παρεῖναι, ἐνεῖναι) this case?' is a very natural way of putting a scientific problem; and 'Here is an "instance" (μίμημα) of such and such a Law (εἶδος) already established and formulated for my guidance (παράδειγμα)' is also a very natural way of speaking when one is concerned, not so much with finding a Law, as with applying it. Of course we must take care that we do not substantiate, or make *Things* of, the Laws which we are seeking for, or have formulated. This is what weak disciples of the Academy evidently did; and Aristotle seems to have regarded their misunderstanding as significant of the real tendency of the Doctrine of Ideas. It tended, he seems to have thought, to fix the minds of its adherents on thing-like abstractions or generalities, and to withdraw them from 'observation and experiment'. His estimate of the weak disciples was, I dare say, pretty correct; but he entirely misrepresents the Doctrine of Ideas as Plato himself teaches it in his Dialogues. One feels that there is poetic justice in Aristotle having to suffer at the hands of Bacon treatment so similar to that which he himself inflicted on Plato.

# PART II

## THE DOCTRINE OF IDEAS AS EXPRESSING AESTHETIC EXPERIENCE

So far the result of our interpretation of the literary data has been to bring out, I hope clearly, the methodological significance of the Doctrine of Ideas. As methodology, we have seen that the Doctrine is a consistent doctrine throughout the whole series of the Dialogues. The question always is: By employing what principles, and following what method, does Human Understanding succeed in explaining the facts of sensible experience? And the answer always is: By bringing its logical categories to bear upon the facts of sensible experience, and so thinking out systematically the various contexts, first immediate, and then wider and wider, in which alone these facts have any significance for conduct and science. Further, the εἴδη, as these categories and the various contexts thought out by means of them are indifferently called, are consistently regarded as having a dynamical, not a statical, existence. For logic, the εἴδη are not 'Things' in a world apart; they are 'points of view' (some of them formal and common to all inquiries, others of a special character) by taking which Human Understanding succeeds in making the facts of the sensible world intelligible. *Per se*, apart from our employment of them, the εἴδη are insignificant and, indeed, unthinkable. This, made especially clear in the *Parmenides* and kindred Dialogues, is the consistent meaning of the Doctrine of Ideas, on its methodological side, throughout the whole series of the Dialogues.

But when common sense and the elementary Psychology on which it rests have exhausted the methodological meaning of the Doctrine, there yet remains something unaccounted for in it—that, in fact, which makes the secret of its perennial attractiveness. Its perennial attractiveness cannot be accounted for by its methodology, insufficiently understood and valued as that has been from the beginning down to the present time, and, so far as understood and valued, appropriated by Aristotle and succeeding logicians, and put down to their own, not to Plato's credit. It is not by his Logician's faculty of connected Discourse, extraordinary as that is, but by his Seer's power of fixed Contemplation that Plato has been, and still is, a living influence. If it is his Logic which exclusively attracts many recent exponents of his Philosophy, this can only be because they are antiquarians, not disciples—because he is, for them, a dead subject of anatomy, not a living man. And expecting to find nothing but Logic in Plato, these exponents find in him much which they can only set down as bad Logic. Aristotle's criticism, as I have contended, is ultimately responsible for this. Aristotle denounces the Ideas as 'Things', unnecessary, impossible 'Things', mere doubles of particulars. This criticism, so characteristic of Plato's great pupil when he reviews his master, is vitiated by two faults: first, it ignores the fact that Plato's Dialogues are a continued protest throughout against the error of making 'Ideas' 'Things' in Logic; and secondly, it shows entire unconsciousness of the experience for which they are veritably 'Things'. That Plato sometimes regarded them as 'Things' there can be no doubt. It is not for Logical Thought, or Discourse, however, but for Contemplation—the attitude of Art and Religion—that they are 'Things'. Aristotle's failure to take note of this distinction is largely responsible for the misunderstanding which has prevailed ever since regarding the Doctrine of Ideas both on its methodological side, which he undervalued, and on its aesthetic—artistic and religious—side, to which he was blind. Finding the Ideas indeed presented as 'Things', but unable to realize the sense in which they were rightly so presented, he assumed that it was in Logic that they were 'Things', shutting his eyes to all the evidence in the Dialogues against his assumption.

In the First Part of this Essay we have seen the misunderstanding, so far as the methodological side of the Doctrine is concerned, removed by psychological interpretation so obvious that one wonders that it was not employed by serious expositors long ago.[1] But the psychological interpretation of the aesthetic—artistic and religious—side of the Doctrine, which we now enter upon in this Second Part, is a very different matter. It is likely to prove as difficult as the other was easy. Omitting all further preface, however, let us begin the work before us with the grammatical rudiments, so to speak, of the proposed interpretation—with the Psychology of Contemplation, as distinguished from Discourse.

The distinction between Qualities and Things which have Qualities is so economical, so convenient for thought, that the plain man assumes that it answers to a real difference present in the external world, while the critical philosopher feels obliged to regard it as imposed upon us *a priori* by the original structure of human understanding. But as Berkeley, anticipating the conclusion of our present-day Psychology, pointed out, 'Things' are nothing but Groups of Qualities. It is Qualities, and only Qualities, that we perceive — sometimes separately, sometimes together in groups. Groups which interest us as groups acquire a coherence which makes them what we call 'Things'. 'Things' are constructions subsequent to Qualities which are the original data of perceptual experience. To borrow

---

[1] 'Plato, we are told,' says Lotze (*Logic*, p. 440, Eng. transl.), 'ascribed to the Ideas of which he had achieved the conception an existence apart from things, and yet, as these same critics tell us, of like kind with the existence of things. It is strange how peacefully the traditional admiration of the profundity of Plato acquiesces in the ascription to him of so absurd an opinion ; we should have to abandon our admiration of him if this really was the doctrine that he taught, and not rather a serious misunderstanding to which in a quite intelligible and pardonable way it has laid itself open.'

Professor Santayana's phrases, 'concretions in existence' are built up out of 'concretions in discourse'.[1] That is, similar sense-stimuli, recurring, produce a single 'idea', or —to express more fully what happens—produce, in the subject experiencing them, a readiness for a certain kind of motor reaction which is the essential condition of what we are conscious of as the 'idea' of, say, whiteness, or hardness, or roundness. This is a 'concretion in discourse': it is the permanent effect of a series of similar sense-stimuli. When several different 'kinds of motor-reaction-readiness', so procured, with their corresponding 'ideas', have often been 'called up' together in a definite group, a 'concretion in existence' is formed—the 'ideas' of, say, whiteness, hardness, roundness, are projected as 'Qualities' coexisting in an 'External Thing': the golf-ball is said to be white, hard, and round. Thus, 'the Thing belongs to the Qualities' is psychologically true; but the economy of thought is well served by the fiction, 'The Qualities belong to the Thing.'

So much for the formation of 'the Thing with its Qualities'.[2] Let us now accept 'the Thing with its Qualities' as finally established for thought, and proceed, from this starting-point, to consider the difference between attending to, or being interested in, a 'Thing' and a 'Quality' respectively.

When we are properly said to attend to, or to be interested in, a 'Thing', it is the 'Thing' *with all (or most of) its 'Qualities'* that we attend to, or are interested in; and our condition is properly that of Contemplation. We acquiesce in the 'Thing' as now present: we do not ask how it came to be what it now is; why its Qualities coexist in it exactly as they do; why there are, it may be, so many other 'Things' like it, all with the same Qualities coexisting in them. The 'Thing' now present takes rank as unique. It is an *individual*, just as *I* am, *you* are, *he* is—a separate

[1] *The Life of Reason: Reason in Common Sense*, ch. vii.
[2] See Professor Stout on the 'Category of Thinghood', *Manual of Psychology*, pp. 315 ff. (ed. 1899).

Self. And a Thing so regarded is not going to be made use of. It is there to be merely gazed at for the sake of its own individuality; it is an end in itself, not a means to something else; it is not a product of anything which went before; it is not the cause or sign of anything to come. This is what something familiar, or beautiful, always is to one whom it fills with love or wonder.

But there is the other and commoner case in which a Thing is regarded not in itself, with all (or most of) its Qualities, as unique, but as exhibiting some one special Quality. Here our interest is not really in the Thing, but in this Quality; the Thing is not an individual but an instance—it is one of a lot, is classed with other Things which have the same interesting Quality. The Things forming the lot, passing before the mind, are all looked at from the one convenient point of view—as having a Quality, say, 'astringency,' which enables us to *do something* with any one of them. Apart from the interest we have in this Common Quality, the Things are uninteresting, that is, they are 'mere particulars'. In technical language we are ready with 'motor reactions' in response to them only as stimulating us by a certain Quality. And this 'readiness', this 'habit of attention', is what comes to be spoken of as the εἶδος in which they all 'participate', and, by participating in which, cease to be 'mere particulars', and become 'instances' of a law or principle. Practical need first picks out the single Quality for 'attention', and makes a provisional class of Things, taking this Quality as *fundamentum classificationis*. Science afterwards comes to the aid of practical need, and begins to help us to do better what we want to do with any one of the Things possessing the Quality by discovering for us the true nature of the Quality, that is, by enabling us to think out its context, immediate and then wider, in the world of experience. And for a long while science contents itself with thus investigating the nature of separate Qualities separately. Then the time comes when, looking beyond the service of immediate need, it becomes interested in the reason why *all the common Qualities* of the things classed together on the ground of the one Quality came to coexist—in how 'Things' come to be exactly what they are. Here the interest, though serving practical ends in the long run, is immediately theoretic, not practical. To use Bacon's terms, science, beginning with the investigation of the *formae* of *simplices naturae* taken separately, advances to the discovery of the *latentes processus* by which the *concretae naturae* (*N. O.* ii. 5) are built up out of the *simplices naturae*—to the discovery of the laws according to which Qualities are organized into the combination called 'the Thing'. But let it be carefully noted— the 'Thing' here, the 'Thing' for Discourse, is still one of a lot, an 'instance of a law', the law namely according to which it and many other similar instances are developed. As an 'interesting instance' the 'Thing' for Discourse is certainly not a 'mere particular'; but, on the other hand, it is not an *individual*, unique, end in itself, as the 'Thing' for Contemplation is. To become that again for the civilized man (the savage[1] easily regards 'Things' as individuals, selves like himself, inspired by the *orenda* or *mana*) the 'Thing' must be taken out of the temporal flux somehow, must be seen through the medium of some elemental emotion—I shall indicate the psychology of 'seeing through the medium of' afterwards—must, whether it be an object sensibly present in nature or in artistic representation, or a memory-picture, be framed apart, to be gazed at in wonder, or sorrow, or melancholy, or love. While Discourse never acquiesces in the Thing itself, but is always busied with its antecedents and consequents, is always 'taking steps' and 'on the move', Contemplation 'rests'— ἠρεμεῖ—confronted by a Real Presence. The Representations of sculpture, painting, and poetry help, in a way to be explained afterwards, to induce and maintain Contemplation;

---

[1] See Baldwin, *Mental Development in the Child and the Race*, p. 335, where it is pointed out that children *make* 'persons' much sooner than 'things' out of groups of experiences.

and we shall see that it is, as thus induced and maintained, that Contemplation is most accessible to the observation of the Psychologist. As otherwise induced, Contemplation, best envisaged as 'concentration',[1] is a psychic condition very difficult to describe and place. Perhaps the consideration which I now propose to give to that mode of 'concentration' characteristic of aesthetic experience may throw some light on the more obscure modes of it which meet us in the abnormal experience of ecstatics such as Plotinus, S. Teresa, and Swedenborg. And it may be that their experience, seen in the light of aesthetic experience, will have something in turn to teach us with regard to the latter experience itself.

So far, then, we have seen that the object of Discourse is primarily the Quality; and, since Qualities always present themselves as attached to Things, secondarily the Thing as vehicle of the Quality: whereas the object of Contemplation is primarily the Thing, and secondarily the Quality—but the Quality only *qua* substantiated (not, let it be noted, by rationalism, but by intense feeling) as a Thing—the object of Contemplation is primarily the Thing itself taken out of the temporal flux and appealing to the mental gaze as individual with all (or most of) its Qualities, there being no thought of how it came to have just these Qualities, common and peculiar, or of what changes it is going to pass through, or purposes it may be made to serve. *Individuality*, in short, is that which marks the object of Contemplation.[2]

Now we may advance a step further, and say that it is *beautiful* Individuality, most especially, that sets a Thing apart thus, 'out of time,' as object of Contemplation. Let this, at least, be accepted provisionally, pending an account of what 'finding a Thing beautiful' is psychologically,

---

[1] See Ribot, *Psychology of Attention*, pp. 96 ff. (Eng. transl.).

[2] 'Der Geniale . . . strebt, die Idee jedes Dinges zu erfassen, nicht dessen Relationen zu anderen Dingen.'—Schopenhauer, *Die Welt als Wille und Vorstellung*, i. 221.

that 'being beautiful' goes with 'being taken out of the temporal flux and made object of Contemplation'.

The 'One Beautiful Body'—whether it be an object presented by Nature, or a representation produced by Art— is all in all to the Contemplation of the artist and of those who fall under his magic. It is there, patent to sense, in 'the world of phenomena': but it is not, like a phenomenon of that world, something to be interpreted and used, and then discarded and passed on from. It is rather a visitant, in sensible guise, come from 'another world' and holding us spell-bound till we lose ourselves in gazing:

> She was most beautiful to see,
> Like a Lady *of a far countree.*

We stand in the presence of nothing appealing to any of the 'habitual motor tendencies' by which we correspond with our temporal environment in detail: we stand in the presence, rather, of something, or some one, come, ἐξαίφνης,[1] with 'Behold, it is I!' and 'Touch me not!' This is always the note of aesthetic experience—the note which it has in common with other modes of ecstasy, as when 'High mountains are a feeling', or when there is 'Love at first sight'. Aesthetic experience is a condition in which concentration, often momentary, never long maintained, *isolates* an object of consciousness: the object stands there itself, alone, peerless: it does not appeal to us as vehicle of some one well-known quality: it is not viewed conveniently, in the light of some one 'concept', or 'universal', or 'expectation'[2]: it does not appeal to some one motor tendency which is straightway actualized—it appeals to so many such tendencies, suddenly and simultaneously, in circumstances so unfavourable to the prevalence of any

---

[1] Ἐξαίφνης κατόψεταί τι θαυμαστὸν τὴν φύσιν καλόν, *Sympos.* 210 E.

[2] 'The "general" or "abstract" is not a content at all; it is an attitude, an expectation, a motor tendency; it is the possibility of a *reaction* which will answer equally for a great many particular experiences.'—Baldwin, *Mental Development in the Child and the Race*, p. 330.

one of them, that they are all 'arrested'[1] together, and a white heat, as it were, of emotion is produced, through which it is seen—perhaps only for a moment—as 'Eternal Idea', unique, 'out of time.' As Eternal Idea? Of what? Of other things 'resembling' it? Surely not: for it is unique, not to be assimilated, albeit perceived by sense, to 'other things' of this sensible world. It is, so we have figured it, a visitant from another world—not a *copy* here of what is there, but the very thing there itself come here. It is the 'Eternal Idea' itself that we see face to face without the mediation of any copy. The 'Eternal Idea' is wholly consubstantial with the 'Beautiful Body' here and now present to sense. They are One, not two.[2]

This, then, is the 'Idea' for Contemplation; and we see already how, as unique Individual confronting us and filling us with the wonder of its real presence, it differs *toto caelo* from the conceptual 'Idea' of Discourse which is but the easy habitual recognition of some familiar quality present in one of the many things which interest us as possessing it—a general point of view from which these things are always regarded, an expectation which any one of them raises, a readiness for some definite motor reaction appealed to by any one of them—in short, a 'universal', not an 'individual'. It is the chief object of this Essay to show

[1] See F. Paulhan, *Les phénomènes affectifs*, pp. 22, 29, 32, 45-6, for the arrest of tendencies as producing affective states.

[2] It is interesting to note that it is by means of the notion of 'influence' exerted by one substance, conceived as 'force', not as extended body, on, or in, another substance similarly conceived—so that the one substance penetrates into the other substance—that Leibniz (*Théod.* §§ 18, 19, and elsewhere) rationalizes the religious experience which Catholics express in the Doctrine of Transubstantiation, and 'Evangelicals' in that of Real Presence (as distinguished both from Transubstantiation and from Consubstantiation), and so endeavours to supply a common philosophical basis on which the two Confessions may be brought to agree. His endeavour really amounts to taking the experience in question out of the extended World of Discourse, and putting it into the intensive World of Contemplation, where interpenetration of Substances—Self and God, Idea of Beauty and beautiful Thing—is accepted without difficulty by the μύστης.

the importance of this distinction for the interpretation of the Doctrine of Ideas as held by Plato and criticized by Aristotle and others—to show that the 'Idea' for Contemplation, of which Aristotle seems to have had no experience, was seldom far out of Plato's sight, and is, indeed, the factor the neglect of which explains why so many attempts at 'solving the Platonic problem' have worked out wrong.[1]

The sensible object fixed and framed apart for Contemplation as 'Eternal Idea' is, it will be understood, a fleeting vision at best, and especially fleeting when presented by mere Nature. In that case the 'real' person, or the 'real' landscape, soon breaks in with familiar associations which bring us back from the still world of rêverie into the waking world of current events. The 'Idea', individual and wonderful, in which Contemplation 'rests', is soon replaced by the 'Idea' of Discourse—by a handy universal, by the recognition of the object as type, or instance, of a class of things interesting as possessing some one quality, or, it may be, a definite group of qualities, inviting us to 'take steps'. But when the object fixed and framed apart for Contemplation as 'Eternal Idea' is not a presentation of mere Nature, but a representation of Art, the inevitable lapse into Discourse, with its 'universal' or 'type of a class', is apt to be deferred for a while, and, when it occurs, may, in certain circumstances, differ, in an important respect, from what it is where the object is one presented by mere Nature. The object supplied to Contemplation by Art is, from the very first, isolated as a presentation of mere Nature cannot be. The action of imitating graphically, or otherwise representing, a natural object, involves, in the agent, 'concentration' on the object represented; and the

---

[1] See an interesting passage in Höffding's *Philosophy of Religion*, p. 123 (Eng. transl.), where it is recognized that Plato's Doctrine of Ideas satisfies two needs—that of thought, for comprehension, that of imagination, for intuitive images: sometimes the one, and sometimes the other, need is the more pressing in Plato's mind.

resulting representation, as such, from the very first, is something set apart and standing by itself, in looking at which we have the artist's original 'concentration' communicated to ourselves.[1] And the object which the artist puts before us by representing Nature is, as compared with that which Nature herself presents for Contemplation, not only of a kind to maintain itself more easily at the level of 'Eternal Idea', individual and unique, but also when we awake from the Contemplation of it into the world of Discourse again and it then lapses to the level of 'universal' or 'type of a class', the awakening which makes it a 'universal' or 'type' yet sometimes retains a 'reminiscence' of it as individual and unique. It is commonly said that the office of Art is to give us types, to 'seize the typical in the individual'. It would be more correct to say that its office is to seize the individual in the typical. The objects—sensible representations of 'real things'—produced by the imitative arts always tend, just as mental images, visual, auditory, motor, always tend, to become 'universals', 'types', 'symbols of classes': and there are, indeed, many products of these arts which seem to exist merely to be types or symbols of classes—for example, the figures in a tailor's fashion-book are such—mere types, not individuals. But where that something, yet to be explained psychologically, which I have called *beautiful* individuality' is present in a product of artistic representation, the product, even when it is become a type, a universal determining the way in which we shall look at a class of objects in the world of Discourse, is nevertheless, though a type, a universal, always reminding us of the 'individual' once seen—of the 'Beautiful Body' the sudden vision of which was the artist's inspiration when he first conceived, and our wonder when we first saw, his work.

Aesthetic experience has now been described provisionally

---

[1] See Schopenhauer, *Parerga und Paralipomena* (*Zur Metaphysik des Schönen und Aesthetik*), § 208, and *Welt als Wille und Vorstellung*, ii. 422.

in terms which, in effect, are these : It is a condition of concentration, the object of which, whether a presentation of Nature or a representation of Art, is framed apart by itself, and characterized by beautiful individuality in such fashion that when, after a longer or shorter period of 'rest' in presence of it, the subject of the experience lapses into the world of discursive movement again, the 'type' or 'universal', into which the 'individual' of the world of rest has now faded, yet often 'doth tease him out of thought' by reminding him, in a distant shadowy way, of that 'individual'.

Such is our description, admittedly provisional, intentionally employing vague, and even impressionist, language to hit off an extraordinarily elusive experience. Now let us take this experience so hit off, and see if, notwithstanding its extraordinary elusiveness, it may not be made to abide further examination under the light of Psychology.

Let us begin, then, with the 'beautiful individuality' ascribed, in our provisional description, to the object of aesthetic experience, and ask—What account has Psychology to give of 'Beauty perceived in an object' ?

The general account is the same for Beauty as for any other Quality in an object : it is a felt condition of the subject projected into the object. So far Psychology is clear. But a special account of the felt condition which, projected into the object, becomes *Beauty* perceived in it is still to seek.

With a view to furthering the search I shall venture to maintain the thesis that the projected feeling which is perceived as Beauty in an object is a state which is causally connected with the condition known to Psychology as 'concentration', the concentration producing the feeling, at least in the first instance, not the feeling the concentration. So we have (1) concentration ; (2) feeling of a certain kind produced by the concentration; (3) projection of this feeling, Beauty perceived in an object; then (by the operation of the law of 'circular reaction' [1]) we have (4) increased concentration caused by the 'Beauty perceived in the object'; (5) heightened feeling produced by the increased concentration; (6) correspondingly greater Beauty perceived in the object—and so on, and so on, till at the extreme pitch of aesthetic, as of religious, ecstasy, subject becomes 'lost' in object.[2]

'Concentration' on the part of the subject, then, is the cause, we say, of Beauty being perceived in the object.

But how does the cause here produce the effect? The answer to this question is to be sought through, or in, the answer to the question, How is 'concentration' induced? That is, In what circumstances does an object, whether a presentation of Nature, or a representation of Art (we assume that objects, 'concretions in existence,' have been formed), get framed apart by itself—get attended to as being simply itself, not as being a link in Discourse?

The answer which recent Psychology, as I read it, points to is, It is in the *Dream-state*, in which mental images take the place of sense-presentations, that 'concentration'— attention fixed on an object as being simply itself—occurs.[3]

---

[1] For the 'Law of circular reaction' see Baldwin, *Mental Development in the Child and the Race*, pp. 178-9 and 334.

[2] See Schopenhauer, *Parerga und Paralipomena* (*Zur Metaphysik des Schönen und Aesthetik*), § 205.

[3] 'Considérons d'abord,' says M. Souriau (*La Rêverie esthétique*, p. 42), 'les impressions que nous recevons de la nature quand nous sommes devant elle en simple contemplation. Nous reposons notre vue sur les choses avec béatitude. Nous ne les scrutons pas du regard, nous ne les étudions pas, nous ne nous posons à leur sujet aucune question. La détente cérébrale est parfaite; et c'est justement de cette détente que nous jouissons ... Notre esprit se donne congé; et il peut se faire que vraiment, pendant un certain temps, nous ne pensions à rien. Mais pour peu que cette contemplation oisive se prolonge, dans cet état de distraction où s'endort l'intelligence, il est impossible que n'apparaissent pas les images; elles se produisent, évoquées spontanément par association d'idées, à peine conscientes, attirant d'autant moins notre attention qu'elles sont plus en harmonie avec les objets que nous avons devant les yeux; et peu à peu notre contemplation devient rêverie.' ... 'Qu'un objet (p. 51) soit naturel ou artificiel, peu importe, il sera poétique dans la mesure où il pourra nous inciter à la rêverie.' ... 'Toujours la poésie commence au moment où l'on cesse de penser et de réfléchir pour ne plus faire que rêver (p. 98).'—'L'objet de l'art,' says M. Bergson (*Les*

The mental images of the dream-state differ from the sense-presentations and mental images of the waking state in being connected with one another either not at all or in the most indefinite manner. Only in the most realistic dreams of continuous sleep, and even there with numerous lacunae, do past-present-future series occur. The general character of the mental images of the dream-state is that of separateness—of not being regarded as representing anything past or as indicating anything future. Each mental image, or small group of mental images, as it comes into light on the screen, is there to be gazed at by itself and for its own sake.[1] And this separateness is especially marked in the case of the mental images which occur in the dream-state which is the condition of aesthetic concentration, as distinguished from the dream-state of continuous sleep.

Now, the dream-state which is the condition of aesthetic concentration coexists with, or alternates rapidly with, the waking state, so that, while the sensible object—landscape, living creature, artistic representation of either—is there for the waking consciousness, its 'image' also is there for the dream-consciousness—or as good as there, for it has just been there, and is just about to be there again. The effect of this overlapping of the dream-state and the waking state is that, for the aesthetic eye, the 'image' stands transparent in front of the sensible object of which it is the

*Données immédiates de la Conscience*, p. 11), 'est d'endormir les puissances actives ou plutôt résistantes de notre personnalité, et de nous amener ainsi à un état de docilité parfaite où nous réalisons l'idée qu'on nous suggère, où nous sympathisons avec le sentiment exprimé. Dans les procédés de l'art on retrouvera sous une forme atténuée, raffinés et en quelque sorte spiritualisés, les procédés par lesquels on obtient ordinairement l'état d'hypnose.'

[1] Since writing this I have read a paper by Mr. M<sup>c</sup>Dougall, in *Brain*, vol. xxxi, pp. 242 ff. (1908), on 'The State of the Brain during Hypnosis', in which the 'separateness' characteristic of dream experiences is explained, in a most interesting manner, in connexion with the hypothesis, or theory, of 'cerebral dissociation'. It is plainly in connexion with some such hypothesis, or theory, that 'concentration' in aesthetic experience must be taken.

image.[1] That object, being presented to the waking consciousness, is apt to be viewed, in the light of some concept, as merely a link in Discourse; but the image of it is there too for the dream-consciousness, and refuses to be so viewed. The image claims Contemplation, and secures it all the more easily that it is such a vivid image, being an image immediately backed by the object of which it is the image —an image through which its original, the actual landscape, or living creature, or artistic representation of either, shines.[2]

I have spoken of 'dream-state', 'concentration', 'object framed apart by itself', as if these were three; but, although it is convenient to speak of them as three, they are really one. When an object is framed apart by itself, that is concentration; and concentration on an object framed apart by itself is the dream-state. The dream-state (whether occurring in continuous sleep, or inserted, it may be only for a moment, in waking consciousness) is a condition marked by extensive arrest of those habitual sensorimotor reactions by which we deal, in the waking state, with the present in view of a future which we expect will resemble the past,[3] that is, sense-presentations are absent

---

[1] This psychic experience, for which many, I doubt not, are able to vouch, may well find its psycho-physical explanation in the condition of '*relative* dissociation' described by Mr. M<sup>c</sup>Dougall in *Brain*, vol. xxxi, p. 251. See also Mr. M<sup>c</sup>Dougall's article on 'Physiological factors of the attention-process', in *Mind*, July, 1902, and Dr. Geley's *L'être subconscient*, p. 26, for the histological theory of 'neurones' with their 'synapses'.

[2] The projection of images or mental representations, with hallucinatory or sensory vividness, upon a card, noted by Mr. M<sup>c</sup>Dougall (*Brain*, vol. xxxi, p. 254), may be compared with this superimposition of its dream-image upon the object of aesthetic contemplation.

[3] 'Le caractère particulier,' says M. Paulhan (*Les Phénomènes affectifs*, pp. 29–30), 'de l'émotion esthétique, c'est que l'objet de l'admiration est considéré en lui-même et pour lui-même; l'émotion est produite par le rapport des différentes parties de l'objet qui la cause ou de l'impression entre elles, non par le rapport de l'objet considéré comme un tout à d'autres objets. L'émotion esthétique ainsi comprise peut être considérée comme due à l'excitation faible d'un grand nombre de tendances. L'excitation est en ce cas trop faible pour aboutir jamais à l'acte, elle est

from the dream-state. And, further, while mental representations are common to the dream-state with the waking state, they are regarded in the former state otherwise than in the latter. They are regarded in the dream-state not as representations—not as images of things which occurred in past experience, but, on the contrary, as presentations: that is, they are not *memory*-images, as the representations of the waking state are. Further, the images of the dream-state are not regarded with the *expectation* which, in the waking state, converts a memory-image into a concept,[1] strips the memory-image of the particularity which it has as memory-image, and leaves it a mere schema applicable to, and interesting only as applicable to, any one of a number of things likely to turn up in the future. The images which arise in the dream-state are regarded without memory and without expectation. Each image, or little group of images, stands for a while by itself framed in the diminutive spot of light to which consciousness has been reduced; and over against it the dreamer stands as a mere spectator, all eye for the one engrossing object, the sensori-motor reactions by which he actively meets the countless stimuli of the waking state all arrested. *Rêverie* (let us use this word to mark the dream-state inserted in the

même trop faible pour être reconnue par le sens intime comme tendance à l'acte, mais elle implique cependant, comme on peut le remarquer facilement, un réveil de sensations et d'idées qui, dans d'autres circonstances, tendent visiblement à faire commettre des actes; et c'est justement le fait que la tendance ne peut en ce cas arriver à sa fin ordinaire, parce qu'elle est absolument enrayée dès qu'elle se produit, qui fait que les phénomènes suscités sont considérés en eux-mêmes et non comme des moyens produits en vue d'une fin quelconque, et c'est là, comme nous l'avons vu, une caractéristique de l'émotion esthétique. . . . Si l'on pense, en voyant un paysage peint, qu'on aurait plaisir à se promener dans le lieu qu'il représente, on n'éprouve pas l'émotion esthétique pure. . . . L'émotion esthétique a donc ceci de particulier qu'elle est due à une excitation complexe, très systématisée, arrêtée au point où la tendance créée par l'excitation donne naissance à des phénomènes de sensation et d'intelligence.'

[1] That is, the thing remembered is one which I am ready to 'react to' again: see Baldwin, *Mental Development in the Child and the Race*, p. 326.

waking consciousness, as distinguished from that occurring in continuous sleep), rêverie so frames an actually present sensible object, natural, or product of one of the useful arts, with more or less difficulty; a mental image of a sensible object it frames with comparative ease; but with great ease, the sensible representation which fine art, graphic or plastic, produces of such an object. Such a representation meets rêverie half way, so to speak: result of the artist's concentration upon a sensible object presented to him, it demands and secures concentration from us too, being that which cannot be regarded as a step from something different to something different again, or used, as its original can be, for some end. The artist who has painted the picture of a spade has made what is, indeed, like a spade, and yet is not like; for he has made a *useless* spade: his picture is an 'individual' to be looked at merely, not a 'universal', not an *instrument always ready* for a certain use, as the real spade is.

Simply by *representation*, then, or image-making, the fine arts—painting and sculpture, at any rate [1]—induce concentration. They provide objects which are not only sensible, and therefore powerfully attractive of attention, but have been translated from the world of movement in which their originals are events, and have been placed for ever, so it seems, in a world of rest—

> Fair youth, beneath the trees, thou canst not leave
>     Thy song, nor ever can those trees be bare;
>         Bold Lover, never, never canst thou kiss,
>     Though winning near the goal—yet, do not grieve;
>         She cannot fade, though thou hast not thy bliss,
>     For ever wilt thou love, and she be fair!

It is now time to ask how our thesis, that concentration is the cause of 'beauty being perceived in an object', has been helped by the foregoing attempt to show the psychological identity of 'object regarded by itself for its own sake', 'concentration', and 'rêverie.'

[1] For poetry see *infra*, pp. 150, 151.

It has been helped, I think, in this way: The object of aesthetic contemplation, we have seen, is something framed apart by itself, and regarded, without memory or expectation, simply as being itself, as end not means, as individual not universal. This something, we have seen further, is not the actual picture, or other sensible product of the artist's workmanship, presented to our waking consciousness, but the dream-image of this, which appears and reappears in quick alternation with the sense-presentation, its original—so that we find ourselves looking at the actual picture with eyes which see, not it, but another within it: and it is that other within it which arrests us by its individuality and amazes us, and is, in fact, the *beauty* of the actual picture on the actual canvas. To be 'beautiful' is to be an object seen thus, that is, to be an object of which rêverie, alternating quickly with waking consciousness, is always making and remaking the dream-image. This dream-image, with its dream-image's quality of self-sufficiency, is conflated with our perception of the sensible object, its original—the perception of the sensible object is 'fringed' by rêverie with a feeling of the self-sufficiency of the object. The object—let us think ourselves away into the presence of Titian's *Amor sagro e profano*, or of some other great work of art well known to us—is there to be gazed at for its own sole sake, as being simply itself, end not means, individual not universal. And to be 'beautiful' is to be so gazed at.[1]

---

[1] See Schopenhauer, *Die Welt als Wille und Vorstellung*, vol. i, pp. 247-8: 'Da nun einerseits jedes vorhandene Ding rein objectiv und ausser aller Relation betrachtet werden kann; da ferner auch andererseits in jedem Dinge der Wille, auf irgend einer Stufe seiner Objektivität, erscheint, und dasselbe sonach Ausdruck einer Idee ist; so ist auch jedes Ding *schön*. Dass auch das Unbedeutendste die rein objektive und willenlose Betrachtung zulässt und dadurch sich als schön bewährt, bezeugt das Stillleben der Niederländer. Schöner ist aber Eines als das Andere dadurch, dass es jene rein objektive Betrachtung erleichtert, ihr entgegenkommt, ja gleichsam dazu zwingt, wo wir es dann sehr schön nennen'— i. e. as expressing its 'Idea' every object is 'beautiful'—more beautiful in proportion as there is that in it which makes the disinterested con-

But, it will be said, concentration may be the cause of 'ugliness', as well as 'beauty', being perceived in an object. This is true: an object may be framed apart by the fascination of aversion or horror: but the rêverie which is the condition of such concentration differs from that which is the condition of aesthetic concentration in this all-important respect that it is a *painful* rêverie, out of which we are rudely waked once for all by the pain of it; whereas the rêverie which is the condition of aesthetic concentration is a *pleasant* state of psychic repose which tends to prolong itself, not, however, continuously, but intermittently, in such a way that we are always waking out of it gently, and then falling back into it again. Of course it is not denied that perception of 'ugliness' may enter, as a subordinate element, into aesthetic experience—in such a way, that is, as to enhance, by contrast, the perception of 'beauty', which must always be the dominating element.

Our thesis, then, will take this form: The beauty which the aesthetic eye perceives in an object is caused by concentration conditioned by a fairly prolonged, but always intermittent, rêverie. Where such fairly prolonged intermittent rêverie does not occur, *aesthetic beauty* is not perceived. In Plato's language, the artist is always looking away from, and we, reproducing the artist's experience as we contemplate his work, are always looking away from the actual picture to the 'ideal pattern', and then again back from the 'pattern' to the picture.[1] Continuous rêverie, mere contemplation of the 'ideal pattern', without recurrent reference, on the part of the artist, to his model and canvas, on the part of the spectator, to the finished picture, would be ordinary dreaming, or ecstatic trance, not aesthetic experience; while, on the other hand, mere 'looking at' model and picture, without recurrent rêverie,

templation of it more easy. Schopenhauer's 'willenlose Betrachtung' is just that regarding of an object as end in itself, not as means, which we have noted as characteristic of aesthetic contemplation.

[1] *Rep.* vi. 501 B ἔπειτα οἶμαι ἀπεργαζόμενοι πυκνὰ ἂν ἑκατέρωσ' ἀποβλέποιεν.

would be sensation, not aesthetic experience. It is essential to aesthetic experience, or perception of beauty in an object of sense, that the object should be regarded as individual, not type, as end not means, and that, as individual and end, it should be lovingly dwelt upon.

No *object of sense* can be regarded thus as end, and lovingly dwelt upon, except as *seen through its dream-image*; and this 'being seen through' requires the quick alternation, or practical simultaneity, of the sense-presentation and its dream-image.[1]

The quick alternation, amounting to the simultaneity, of the waking state and the rêverie-state is possible only when calls made upon the habitual sensori-motor tendencies are few and not pressing. This is notably the case in the circumstances peculiar to aesthetic experience. In the subject of that experience sensori-motor tendencies are appealed to mainly by objects which 'don't matter', by 'representations', not 'real things'. 'Real things' are apt to keep us awake; but 'representations' are the stuff that dreams are made on. The artist's representations, while, indeed, suggesting the sensori-motor reactions habitually called for by the 'real things' which they resemble, are, at the same time, so different from these 'real things', in material, in setting, and in atmosphere, that the habitual reactions are no sooner suggested than they are arrested.[2]

[1] 'Telle est l'illusion théâtrale,' says M. Taine (*De l'Intelligence*, i. 442-3), ' incessamment défaite et renaissante; en cela consiste le plaisir du spectateur ... On se dit tour à tour : "Pauvre femme, comme elle est malheureuse!" et presque aussitôt : "Mais c'est une actrice, elle joue très-bien son rôle!"'

[2] M. Paulhan (*Les Phénomènes affectifs*, p. 100), speaking of the affective result of arrested tendencies, remarks that this result may be produced in music by putting a *motif*, well known to the audience in one situation, into another situation new to them.

The tendencies suggested by the objects of aesthetic contemplation being, from the nature of the case, feeble, are necessarily 'arrested' by collision with the realities of waking sense, with the result that our perception of the realities is 'fringed' with what I have elsewhere (*Myths of Plato*, pp. 33 ff. and 382 ff.) called 'Transcendental Feeling', arguing that it is at the moment of waking that the flash of this feeling

As the result of their sudden arrest an emotional state supervenes—the emotional state experienced as Wonder at seeing objects translated out of the ordinary world into another world, into the fairyland of artistic representation. There are the horses galloping over the snow under the sleigh-driver's lash, their bells jangling, and the wolves barking close behind: there they are, all motion and sound, in a strange world of rest and silence!

And the emotional state, which we may call 'aesthetic wonder' of the first degree, caused by the sudden arrest of habitual reactions, which takes place when an object is translated by representation out of the real world into the mimic world of art, is again, itself, in its turn, the cause of a further arrest of reactions and a further development of emotion. The aesthetic wonder, produced in the way described, isolates its object more and more, till, at last, we pass into rêverie and see, not that object—the picture on the canvas—but its dream-image: new reactions—those constitutive of this dream-image—come into play, and arrest those concerned in our perception of the picture on the canvas; a new emotional state is produced—aesthetic wonder of the second degree, wonder at the transfiguration of the picture on the canvas into a picture (I can hardly find words to express an experience which is, nevertheless, most real), into a picture which is a picture, and yet not a picture but 'an imaginary vision in the interior of the

occurs, and that out of the feeling a crop of images or ideas is produced (see Paulhan, op. cit. pp. 45–6) which, becoming objects of contemplation, again induce the state of rêverie, soon again to give place to the waking state. Plato has, indeed, the support of recent Psychology when he tells us that the vision of the ἰδέαι is for the eye of the μαινόμενος : but we must be careful to observe that the ἰδέαι of this vision are not 'scientific points of view', but *images*—beautiful individuals, shapes, or even only colours, or lustres, seen, somewhere, like the personages appearing, to the eye of Dante, in the Heavenly Spheres, as *fulgor vivi e vincenti*. The *Paradiso*, with its glory of light and colour, is next of kin to the Doctrine of Ideas as it is before us in this Second Part. Ἔρως, Amor, and bright visions—that is the experience of both Plato and Dante; and the psychological account in both cases is the same.

soul'. Then one wakes from one's rêverie into the presence of the picture on the canvas again; and the reactions of the 'psychic system' to which the dream-image of the picture on the canvas belongs are arrested by the prevalence of those of the other 'psychic system' to which that picture itself, as already object of aesthetic wonder of the first degree, belongs. Finally, out of this new arrest arises another development of the emotional state—what we shall call aesthetic wonder of the third degree: the picture on the canvas is now, not something translated out of the ordinary world, for *it never was in that world*—it comes from an 'ideal world'; for *did I not see it there a moment ago*? And now it is here on the canvas, if I could only see it clearly—here *itself*, on *this* canvas, a real presence: at any rate (this is what the *rêveur* says, as his wonder abates) what I see before me is a copy of the 'ideal' picture, not a copy of anything in the world of sense.

Thus, in aesthetic experience, or perception of beautiful individuality, there is involved the concurrence of three 'psychic systems'[1] always suffering arrest from one another, the arrest producing an emotional state of great complexity, in which three degrees of wonder succeed, alternate with, become conflated with, one another. The first psychic system is that to which our perception of the actual object represented belongs: the second is that to which our perception of the representation belongs: the third is that to which the dream-image of the representation belongs. It is in this third psychic system that the soul, so to speak, of Art is realized; the other psychic systems are body to that soul, and are 'for the sake of' it. The artist,

Ch' ha l' abito dell' arte, e man che trema,[2]

and we who follow his leading are always trying to get at

---

[1] See Paulhan (*Phénomènes affectifs*, pp. 121 ff.) for an interesting illustration of the affective result produced by the clashing of 'psychic systems'. The existence of these 'systems', he remarks, is demonstrated by the investigations of Psychology and Pathology.

[2] *Par.* xiii. 78.

something 'better than' the actual achievement on canvas, in stone, in verse—to get at something which shall justify the attempt, in itself, perhaps, indifferently successful, made to represent some, perhaps, very common-place object—we are always trying to get at some Beauty, not to be found in that object, or in the representation of it, but beyond both. 'Ce n'est pas tant,' writes Millet,[1] 'les choses représentées, qui font le beau, que le besoin qu'on a eu de les représenter, et ce besoin lui-même a créé le degré de puissance avec lequel on s'en est acquitté.'

It may perhaps be asked how this account, accommodated plainly to the experience of the painter or sculptor and of those who contemplate his works, squares with the experience of the poet and his patients. The experience procured by the painter or sculptor exhibits, as we have seen, three 'psychic systems' answering to sensible object presented (say, landscape), sensible representation of that sensible object (say, picture of landscape), and mental representation, rêverie image, of that sensible representation. But, in poetic experience, we seem to have only two 'psychic systems', answering to sensible object and mental representation of it. To this I would reply: in poetic experience there are still two distinct 'representations', both, however, *mental*, one being a waking mental representation of the sensible object—this corresponds to the painter's picture on the canvas—and the other a rêverie representation of the waking mental representation of the sensible object—this corresponds to the 'ideal picture' present, for rêverie, 'within' the picture on the canvas. In reading Wordsworth's Poem, we begin by seeing the Solitary Reaper with the mind's eye, and we even hear her singing: it is, at first, simply as if we remembered something that we had actually seen and heard—our mental representation is a waking one; and this was, doubtless, how the Poet himself began. But, as we read, suddenly the waking

[1] Letter to Pelloquet, quoted by L. Arréat, *Psychologie du Peintre*, p. 48.

image is superseded by its own rêverie image: we still see her 'o'er the sickle bending', but no longer in this world: we see her as one translated into another world (this is the experience which we 'remember' when we wake again from our momentary rêverie), we see her translated into a world of 'emblems': and we still hear her 'singing by herself'—but, through her prevailing song, we hear the nightingale from his 'shady haunt', and the voice of 'the cuckoo-bird breaking the silence of the seas among the farthest Hebrides'; while the mystery of it all—'will no one tell me what she sings?'—fills us with amazement, so that we are lost in gazing and listening; and the rhythm, too, of the poet's words has, all the time, been lulling us into rêverie—for it is, after all, by means of words that the poet makes us see the reaper and hear her song—the rhythm of his words, passing, in some subtle way, into the images which the words raise up, predisposes them to suffer the poetic change when the 'psychological moment' comes: suddenly, as we read, the complex of waking mental images is transfigured into a complex of rêverie images.

In the foregoing sketch of the Psychology of Aesthetic Experience, which I have endeavoured to explain as a variety of ecstatic experience, as a case of 'concentration', I have had in mind the experience of the painter and sculptor, and of those who contemplate the originals and representations belonging to the departments of these artists, and also the experience of the poet and his patients, so far, at least, as poetry is the making of images, more especially of visual images [1]; let me now add some remarks

[1] 'Ce qu'il y a de vraiment poétique dans un poème,' says Professor Souriau (*La Rêverie esthétique*, p. 96), 'ce ne sont pas les idées, mais les images.' . . . 'Nous ne parlons pas nos rêveries (pp. 99-101). Les images passent; et silencieux, charmés, nous les suivons du regard. Nous avons donc ici un signe qui nous permet d'isoler par analyse dans une œuvre littéraire l'élément purement poétique. Seules sont poétiques les pensées qui pourraient être aussi bien conçues sans le secours d'aucune expression verbale. Laissez tomber tout ce qui doit être dit

on the experience of the musician, which seems to me[1] to occupy a middle position between the aesthetic experience of the practitioners and patients of the other fine arts—painting, sculpture, poetry—and that type of concentration, found in a Plotinus or a Teresa, to which the expression 'ecstatic experience' is commonly appropriated. The tendency to look for some Beauty not to be found in a natural object, or in the representation of it, but beyond both, which we have detected in the experience of other artists—the painter, the sculptor, the poet—is much more pronounced in the musician. There is a remarkable consensus in the evidence furnished by musicians to the effect that musical experience, at its deepest, is something which cannot be put into thoughts, or expressed in the language of images or words: something which can hardly be expressed even in 'musical sounds'. It is true of course, as a matter of fact, that it does get expressed somehow in 'musical sounds', and, so far, is an aesthetic experience parallel to that of the painter whose 'ideal picture' is somehow rendered on canvas: yet, it is also a fact that musicians speak about the incommunicability of their experience in a way we do not find painters or poets, but do find such ecstatics as Plotinus and Teresa, speaking. Plotinus speaks of the 'ineffable sights', and Teresa says, 'Although I often see Angels, it is without seeing them': similarly Mlle Blanche Lucas, a talented musician whose experience, described by herself, is recorded by M. Arréat,[2] speaks of an 'absolute music', 'music in her head', 'music with a sound which she cannot quite hear', music which it

pour être pensé; conservez ce qu'il est plus facile de se représenter que d'exprimer : ce qui restera sera précisément l'élément poétique ... nous nous rappellerons qu'en poésie surtout les mots ne doivent pas attirer l'attention ; ils sont faits pour être oubliés; seule importe la qualité poétique des représentations qu'ils nous auront suggérées, après leur passage dans l'esprit.'

[1] I judge entirely from the accounts of this experience given by musicians, for unfortunately I have no personal experience of my own to fall back upon here.

[2] *Art et psychologie individuelle*, pp. 141 ff.

often 'annoys her to have to embody (so imperfectly!) in the actual sounds of voice or instrument': and it is the same experience that Mozart describes: The piece, he tells us,[1] came to him as a whole, often in bed, or when he was walking. It articulated itself in his head, till he 'heard' it, not as a succession of sounds, but, as it were, 'all together', *Alles zusammen*: 'That was a feast!' he exclaims, 'That kind of "hearing" was the best!' Once having got it in that way, as something grasped, 'like a picture or a beautiful person,' in a single intuition,[2] he could write it out without much trouble, even amid interruptions. Again, Mendelssohn, in a letter quoted by M. Arréat,[3] says, ' Music is more definite than speech, and to try to explain its meaning by words is to obscure it. . . .

[1] In a letter (Jahn's *Mozart*, vol. iii, pp. 423-5) quoted by von Hartmann, *Philosophie des Unbewussten*, p. 242 (second edition). On this letter, see Note appended *infra*, p. 198.

[2] In such an intuition the musical genius seems to apprehend, with abnormal strength of grasp, what M. Bergson calls 'la durée vraie' (une durée dont les moments hétérogènes se pénètrent); and the following passage in his *Les Données immédiates de la Conscience*, pp. 76-7, is certainly not without bearing upon our present subject: 'Ne pourrait-on pas dire que, si ces notes se succèdent, nous les apercevons néanmoins les unes dans les autres, et que leur ensemble est comparable à un être vivant, dont les parties, quoique distinctes, se pénètrent par l'effet même de leur solidarité? La preuve en est que si nous rompons la mesure en insistant plus que de raison sur une note de la mélodie, ce n'est pas sa longueur exagérée, en tant que longueur, qui nous avertira de notre faute, mais le changement qualitatif apporté par là à l'ensemble de la phrase musicale. On peut donc concevoir la succession sans la distinction, et comme une pénétration mutuelle, une solidarité, une organisation intime d'éléments, dont chacun, représentatif du tout, ne s'en distingue et ne s'en isole que pour une pensée capable d'abstraire. Telle est sans aucun doute la représentation que se ferait de la durée un être à la fois identique et changeant, qui n'aurait aucune idée de l'espace. Mais familiarisés avec cette dernière idée, obsédés même par elle, nous l'introduisons à notre insu dans notre représentation de la succession pure; nous juxtaposons nos états de conscience de manière à les apercevoir simultanément, non plus l'un dans l'autre, mais l'un à côté de l'autre; bref, nous projetons le temps dans l'espace, nous exprimons la durée en étendue, et la succession prend pour nous la forme d'une ligne continue ou d'une chaîne, dont les parties se touchent sans se pénétrer.'

[3] *Mémoire et Imagination*, pp. 88-9.

If I thought that words could explain its meaning, I should compose no more music. There are people who accuse music of ambiguity, and maintain that speech is always intelligible. For me it is the very opposite: words seem to me to be ambiguous, vague, unintelligible, if one compares them with true music which fills the soul with a thousand things better than words. What music that I love expresses for me seems to me to be rather too *definite*, than too indefinite, to be put into words. If I had in my mind definite words for one or several of my *Lieder*, I would not reveal them, because words have never the same meaning for different people, whereas music stands alone in awakening the same ideas and the same feelings in all minds.' And that Schopenhauer's experience was that recorded by these musicians seems to be a safe inference from his Theory of Music. Music he puts apart by itself, above the other fine arts: while the other fine arts produce *copies* of the Ideas, music is on the same level with the Ideas themselves, being an 'immediate objectivation of Will as a whole ',[1] being, in fact, itself an Idea, or, rather, System of Ideas, not the copying of Ideas.

Having now got before us, in outline, a Psychology which explains aesthetic experience, or perception of Beauty in an object of sense, as a variety of ecstatic experience, let us look at the other variety or case—the experience of a Plotinus or Teresa (upon which the experience of the musician, though still aesthetic, seems to border closely)—in the light of this Psychology: 'Often waking to myself from the body,' says Plotinus,[2] 'and going out from the world into myself, and beholding a wondrous Beauty, and feeling most sure that I am partaker of the Better Lot, and that I live the Highest Life, and that I am become one with God, and that, established in Him, I have attained unto that Function

---

[1] *Die Welt als Wille und Vorstellung*, vol. i, p. 304.

[2] *Enn.* iv. 8. 1. For Ecstasy, from the Prophets of the Old Testament down to Plotinus, M. Guyot's work *L'Infinité divine* (1906) may be consulted: see especially pp. 85 ff.

of His, and have established myself above all else that is Intelligible; and then, after thus dwelling in the Godhead, coming down from Contemplation to Discourse, I am at a loss how to explain the manner of my coming down and of my soul's having entered into my body.' 'This [1] is why Eros is united to Psyche in painting and story—because the Soul is different from God, yet proceeded from Him; therefore she loves Him of necessity. When she is There, with Him, she has the Heavenly Love; for There Aphrodite is heavenly, but here she becomes common and a harlot. Yea, every Soul is Aphrodite: this is the hidden meaning of the story about the birthday of Aphrodite, and Eros being born with her. The Soul, then, naturally loves God, wishing to be made one with Him, as a Virgin loves her noble Father with a noble love; but when the Virgin-Soul comes to birth in the flesh, and is deceived by the seductions of the flesh, she changes from one mortal love to another, and, being without her Father's protection, is mastered by lusts. Then, in time, she comes to hate the lusts of the flesh, and, having purified herself from earthly things, returns to her Father and has comfort. They to whom this condition is unknown may judge of it from the loves here, calling to mind what it is to get what one loves most, but remembering always that the things loved here are mortal, and harmful, and variable—mere shadows; for they are not the true object of Love, nor our true Good, nor that which we seek; whereas There abides the True Object of Love, to which a man may be united, laying hold of It and having It truly.... He who has seen It knows what I mean: he knows that the Soul then possesses Another Life, and draws near to, and actually reaches, and has part in, It; he knows that the Leader of the True Life is present, and that there is need of nought else—on the contrary, that he must put off all else and stand in This alone, and become This alone, having stripped off all that wherewith we are enveloped:

---

[1] *Enn.* vi. 9. 9.

wherefore he must make haste to depart hence, chafing at being bound to the things of this world, so that he may embrace God with the whole of himself, and have no part of himself with which he does not touch God. Then, indeed, may he see both Him and himself, as it is given unto him to see them—himself lit up, full of Intelligible Light, or rather become Light, pure, without weight; that is, become God, or rather *being* God [1]—for a moment, indeed, kindled, but afterwards weighed down and quenched.'

'Seeing himself,[2] he shall see himself as such, and shall perceive himself as such, having become single : but perhaps we ought not to say even "He shall see". As for That which is seen—if we may venture to speak of seer and seen as two, and not as both one—the seer, then, neither sees It, nor distinguishes It, nor imagines It, as separate from himself; but has, as it were, become another, and is not himself; nor does he *There* belong to himself, but belongs to It, is one with It, having joined his centre to It as to a centre: for even *here*, when things are come together, they are one, and are two when they are apart. Wherefore this Vision of his is hard to describe; for how could he report as different what he did not see as different, when he saw it, but as one with himself ? '

'What, then, is the One,[3] and what nature has it ? Indeed it is no wonder that it is not easy to tell; for neither is it easy to explain Existence or the Formal Idea, our knowledge being based on Forms. The farther the Soul goes towards that which is without Form, being entirely unable to comprehend it, inasmuch as she is no longer being determined and moulded by an agency which is manifold, the more does she glance aside from her mark, and is filled with

---

[1] 'All theories,' writes Professor Leuba ('The Psychology of Religious Phenomena,' in *American Journal of Psychology*, vol. vii, 315, April, 1896), 'making religion depend upon a *desire to know*, instead of upon the *desire to be*, are belied by the biographies of the great founders or promoters of religions. . . . Christ expresses his inner condition in august words like these, "I and my Father are one".'

[2] *Enn.* vi. 9. 10.                                   [3] *Enn.* vi. 9. 3.

fear lest she should have nought. Wherefore, in such a case, she becomes weary, and gladly descends. . . . When, however, the Soul sees for, and by, herself—that is, sees only by communion and as being one—she then is fain to suppose, being one with It, that she has not that which she seeks; for she is not different from that which is the object of her thought. Yet he who would attain to the Philosophy of the One must enter into this close thought-baffling communion with It.[1] . . . It is before Reason, for Reason is one of the existing things: It is not a thing, but before any thing: It is not " existent ", for the existent has, as it were, the Form of existence: but It is without Form, yea, even without Intelligible Form. Being That which produces all things, It is not one of them : It is neither thing, nor quality, nor quantity, nor Reason, nor Soul, nor in motion, nor, again, at rest: It is not in place, not in time; but is That which is in-Itself, unique in Form—or rather, without Form, being before any Form, before motion, before rest; for these are attributes of the existent. . . . But may we call It " The Cause "? Yes, for to call It " The Cause " is to ascribe an attribute, not to It, but to ourselves who have something from It, while It abides in Itself. Speaking strictly we must not call It either " that " or " this " : 'tis we who, as it were, beat round about It, and interpret our own affections, according as we sometimes come near to It, sometimes fall away from It, by reason of the difficulties involved in the contemplation of It.'

' The One is " one "[2] in an ampler sense than " unit " and " point " are " ones "; for in the case of these the Soul abstracts magnitude and multiplicity, and acquiesces in

---

[1] The One which cannot be thought, cannot be described in words, is the Self. This *is*, but is not *known*. And God too, 'reproduced' in me, is not *known*, as something external may be *known*, but *is*, as I *am* : is therefore realized by me as a *Person* with whom I, a Person, am one. It is in 'concentration', or ecstasy, that God as Person is revealed: for Discourse, or scientific thought, as distinguished from ecstatic concentration, the One is a system of laws, not a Person.

[2] *Enn.* vi. 9. 6.

that which is smallest, taking as basis something which, indeed, is without parts, but was in that which is divisible into parts—something, too, which is in another. But the One is neither in another nor in that which is divisible into parts, nor is it so without parts as a *minimum* is; for It is the greatest of all, not in magnitude, but in power—It is without magnitude, Its greatness consisting in power; for even the things which are after It are in their powers indivisible and without parts, although not in their bulks. We must assume also that It is infinite—not in the sense that Its size or number cannot be traversed, but because Its power cannot be comprehended.'[1]

With the experience revealed in these passages—the raw material, so to speak, to which the philosophical technique of Plotinus gives form—the experience expressed in the teaching of Algazel, Avicenna, and other representatives of Moslem mysticism, may be compared. According to this teaching (in which Christian, Neoplatonic, and ascetic influences are noticeable), ecstasy, or intuitive knowledge, is at once the gift of God, and procurable by ascetic practices. 'Times' are distinguished from 'Places', or 'Stations'. 'Times' are moments which God selects for touching chosen souls; while 'Places', or 'Stations' are 'stable states of the soul, in which it sojourns in the course of its mystic progress'[2]—what S. Teresa calls 'Castles of the Soul',[3] what Diotima indicates in the stages of her κλῖμαξ—καλὰ σώματα, καλὰ ἐπιτηδεύματα, καλὰ μαθήματα, αὐτὸ τὸ κάλλος. These 'Places', or 'Stations', according to the teaching of the Moslem mystics, are reached only by *effort* on the part of the μύστης. Each 'Place', or 'Station', has its own proper work, and a man does not pass up to the one next above until he has attained to perfection in the work of the

[1] M. Bergson's 'pure duration' (an 'intensive magnitude') given in the self-consciousness of the 'fundamental ego' is very like the One of Plotinus (see *Les Données immédiates de la Conscience*, pp. 80 ff.). It is not expressible in words without falsification.
[2] M. le Baron Carra de Vaux, *Gazali* (Paris, 1902), p. 185.
[3] See *infra*, p. 160 f.

one beneath; we are reminded of the passing of the soul of
Statius to a higher terrace of the Mount of Purgatory.[1]
The three chief stations are Faith in God, Discovery of God,
and Life in God, i. e. union with Him.[2] And of what nature
is He with Whom the μύστης is finally united? He is Light
of Lights. To the World of Light, according to the doctrine
of the school of Avicenna,[3] is opposed that of Darkness, or
Body. Bodies are symbols, idols, of the Invisible Intelligences. From God proceeds an Illumination by means of
which Intelligences—'victorious lights'—are multiplied.
The Light nearest to the Light of Lights, looking upon
Him, is aware of itself as a Shadow in comparison with
Him; and, *qua* Shadow, produces the First Body, the Sphere
which limits the Cosmos; then are produced, in their order,
the other Lights and the other Bodies (Intelligences and
celestial Spheres), the Bodies moving under the control of
the Lights, which are thus said to be 'victorious' (one is
reminded of Dante's *fulgor vivi e vincenti*[4]), while the
Bodies are said to be 'conquered'. Thus the Light of
Lights comes down through the intermediation of the
various Lights to this world, which is a Shadow cast by
them; and the individuals here are Shadows cast by these
Lights, which in this Philosophy play the part of universals:
all the individuals of a species are shadow-manifesta-
tions of some one 'Light', 'a " victorious light " which, with
other " Lights ", resides in the world of Pure Light, where
it is characterized by its own peculiar dispositions, its own
peculiar forms of Love, Pleasure, Domination; and when
the Shadow cast by it falls upon our world, visible individuals are produced, idols—man with his diverse members,
animal with its special structure, mineral, taste of sugar,
perfume of musk—all according to the mysterious dispositions which prepare the matter of these beings to be informed

---

[1] *Purg.* xxi. 58 ff. : on which I venture to refer to my *Myths of Plato*,
p. 159.
[2] de Vaux, *Gazali*, p. 186.   [3] *Gazali*, pp. 232-3.   [4] *Par.* x. 64.

by this Light.'[1] What, it may be asked, does this 'Illuminative Philosophy'[2] mean with its doctrine of 'a Light casting a Shadow'? The train of thought seems to be as follows : a lower Light is *conscious* of itself as Shadow compared with the Light above from which it flows. The *consciousness* of being a Shadow 'precipitates' itself as Body ; Body is that Shadow manifest—a Shadow of something *in the light*, of something which is still *a mode of light*, although dark as compared with the Light of Lights, and, indeed, as compared with any Light above itself. The Light of Lights, which is One and Uniform, multiplies Itself in a World of Lights, each one of which is darker than Itself. There is much in this Illuminative Philosophy to remind one of the Intelligible World of ' Essences ' or ' Possibilities ' set forth by Leibniz; while its presentation of Essences as forms of 'Light' marks the ecstatic origin of the whole system. The experience of Saul, when 'suddenly there shined round about him a light from heaven', is at the bottom of the philosophy of Algazel and Avicenna, as it is at the bottom of the philosophy of Plotinus—the 'philosophy' is nothing more than the ecstatic experience rationalized—διαφανῆ γὰρ πάντα καὶ σκοτεινὸν οὐδὲ ἀντίτυπον οὐδέν, ἀλλὰ πᾶς παντὶ φανερὸς εἰς τὸ εἴσω καὶ πάντα· φῶς γὰρ φωτί. καὶ γὰρ ἔχει πᾶς πάντα ἐν αὑτῷ καὶ αὖ ὁρᾷ ἐν ἄλλῳ πάντα, ὥστε πανταχοῦ πάντα καὶ πᾶν πᾶν καὶ ἕκαστον πᾶν καὶ ἄπειρος ἡ αἴγλη [3]. . . ἐκεῖ δὲ χρόα ἡ ἐπανθοῦσα κάλλος ἐστί, μᾶλλον δὲ πᾶν χρόα καὶ κάλλος ἐκ βάθους—the Beauty there is Colour ' in three dimensions'.[4]

The same experience is recorded by S. Teresa—stations, or stages of progressive concentration of consciousness, from the ordinary state of diffusion up to the perfect unity of intuition.[5] There exists, she says, a Castle built of a solitary Diamond of matchless beauty and incomparable purity ; to enter, and to dwell in, that Castle is the end of all endeavour. The Castle is within us, within the Soul,

[1] *Gazali*, p. 234.     [2] The title of a work of Avicenna.
[3] *Enn.* v. 8. 4.     [4] *Enn.* v. 8. 10.
[5] See Ribot, *Psychology of Attention*, pp. 96 ff. (Eng. transl.).

and to reach it we have to pass through seven stations,[1] the seven degrees of 'prayer'—(1) oral, (2) mental, (3) of recollection, (4) of quietude, (5) of union, (6) of rapture, (7) of ecstasy when the spirit takes flight and attains to union with God; will and understanding are in abeyance, and the soul enters into the Diamond Castle. 'Being once in prayer,' she says,[2] 'the Diamond was represented to me like a flash, although I saw nothing formed,[3] still it was a representation with all clearness, how all things are seen in God, and how all are contained in Him. . . . Let us say that the Divinity is like a very lustrous Diamond, larger than all the World, or like a Mirror . . . and that all we do is seen in this Diamond, it being so fashioned that it includes everything within itself, because there is nothing but what is contained in this magnitude. It was a fearful thing for me to see, in so brief a space, so many things together in this clear Diamond, and most grievous, whenever I think on it, to see what ugly things are represented in that lovely clearness, as were my Sins.'[4] How near this Diamond stands to the Leibnizian world of Eternal Possibilities! There, in the Understanding of God, are the patterns of all things, evil as well as good: God saw, among the Eternal Possibilities, Adam sinning freely, and decreed to admit him, such as He had seen him from all eternity, into actual existence at the time foreordained.[5]

[1] Cf. the Mithraic κλῖμαξ ἑπτάπυλος, and the seven terraces of Dante's Mount of Purgatory.
[2] Quoted by G. Cunninghame-Graham, *Teresa*, p. 410.
[3] Cf. description of the One as ἄμορφον εἶδος given by Plotinus, *Enn.* vi. 7. 33.
[4] Teresa had her visions very often after communicating. She saw in one vision her soul as a mirror, in the midst of which was Christ. Description, she says, could not render what she saw—but the vision 'did her great good': see G. Cunninghame-Graham, *Teresa*, p. 410. Her visions seem often to have had their occasion in religious pictures gazed at, or mentally recalled: see Professor W. James, *Varieties of Religious Experience*, p. 407, on the importance of symbols and pictures for the production of the mystic consciousness. There is, I take it, a close connexion between power of visualization and the mystic consciousness.
[5] Leibniz, *Théodicée*, §§ 231, 350.

It is chiefly by the comparatively unimportant place which mental images occupy in it, that the variety of ecstatic experience illustrated in the foregoing examples is distinguished from the other—the aesthetic variety. In aesthetic experience, images, carefully procured, and pretty well defined, are the primary objects of contemplation, the affective state being merely the atmosphere, so to speak, in which these objects are seen; but in the ecstasy of a Plotinus or a Teresa, it is the affective state which is the primary object of contemplation, and often the only object: the subject of such ecstasy contemplates his state, and sees nothing but it, as one might contemplate a thick fog, and see nothing but it; and images, when they arise, are, for the most part, hardly independent objects in the affective fog: they are rather fantastic condensations of the fog itself flitting past—they are so vague and elusive that the subject has generally to report that he is sure that he saw something, but cannot remember what it was. What is 'remembered' is, not the image, but the affective state which accompanied the image [1]—

> La forma universal di questo nodo
> Credo ch' io vidi, perchè più di largo,
> Dicendo questo, mi sento ch' io godo [2]—

and Teresa says that, although she hardly remembered, and could not describe, her visions, yet she felt that they 'did her great good'.

In other words, the arrest of sensori-motor tendencies by which the affective state characteristic of this variety of ecstasy is produced is much more complete than the arrest which occurs in the other variety—in aesthetic experience: it is a prolonged and monotonous arrest, very different from the discontinuous arrest, or rhythm of alter-

---

[1] See Ribot, *Psychology of the Emotions* (chapter on 'The Memory of Feelings'), p. 171 (Eng. transl.); Arréat, *Art et psychologie individuelle*, pp. 39 and 79, on 'mémoire affective'; and J. R. Angell, *Psychology*, pp. 266-7.
[2] *Par.* xxxiii. 91-3.

nating arrests, by which I have accounted for the special character of aesthetic experience. And when the congestion [1] of this monotonous arrest is relieved for a moment at some point, the image which results, if it persists long enough to be apprehended distinctly and remembered at all, seems to come out of the surrounding affective fog with a message from within: it is accepted at once as explaining the mystery with which the affective state is charged: it is a symbol, the mere seeing of which is the explanation longed for. Such is the image, or system of images—Ezekiel's Cherubim and Wheels, Teresa's Diamond—which rises up, on a sudden, into the dream-consciousness of a Prophet: very different from the image, or system of images, suggested by a present object of sense, and hardly differing from it, which the Artist and his patient now look at, and then look away from, and then look at again, in waking rêverie, the landscape, or the picture of it, confronting them all the while. The Prophet's dream looms darkling in his head; the Artist's is in the outer daylight somewhere. But, while contrasting the deep ecstatic trance of the Prophet and the superficial rêverie of the Artist, we must remember that the genius, as distinguished from the talent, of the Artist consists in his having, now and then,

[1] 'Les phénomènes affectifs sont l'indice d'un trouble plus considérable que celui qu'indiquent les autres faits de conscience . . . toutes les circonstances qui accompagnent la production de l'émotion—l'arrêt des tendances, l'afflux du sang au cerveau, l'augmentation de température, la multiplicité des phénomènes, leur incoordination relative, etc., doivent s'interpréter dans ce sens. En les ramenant au point de vue de la psychologie synthétique, nous voyons que l'on peut les ramener à trois faits principaux : éveil de systèmes ou de parties de systèmes psychiques ou psycho-organiques mal coordonnés avec la tendance dominante; défaut de coordination des éléments ou des systèmes mis en jeu simultanément et avec une importance égale, enfin manque de certains éléments psychiques nécessaires au fonctionnement harmonique de l'esprit. Ces phénomènes doivent être assez marqués pour produire le fait affectif, ils sont toujours la conséquence du fait principal que nous avons désigné, la mise en jeu d'une force psychique relativement considérable qui ne peut s'employer harmoniquement.'—Paulhan, *Les Phénomènes affectifs*, pp. 160-1

sudden visitations like those of the Prophet—images which arise suddenly out of intense feeling, and, because they arise suddenly out of intense feeling, seem to explain the mystery which it indicates but does not explain. At the same time, the Artist's condition is not, like the Prophet's, one of extensive psychic congestion, and the image risen from the depth is not the only image which engages his attention: his mind is always being visited and revisited by rêverie-images of objects actually present to sense, or once present, and his rank, as a good painter or poet, is shown mainly by the way in which these rêverie-images so cluster round the image which is risen from the depth, as to form a beautiful system, which often, indeed very often, remains and finds artistic expression after the central image has been 'forgotten'—after it has returned, as it is apt soon to do, into the depth, leaving the clustered rêverie-images with a magic beauty about them—the beauty of a grouping which one accepts without demur as an exquisite grouping, while one recognizes, at the same moment, that the key of it is lost. This 'magic of the lost key' is illustrated perhaps better in Poetry than in Painting, inasmuch as the images of the former, not being controlled, as those of the latter are, by the presence of sensible originals, are more mobile and more ready to group themselves suddenly round some prophetic image which emerges from the depth of the affective state just for a moment—and then is gone for ever: and when it is gone, there stands the result of its coming—the cluster of images which composes the bit of poetic experience which the Poet expresses in his sonnet, or other unit—there stands the result, beautiful: but the secret of its beauty—for most surely its beauty has a secret—is past finding out.[1]

[1] The psychological theory advanced above seems to me to be supported by the evidence of poets themselves where they venture to speak about poetic inspiration—as Dante does in *Par.* xxxiii. 82 ff., and in the twenty-fifth sonnet of the *V. N.*; and Coleridge does in the following passages—*Biog. Lit.* ch. xv: 'Images, however beautiful, though faithfully copied from nature, and as accurately represented in words, do not of themselves

This clustering of the feebler images of aesthetic rêverie round an imposing trance-image is closely parallel to, indeed probably consequential upon, what psychologists, from Plato downwards, have noted as the law holding between affective states themselves—that one ἔρως τις τύραννος,[1] is apt to compel into its service, to make satellites of, all other affective states—

> All thoughts, all passions, all delights,
> Whatever stirs this mortal frame,
> All are but ministers of Love,
> And feed his sacred flame.

characterize the poet. They become proofs of original genius only as far as they are modified by a predominant passion, or when they have the effect of reducing multitude to unity, or succession to an instant; or lastly, when a human and intellectual life is transferred to them from the poet's own spirit,

> Which shoots its being through earth, sea, and air.'

*Biog. Lit.* ch. x : 'Most interesting is it to consider the effect, when the feelings are wrought above the natural pitch by the belief of something mysterious, while all the images are purely natural. Then it is that religion and poetry strike deepest.' Wordsworth, too, speaks to the same effect, in *The Prelude*, at the end of the Fifth Book—

> Visionary power
> Attends the motions of the viewless winds,
> Embodied in the mystery of words:
> There, darkness makes abode, and all the host
> Of shadowy things work endless changes—there,
> As in a mansion like their proper home,
> Even forms and substances are circumfused
> By that transparent veil with light divine,
> And, through the turnings intricate of verse,
> Present themselves as objects recognized,
> In flashes, and with glory not their own—

and in *The Preface to the Edition of* 1815, speaking of Milton, he says— 'The anthropomorphism of the Pagan religion subjected the minds of the greatest poets of ancient Greece and Rome too much to the bondage of definite form; from which the Hebrews were preserved by their abhorrence of idolatry. This abhorrence was almost as strong in our great Epic Poet, both from circumstances of his life, and from the constitution of his mind. However imbued the surface might be with classical literature, he was a Hebrew in soul; and all things tended in him towards the sublime.'

[1] *Rep.* ix. 573 ff., and cf. Hume's *Dissertation* ii, of the *Passions*, and *Dissertation* iii, of *Tragedy*; Paulhan, *Les Phénomènes affectifs*, p. 76; and Guyau, *Les Problèmes de l'esthétique contemp.*, p. 20.

The result, so far, of our psychological examination of the conditions underlying aesthetic experience may now be stated summarily as follows: We have a series of substitutions: (1) an affective state due to extensive arrest of habitual reactions; (2) an imposing image rising suddenly out of the affective state, and received as symbol explanatory of the mystery indicated by the affective state—it is at this point that the subject of 'prophetic', as distinguished from aesthetic, ecstasy stops; (3) a grouping of aesthetic rêverie-images round the imposing trance-image, or symbol, which, soon disappearing from consciousness, leaves the rêverie-images grouped in the fashion which aesthetic contemplation finds 'beautiful' with that magical Beauty peculiar to works of artistic genius [1]—that Beauty the 'secret' of which is always eluding us, just when we seem to have discovered it—

We ask and ask: it smileth and is still.

I have now said, or suggested, enough to make it at last possible to come to close quarters with the question: What light does this Psychology of ecstatic experience, and especially of the aesthetic variety of it, throw on that side

---

[1] 'Das gewöhnliche Talent,' writes von Hartmann (*Phil. des Unbewussten*, pp. 240-1, 2nd ed.), 'producirt künstlerisch durch verständige Auswahl und Combination, geleitet durch sein ästhetisches Urtheil. Auf diesem Standpuncte steht der gemeine Dilettantismus und der grösste Theil der Künstler von Fach: sie alle können aus sich heraus nicht begreifen, dass diese Mittel, unterstützt durch technische Routine, wohl recht Tüchtiges leisten können, aber nie etwas Grosses zu erreichen, nie aus dem gebahnten Geleise der Nachahmung zu schreiten, nie ein Original zu schaffen im Stande sind . . . es fehlt der göttliche Wahnsinn, der belebende Hauch des Unbewussten, der dem Bewusstsein als höhere unerklärliche Eingebung erscheint . . . die Conception des Genies ist eine willenlose leidende Empfängniss, sie kommt ihm beim angestrengtesten Suchen gerade nicht, sondern ganz unvermuthet wie vom Himmel gefallen, auf Reisen, im Theater, im Gespräch, überall wo es sie am wenigsten erwartet und immer plötzlich und momentan'—works of genius are 'originals', not 'copies'. They come up from the 'unconscious' as 'wholes'—and *organic* wholes, unlike the works of selective diligence in which the parts are always more or less to be seen as bits of a conglomerate.

of Plato's Doctrine of Ideas which is not methodological, which refers, not to the world of Discourse, but to the world of Contemplation?

We have seen that the object of Contemplation is an Individual Thing, not a common aspect or quality of things; and that it is a Thing which always tends, as the Contemplation, or Concentration, becomes more intense, to shine out as a *beautiful* Thing. We have also seen that it is in being looked at through the transparency of its rêverie-image that the object of Contemplation shines out as a beautiful Thing.

Let us begin by connecting this with what Plato insists on with such evident conviction—the pre-eminent clearness of the Idea of Beauty, its presence, visible, not notional, in the particular of sense.[1] The Idea of Beauty which is present in the particular of sense is not a common quality which would fit another particular just as well as it fits this one. It is something which appeals to the beholder's *Love*, and is therefore individual, not common.[2] It is the sensible object's *own beauty*—its beautiful individuality. This, I take it, is what Plato feels when he insists on the visible presence of the Idea of Beauty in the sensible object. His aesthetic experience has taught him that, as a modern psychologist puts it,[3] a natural object, or its artistic representation, is not the 'expression', or 'symbol', of the Beautiful, but *is itself the Beautiful*; whereas the

[1] *Phaedrus* 250 D.

[2] As Individuality appealing to Love, the Idea of Beauty comes most often in Human Form, and when not actually in Human Form, always with some more or less intimate claim upon Human Sympathy: 'Si dans les règnes inférieurs,' says M. Ribot, explaining Schopenhauer's theory of fine art (*La Philosophie de Schopenhauer*, p. 112), 'l'idée se confond avec le caractère spécifique, c'est qu'en réalité, malgré les principes leibniziens, les êtres ne forment pas de véritables individus, du moins au sens esthétique, et qu'ils ne dérogent pas au type commun : dans le monde humain, au contraire, il n'y a que des individus, la personne est son type à elle-même, elle a la valeur d'une idée, et, comme dit Winckelmann, " le portrait même doit être l'idéal de l'individu."'

[3] Wundt, *Vorlesungen über die Menschen- und Thierseele*, vol. ii, p. 55 (1st ed.).

Ideas which reign in the regions of Religion, Morals, and Science, are never identical with the objects which express them.

But the sensible object's *own beauty*, its beautiful individuality, we have seen, is its rêverie-image rising up, for a moment, again and again, now becoming conflated with our perception of that object as actually presented and then again distinguished from it. Here it is no case of a Quality being attributed to a Thing. Two individual Things—the object of sense, and its rêverie-image—are united together as one Thing. The 'beautiful body', in the contemplation of which the aesthetic beholder is lost, is now present object of sense, now rêverie-image of that object, now both in one. This 'beautiful body' is seen afar, though so near, and near, though far off. Its beauty is, at once, its own individual beauty, and yet 'cometh from afar'— from a transcendental source, from 'The Eternal Beauty'. This is the experience which Plato expresses in the *Phaedrus* and *Symposium*; and the psychological account of the reference always made in that experience to a transcendental source is, according to the theory which I advance, that the rêverie-image, first apprehended as distinct from the sensible object of which it is the image, is, for a reason about which I shall have something to say afterwards, figured as the *archetype* of that object; and then, when conflated with the object, is still figured as archetype, but as archetype really present in its ectype. In so far as sensible object perceived and rêverie-image of it are felt to differ, we have χωρισμός; in so far as they coalesce, we have παρουσία. And—as I have said, and would repeat, because it is a matter of first-rate importance for the understanding of this part of Plato's Doctrine of Ideas—it is the παρουσία of an individual substance, not of a common quality: a common quality, such as 'wisdom', *cannot be seen*, whereas this lovely Presence is seen most clearly.[1] The Idea of Beauty is always a beautiful *body*

---
[1] *Phaedrus* 250 D.

## PART II

present in rêverie consubstantial with a beautiful body present in sense.

Thus it is in the psychology of the relation of the Idea of Beauty to the beautiful body that we have the solution of the difficulty, made so much of by Aristotle, and indeed insuperable, if the Doctrine of Ideas is regarded as having only a logical significance—the difficulty about one substantial Thing 'participating in' another substantial Thing, or having that other Thing ' present in ' it. ̬This is no difficulty where aesthetic experience is concerned, for aesthetic experience is just the being conscious of one Thing ' participating in ', or ' having present in it ' another Thing.[1]

We may now proceed a step further to observe that the transfiguration of the rêverie-image of a sensible object into the archetype of that object, which has just been mentioned as taking place in aesthetic experience, is, after all, not peculiar to that region of experience, although,

---

[1] According to Professor Lipps what 'is present in' the object of aesthetic regard is *myself*. The *object* of aesthetic regard, according to his view, is always a sensible object, perceived or represented : but this *object* is not the *ground* of aesthetic pleasure ; *I myself* am the ground— I feel myself active or pleased, not *over-against* the object, but *in* it. 'Die spezifische Eigenart des aesthetischen Genusses besteht darin, dass dieser Genuss ist eines Gegenstandes, der doch, ebensofern er Gegenstand des *Genusses* ist, nicht Gegenstand ist, sondern ich . . . Die Einfühlung ist die Thatsache dass der Gegenstand Ich ist, und ebendamit das Ich Gegenstand.' This 'Einfühlung' is effected by what is called 'innere Nachahmung' : when I involuntarily imitate the movements of another, my feeling of activity is bound up, not with *my* movement, but with *that of the other* which I see : with my feeling of activity I am entirely in the moving form which I see ; I am spatially in its place, as it were ; I am identical with it ; 'I feel myself free, light, proud.' This is aesthetic imitation, and, at the same time, 'Einfühlung' —it being always remembered, however, that the *ego* here is an ideal, not a practically operative, *ego* : see 'Einfühlung, innere Nachahmung, und Organempfindungen' in the *Archiv für die gesammte Psychologie*, vol. i, pp. 185 ff. (1903). The theory of 'Einfühlung' advanced by Professor Lipps differs from the view which I am advancing, in laying more stress on 'activity'. My view, while, of course, recognizing the motor element involved in all ideation, dwells chiefly on the superimposition of mental images upon the objects of aesthetic regard.

doubtless, more remarkable in it than elsewhere. Mental images, being products of that *imitation*,[1] organic or consciously designed, by which we adapt ourselves to a uniform environment, or, rather, make for ourselves an environment suitable to our permanent nature, always tend to assume the character of archetypes over against sensible particulars. A sensible particular is a system of stimuli which calls for, and is answered by, and, indeed, is maintained as a definite system by, a system of habitual sensori-motor reactions corresponding. And the 'image' of the sensible particular is just this system of reactions, somewhere below sensation-par, preparing to rise to that level, or having fallen from it: that is, the image is the sense-particular, either expected, or remembered. In the latter case, the image doubtless often appears as an otiose imitation of reality; but, in the former case, is easily figured, and indeed rightly figured, as itself the reality, for it stands for our permanent attitude towards all particulars of a certain kind.[2] The image, in this case, appears, no longer as the copy of a real thing, but as itself the real thing which must enter into, be present in, the particular, if the particular is to have existence at all. And this image, although it may appear to subsequent psychological observation as a concept, a universal, a general rule, is, as actually experienced, an individual thing, and an individual thing which is not a mere pattern hanging idly in the mental chamber waiting to be copied by some one,[3] but has, in itself, the force—'the intrinsic motor force of an idea'[4]—whereby

---

[1] 'The adaptation of all organisms,' says Professor Baldwin (*Mental Development in the Child and the Race*, p. 278), 'is secured by their tendency to act so as to reproduce or maintain stimulations which are beneficial'—this he calls 'organic imitation'; 'Contractility (p. 307), exhibiting itself in "organic imitation", is the original form of adaptive reaction which works through the whole process of development'; and see also pp. 350 ff.

[2] 'All our higher conceptions,' says Professor Royce (*Outlines of Psychology*, p. 291), 'involve conscious imitations of things'—and are well expressed in diagrams applicable to a great number of objects.

[3] Cf. Spinoza, *Eth.* ii. 43, scholium.

[4] Baldwin, *Mental Development in the Child and the Race*, p. 5.

it penetrates with its individuality into particulars, and, by so penetrating, makes them integral parts of the 'intelligible world'.

Image, then, as Image, is naturally enough figured as creative archetype. In discursive experience it is only occasionally so figured, its normal function there being that of a universal, or general point of view, which it performs as having had its individuality worn off by common use. But in Contemplation, especially in that which occurs in aesthetic experience, the Image is, not occasionally, but normally, figured as archetype; and I take it that in minds, like Plato's, in which aesthetic experience bulks largely, the peculiarities of that experience are apt to be reflected in the discursive section of their experience. Such minds will show a more than ordinary tendency to figure images occurring in Discourse as individuals with creative force, rather than as universals or types. In Plato the tendency is marked; but, as its origin in aesthetic experience has not been clearly recognized, its scope has been misapprehended. The Critics, most of whom have attended too much to the letter of Plato's text, where the εἴδη are concerned, and too little to its psychological interpretation, point to passages in which the separate thinghood of the εἴδη *as objects of Science* is affirmed,[1] and meet the suggestion, that, in Science, Plato conceives them as 'points of view', with flat denial; at the same time ruling out of court, as 'Socratic, not Platonic', the doctrine of the early Dialogues, in which the εἴδη undoubtedly are, not separate things statically existent, but scientific points of view, concepts-in-use, dynamically existent. If the First Part of

[1] Of these passages *Phaedrus* 247 D may be taken as a typical instance; and of the way in which their meaning is commonly conceived, Professor Burnet's words may be taken as an authoritative expression: 'The Ideas,' he says (*Mind*, January, 1906, p. 98), 'as such, never enter into a myth at all. Even in the *Phaedrus* myth, they appear but for a moment, and then with their usual technical names. There is no attempt to represent them mythically or even allegorically.'

this Essay, with its psychological interpretation of the εἶδος in discursive experience, has succeeded in making out its case, the early Dialogues cannot be ruled out of court, for the view of the nature and function of the εἶδος found in them is essentially that advanced throughout the whole series of the Dialogues—viz. that, in Discourse, the εἶδος is a point of view, either special to a particular inquiry (e.g. the notion of courage, or of ox, or of bed), or common to all inquiries (e.g. the form or category, of same-different)—a point of view which makes *sensibilia* intelligible in this world of Becoming, not a transcendental object of knowledge in another world of Being beyond. Psychology, having opened our eyes to this as Plato's doctrine of the εἶδος in discursive experience, and having also shown how statements affirming its separate thinghood may be explained by reference to aesthetic experience, has, I venture to think, set us on the way towards a point of vantage, our occupation of which is likely to put a good many textualists out of action. As it is, enough has been done already, I think, to relegate Plato's statements about the separate thinghood of the εἶδος to their proper place. These statements can no longer be regarded as making it impossible to credit him with full recognition of the point-of-view character of the εἶδος in Discourse; for we now see how natural it is that aesthetic experience should 'contaminate' the discursive experience of a man of his temperament and calibre, without at all vitiating his conception of the method of Discourse—without causing him for a moment to forget that, in Discourse, the εἶδος is not an individual Thing apart, but a point of view generally applicable. Plato was too much at home in the world of aesthetic experience not to be aware of its unique character—not to know that *only in it* are there 'Eternal and Immutable Archetypes', beautiful individuals—not to know that these, and their Beauty (it too being an individual, now 'separate' from them, now 'present' in them), are existent only for Contemplation.

Recognizing then, first, that the tendency to figure the plastic type, the generalized image, the concept-in-use, of discursive experience as an immutable archetype, is due largely to the 'contamination' of that experience by aesthetic experience; and secondly, that Plato's familiarity with aesthetic experience was of the most intimate kind, we can say with confidence that he was not deceived when this tendency had its way in him. He knew well that the immutable thinghood, the beautiful individuality, which he sometimes felt himself constrained to ascribe to the concept-in-use of Discourse, exists only for aesthetic experience. He did not suppose that Discourse has its own eternal and immutable εἴδη as well as Contemplation. He knew the unique products of Contemplation when he saw them afield in the region of Discourse. But not only was Plato deeply initiated in the mysteries of aesthetic experience; he had also a grasp of scientific method which astonishes one more and more as one learns to read him candidly without the prejudice created by the Aristotelian Criticism of the Doctrine of Ideas: and it is exactly because he had, at once, this extraordinary grasp of scientific method, and this profound acquaintance with aesthetic experience, that we are justified in saying that, while it was natural that he should sometimes think and speak of the conceptual instruments of science as eternal and immutable archetypes, he never allowed himself to make a 'constitutive use' of them as such in science. He always sets forth, and employs, the method of science in a manner which implies that εἴδη are plastic, not immutable—points of view taken in this world, not things apart by themselves in another world. It is a 'regulative use' in Discourse of the archetypes of Contemplation that Plato makes.[1] He feels so sure of his ground as man of science, and critic of scientific method, that he is not afraid sometimes to look at scientific concepts *en artiste*, especially—and it is here

[1] So 'Goethe explained the metamorphoses of plants by reference to a sort of Platonic idea of the absolute plant.'—Prof. W. P. Ker, *On the Philosophy of History* (Glasgow, 1909), p. 18.

chiefly that 'regulative use' comes in—where they are the concepts of the *moral* sciences. These concepts (his method of acquiring which, and handling as instruments of investigation, defined once for all the procedure proper to the sciences in question) are something more than instruments of scientific investigation: they stand also for aims of endeavour: each one is a *mot d'ordre* for conduct, as well as a point of view for science, in evidence of which let such utterances serve as:—'The beauty of *Holiness*;'—'The greatest of these is *Charity*;'—'*Justice* is fairer than Morning or Evening Star;'—'Starry Heaven above, and *Moral Law* within;'—'*Liberté, Égalité, Fraternité.*' The 'moral sciences' differ from the 'natural sciences' in being more than 'sciences' addressed to the discursive intellect; they appeal, at every turn, to imagination and feeling, and their 'concepts' easily become objects of Contemplation—beautiful individuals, eternal archetypes, haunting this world of daily work with their real presence.

And it is because they mark 'values' of supreme importance for man's life that the concepts of the 'moral sciences' appeal as they do to imagination and feeling, and become, at least in the eyes of a prophetic genius like Plato, objects of contemplation, beautiful individuals 'out of time'. This out-of-timeness which the value-concepts of morals and theology tend to assume, more readily than other concepts, in the eyes of the Prophet, while explaining, as it evidently does, much that it is otherwise difficult to understand in the Doctrine of Ideas, is, at the same time, a psychological fact of the greatest importance for the interpretation of such deliverances of the moral and religious consciousness as 'Eternal and Immutable Morality', 'Immortality of the Soul', 'Personality of God'. In affirming these, the moral and religious consciousness is making certain concepts objects of 'Contemplation', treating them as 'beautiful individuals', taking them 'out of time'. It is not to the point, where 'values' of such moment are concerned, to say that these 'beautiful individuals' are *mere creations* of 'Contemplation'. Let them be such; yet they are creations without which Human Nature would sink into accidie and pessimism, and come to nought. 'It is not surprising,' says Professor Höffding,[1] 'that the religious consciousness should regard the time-relation as an imperfection. The misfortune of development in time is due, more or less, to the fact that one period of life is looked upon merely as a means to another. Means and end are separated, and life is divided between work without any enjoyment and enjoyment without any work. Time is, for the most part, filled out with something which only has value *because of*, and *in*, its effects. Every advance in the art of education, in ethics and in sociology, implies an attempt to annul this, the worst of all dualisms. Just as no one man ought to be treated merely as a means for other men, so no single moment in a man's life ought to be regarded merely as a means for the future. This will be avoided if work and development themselves acquire immediate value, and can thus themselves become ends or parts of an end. The child is something more than a man in the making; childhood becomes an independent period of life, with its own special tasks and its own peculiar value. Every period of life, every piece of the course of time, must be thus conceived. Then, at last, it will be possible, in the midst of time, to live in Eternity, yet without sinking into mystic contemplation. The externality of the time-relation disappears. "Eternity" no longer appears as a continuation of Time, or as a distant time, but as the expression of the permanence of value throughout time's changes.' It is this 'permanence of value throughout time's changes', revealed only to ' Contemplation', that Prophets since the world began have been continually preaching to the men of their own, and of all, generations, in myth, in allegory, in dogma—and Plato's Doctrine of an Eternal and Immutable Good, variously

[1] *Philosophy of Religion*, pp. 56-7 (Eng. transl.).

manifested in Justice Itself, Temperance Itself, Courage Itself, and the other Forms of Moral Beauty, is his peculiar version of this one prophetic gospel which rests on 'faith in the preservation of values'.[1]

So much by way of accounting psychologically for the intrusion of Eternal Archetypes into the region of Discourse; and so much by way of showing that their intrusion does not vitiate Plato's view of the method required in that region. His double eminence, as artist and as man of science, guarantees the correctness of his use of Eternal Archetypes in Discourse: his use of them there is such that, while it satisfies the imaginative and emotional needs stimulated by contact with the subject-matter of the moral sciences—the sciences, after all, in which, together with the mathematical sciences, he was chiefly interested—it does not interfere with the conduct of the understanding proper to these, as to all other sciences. As I have put it, his use of Eternal Archetypes in Discourse is regulative, not constitutive.

Let us now digress for a while from the psychology of the εἶδος as Eternal Archetype, object of aesthetic Contemplation, with a regulative value in scientific Discourse, and consider the psychology of the εἶδος as Ideogram, with, as we shall see, a value in science distinct both from that of the Eternal Archetype and from that of the Concept. My reasons for discussing the εἶδος as Ideogram here, in this Second Part, not in the First Part alongside of the εἶδος as Concept, are the following: the εἶδος as Ideogram, although its function is almost entirely in the region of Discourse, cannot be understood without a good deal of the psychology of aesthetic experience which is in place only in this Second Part: it resembles the εἶδος of aesthetic Contemplation, and differs from that of Discourse, in being

---

[1] 'The relation between religion and ethics is a very simple one; religion is faith in the preservation of values, and ethics investigates the principles according to which the discovery and production of values take place.'—Höffding, *Philosophy of Religion*, pp. 373-4.

an individual, not a universal: and the experience in which its individuality is perceived sometimes 'contaminates' that in which the individuality of the εἶδος as object of aesthetic Contemplation is perceived, that is, the rêverie-image of aesthetic Contemplation is sometimes upheld by the motor force of the Ideogram—but, it must be added, only when that force is not strongly exerted; for when it is strongly exerted, the experience is not that of Contemplation, but of Discourse—the artist is no longer in the rêverie-state, but is thinking of how he is going to execute the work, and we, with his finished work before us, no longer see it through a dream, but are thinking out the process by which he executed it. These are my reasons for taking the εἶδος as Ideogram, although its function is mainly within the region of Discourse, here, rather than in the First Part of this Essay; the force of my reasons will be appreciated, I hope, in the perusal of what now follows.

Let us, then, digress, for a while, from the εἶδος for aesthetic Contemplation to the εἶδος as Ideogram with a function operative almost entirely within the region of Discourse.

Here, again, it is the psychology of art, especially of graphic art, that throws light upon Plato's doctrine. There is a function performed by the εἴδη in science which is closely akin to that performed by ideograms in art. For the function of 'ideograms', 'ideographic figures', 'schemata', 'active symbols', 'images of interpretation or of traduction', it will be sufficient to quote the words of a distinguished French writer on the psychology of art, M. Arréat:—

'Un peintre figuriste,' he writes,[1] 'qui ne *sait* pas l'animal, a des chevaux à placer dans une composition. Il s'applique alors à l'étude du cheval; il prend des croquis, et se met dans la tête des "images". Un cavalier expert pourra ensuite critiquer son tableau en connaisseur. Il garde donc en mémoire, lui aussi, des images précises, auxquelles il a comparé celles du peintre. Il ne serait pas capable

---

[1] *Mémoire et Imagination*, pp. 28-9.

cependant de dessiner un cheval ni de le peindre. A quoi tient précisément cette différence ? Il ne suffit pas de dire que c'est faute d'exercice, car la faculté même d'apprendre marque un véritable privilège. C'est d'abord faute d'images d'*interprétation*, ou de *traduction* : j'entends par là des schémas visuo-moteurs, laissés par l'étude dans le cerveau du peintre, et grâce auxquels sa représentation mentale peut prendre figure aussitôt sur le papier ou la toile—des symboles actifs, en quelque sorte, qui sont comme les idées générales " pittoresques ". Faire l'éducation des yeux et de la main consiste en somme à affiner la perception et à pourvoir la mémoire de ces idées générales pittoresques, de ces symboles, où s'agrégeront à mesure les images actuelles. ... Il faut que le peintre dispose, en définitive, de nombreuses images d'interprétation, et qu'il les trouve au bout de ses doigts ; mais il faut encore qu'il ait assez de souplesse pour les ajuster continuellement à la réalité vivante.' Again M. Arréat writes,[1] 'Comparons les images visuelles dans un homme ordinaire et dans le peintre. Pour celui-là, ses images concrètes—figure d'une personne, forme et coloration d'un objet déterminé—restent le plus souvent vagues et fuyantes, ses images abstraites à peu près vides : *rouge, bleu, noir, blanc, arbre, animal, tête, bouche, bras*, &c., ne sont guère que des mots, des symboles qui expriment une synthèse grossière. Pour le peintre, au contraire, les images ont une précision de détails bien supérieure, et ce qui vit sous les mots ou dans les objets réels, ce sont des faits analysés, des éléments positifs de perception et de mouvement. La bouche, les yeux, le nez, les membres, les attitudes du corps, existent pour lui à l'état de représentations ayant un certain dessin ; il ramène toute chose vue à des schémas, que son œil a appris à voir et sa main à dessiner. Apprendre à dessiner revient à se mettre dans les yeux et dans les doigts ces formes potentielles, sur lesquelles s'établiront les formes, vivantes, diverses à l'infini. L'étude ne profite que dans la mesure où elle aboutit à produire ces sortes de figures idéo-graphiques, résidu de l'observation patiente. On dit d'un artiste, qu'il a " l'éducation première ", quand il les possède ; et celui qui ne réussit jamais à les acquérir aura manqué de génie.'

The function of sensori-motor (visual and auditory) ideographic forms in the other arts—in poetry and music—is

[1] op. cit. pp. 115–16.

similar. What it concerns us to note is that these ideographic forms are *individuals*, and *active*, and, as such, correspond closely to the εἴδη as Plato often describes them, especially in passages relating to their employment, in Discourse, as παραδείγματα. Just as an individual—the rêverie-image of an object natural or artefact, coming in with its transparency between us and that object, covers it, and transfigures it, in Contemplation, so, in Discourse too, there is a covering and transfiguration of the particular of sense by an individual of another kind—by the ideogram, which is a mental image, differing from the rêverie-image in being more active: being a waking, not a dream image, and involving motor tendencies not constantly arrested, but always realizing themselves in the particular of sense, which, as finally apprehended, is, in fact, this sensori-motor image realized, this ideogram, or παράδειγμα, getting, and in due course having got, itself 'copied'. That Plato transferred to his description of the procedure of the man of science language descriptive of the procedure of the painter who copies an original is quite plain. The Idea is a παράδειγμα which the man of science 'looks steadily at'—ἀποβλέπει πρός—and then recognizes again in the particulars of sense which are 'copied' from it. Just as the eye and hand of the painter are guided by an ideographic form existing somewhere 'at the back of his mind'—something 'without shape and without colour', a picture in his head which is yet not a picture—while he copies the sensible object, the ostensible original of his work, so is the scientific man's interpretation of the particulars of sense which pass before him in Discourse effected under the control of an outline-individual—not a concept, which is attention fixed directly on some interesting quality common to the particulars, but a rough sketch, as it were, in his mind's eye, which serves at least the negative purpose of securing the immediate rejection of any one of these particulars which does not possess the quality in question: any particular which the ideogram does not cover is seen at once to be irrelevant. Just as we have ideograms in our heads—a mental square, a mental circle, a mental triangle—corresponding to the various determinations of space which are presented in sense, so, but generally realized in less definite forms, we have mental sketches—as the pathological condition known as apraxia makes evident—without which we should not recognize particulars as likely to subserve any purpose whatever, that is, should not receive them as data of experience at all. 'The objects of the external world,' writes Professor Baldwin,[1] 'are very complex mental constructions. They are for the most part made by association . . . the motor contribution to each presented object is just beginning to be recognized in cases of disease called by a general term *apraxia*, i.e. loss of the sense of the use, function, utility, of objects. A knife is no longer recognized by these patients as a knife, because the patient does not know *how to use it*, or what its purpose is. The complex system of elements is still there to the eye, all together: the knife is a thing that looks, feels, &c., so and so. This is accomplished by the simple contiguous association of these elements, which has hardened into nervous habit. But the central link by which the object is made complete, by which, that is, these different elements were originally reproduced together, by being imitated[2] together in a simple *act*, this has fallen away. So the *apperception*, the synthesis which made the whole complex content a thing for recognition and use, this is gone.'

That which is lacking to the apraxia patient—the ideogram of 'knife', or whatever the instrument may be—the sensori-motor image, without the presence and operation of which, as recent psychology teaches us, sense is blind—this is just what Plato, in the *Cratylus*, calls the knowledge of the use of an instrument, and identifies with knowledge of its Idea, or Pattern—for the expression

---

[1] *Mental Development in the Child and the Race*, pp. 310-11.
[2] Cf. op. cit. p. 307, for 'organic imitation'.

ἀποβλέπων πρός implies that the term παράδειγμα is in his mind. And it is sometimes truer to our actual experience to present, as Plato does, this ideogram, or sensori-motor image, as an individual, as the Real Knife itself, than to present it as a common quality, or universal, inhering in particular knives. At the same time, this ideogram, or sensori-motor image, although an individual, and source of energy, may well be described in the terms which Plato applies to the εἴδη in the *Phaedrus*, as having no sensible qualities—247 c ἡ γὰρ ἀχρώματός τε καὶ ἀσχημάτιστος καὶ ἀναφὴς οὐσία: for it is as an *anticipation* of a sensible experience not yet actually present that this ideogram appears in consciousness: it is of the nature of the 'absolute music in her head' described by Mlle Blanche Lucas, or of those angels whom Teresa 'saw, without seeing them'. The student of recent Psychology has, therefore, no difficulty in understanding how Plato can present the Idea, even in Discourse, as an individual, and an individual without sensible qualities. His μόνῳ θεατὸν νῷ is, after all, as applicable to such an individual as it is to the content of a concept. But, while the Idea as sensori-motor image, or ideogram, and the Idea as scientific point of view, or concept, certainly appear as two distinguishable *aperçus* in Plato's methodology—the latter being, perhaps, more prominent in the Dialogues of the 'Socratic Group', the former gaining ground afterwards—yet these two are constantly blended in his mind into one composite whole—into the Idea apprehended as centre of an individual force which is in the act of distributing itself among particulars, so that it appears in them as a common quality—this common quality being seized in them by the scientific inquirer just in so far as he is also aware of the individual force which manifests itself in the common quality. This tendency in Plato's mind to combine concept and ideogram, so that the Idea in Discourse appeared to him at once as general point of view and as individual—at once as καθόλου and as οὐσία, a conjunction which Aristotle could make nothing of [1]—did not, however, stop at the stage where the ideogram is experienced, as an individual indeed, but without sensible qualities. Plato was pre-eminently a visualizer, and his ideograms were always apt to become eye-images; while his concepts, although reached by dialectic, were apt to become in the end closely associated with these eye-images. The Idea was at once a scientific point of view, and a visible thing. And a *beautiful* visible thing. We have seen how he perceived the Idea of Beauty as some sensible object's own Beauty—as the sensible object itself seen in a dream—seen afar, though so near. But, in truth, other Ideas were often envisaged by him in the same way, as sensible things after a fashion. Of course he tells us that they are 'intelligible', not 'sensible', that they are 'without shape or colour' (a statement which the psychology of the ideogram enables us to understand); but how difficult he finds it to keep them true to this description! They are always just taking on the form of visual images: even while he is telling us that those nurslings of the Plain of Truth are invisible, how he makes us see them growing there like flowers all in bright array! And the Idea of the Good, how it shines in the Intelligible Heaven! Relations, which are, of course, intelligible, not sensible, are always materializing themselves as visible symbols— symbols which, for a mind so enamoured of beauty as Plato's, have a charm in themselves, apart from their utility as symbols.[2] A parallel (I mention it only as a

[1] See *Met.* B. 6. 1003 a 8, and M. 9. 1086 a 32.

[2] Those for whom the Doctrine of Ideas has a fascination are not 'motors'—'les moteurs,' says M. Queyrat (*L'Imagination chez l'enfant*, p. 81), 'ne voient pas, n'entendent pas leur pensée, mais ils la *parlent*.' 'Handy,' 'mechanical' people, and very 'fluent' people, do not ' rest ', or 'contemplate', or 'concentrate': they have *habit*, as opposed to *interest* (see Baldwin, *Mental Development in the Child and the Race*, p. 292); they are deficient in ἔρως: see also M. Queyrat (op. cit. p. 109) for the independence of the motor and the visual tendencies, and how one tendency may dominate a man, so that when he loses it, by disease, he is helpless. Thus Dr. Charcot records the case of a man with highly developed power of visualization who lost it entirely, and could not remember or recognize places, faces, or colours when he saw them.

*parallel*) to Plato's experience here may be found in cases recorded [1] of the visualization of the numbers 1, 2, 3, 4, &c. The passage from one number to another—a relation 'apprehended by intellect only', a relation 'without shape, or colour, or any sensible quality'—appears in sensible form, and only in sensible form, to certain minds: appears as a passage over definitely qualified ground—in one case known to me the passage from 12 to 13 takes, 'always and necessarily,' the form of a steep slope down to a dark ditch at the bottom; and on the farther side of the ditch there is a reddish-coloured rising ground, recognized as answering to the other 'teens, with what answers to 20 making the top of the hill—no 'figures' being seen anywhere, only ground. This picture always and necessarily rising up when the patient 'thinks' 12-13, might be called the 'Idea', or 'Pattern', which gives reality and significance to all 12-13's. *In some such way*, one may surmise, Plato tended to visualize all relations—Identity, Equality, Justice. He knew well that for science, and even for artistic experience, the Ideas are not *sensibilia*; but his language, psychologically interpreted, indicates that, as a matter of fact, he visualized them—some of them more clearly, some less clearly—as *sensibilia*. And, in visualizing them, he only did, perhaps with more vivid results than occur in the experience of most people, what we are all bound, in some fashion or other, to do when we 'think relations'. Relations, such as Identity, Equality, Justice, are, after all, *ideals*; and, just because they have no adequate *sensible* embodiments, we are fain to clothe them in *fantastical* embodiments, which, by an easy act of make-believe, we regard as adequate: the effort of holding them up as ideals produces a state of fatigue and puzzlement, which finds relief in images: we symbolize our ideals—some of us, in the form of words imaged, for the eye of reader, or ear of

---

[1] See Mr. Francis Galton's *Inquiries into Human Faculty and its Development*: section on 'Number-Forms'.

listener, or vocal organs of speaker, or hand of writer,[1] some of us in the form of objects behind these words, so that Identity, Equality, Justice, and the like, become colours, or things, or persons, or places, somewhere—somewhere, perhaps, in the undiscovered region of Mount Abora, or, it may be, nearer home. And yet they are, all the while, the conceptual instruments by employing which science is enabled to handle the data of sense: their fantastical embodiment, if kept within due bounds, hinders their employment as instruments of science not in the least, indeed, may be thought to make that employment possible; for, without the support of the make-believe which I have referred to, they could hardly long survive the ordeal of being confronted with 'facts' and always found not to correspond with them. It is the make-believe of 'Let line $AB$ equal line $CD$' in that 'fantastical' thing, the geometer's diagram, which renders possible the use of the Idea, Ideal, or Concept, of 'Equality' as an instrument of geometrical science: here the fantastical object is near home, and its ideal-sustaining power is plain and easily understood; but an object of make-believe situated somewhere in the region of Mount Abora may exercise the same power—the power, be it noted, of an Individual. The concept, the steady point of view from which the sensible data are regarded, is, indeed, a 'universal'; but this universal, this steady point of view, would never have been gained, and, gained, could not be held fast, except from the standing-ground of the $παράδειγμα$, an Individual: an Individual, however, which, since it sustains the

[1] 'M. Charcot,' says M. Arréat (*Mémoire et Imagination*, pp. 1-2), 'lorsqu'il introduisit dans la langue psychologique les qualificatifs de *visuel, auditif, moteur*, qui depuis ont eu si grande fortune, les avait appliqués à une mémoire restreinte, celle des mots. On ne pouvait s'en tenir là. Si les mots reviennent plutôt à la mémoire, chez certains malades, sous la forme d'images visuelles (le mot *vu*), auditives (le mot *entendu*), ou motrices (le mot *articulé* ou *écrit*), il est clair pourtant que ces cas pathologiques nous donnent à la fois une analyse curieuse du fait normal et la possibilité de dispositions individuelles affectant l'ensemble de l'intelligence.'

'universal', cannot, we say to ourselves, be any 'imperfect' object of sense-presentation: it must be an object, belonging to the realm of mental representation, which make-believe can posit as 'perfect'. There is really nothing to surprise the student of modern Psychology in Plato's insistence on a world of perfect Individual Forms, a *mundus intelligibilis*, beyond this *mundus sensibilis* of imperfect manifestations; and no difficulty in seeing how these two worlds come into touch with each other.

Hitherto my main object, in this Second Part, has been to show how the influence of the rêverie-image of Contemplation (the ideogram of waking experience often co-operating with it) accounts for Plato's tendency to substantiate the concept of Discourse; and, at the same time, explains the sharp separation, which he is so fond of insisting upon, between the νοητόν and the αἰσθητόν. No mere scientific concept could be separated by any methodologist from the *sensibilia* which it renders intelligible, as the νοητόν seems to be separated from the αἰσθητόν in passages to be found throughout the whole range of the Dialogues; and, as we have seen in the First Part of this Essay, Plato, indeed, takes the greatest pains—devoting whole Dialogues to the task—to show that science is impossible, if the separation is insisted upon. Yet he is always falling into phrases in which he seems to insist upon it. This inconsistency we have traced to the contamination of the experience of Discourse by that of aesthetic Contemplation: the νοητόν, qua '*separate from*' the αἰσθητόν, is, we have seen, a mental representation, while the αἰσθητόν is a sense-presentation—and what greater difference can there be, for the mind endowed with aesthetic susceptibility, than that between these two![1] The sense-presentation is a transient event;

[1] The following passage in M. Arréat's *Mémoire et Imagination*, pp. 106–7, may be quoted for the truth—of far-reaching import, I hold, for aesthetic theory—that it is the imaged, not the actually presented, landscape which inspires the artist, especially the musical and poetical artist: 'Ernest Reyer (*Notes de musique*, p. 150) n'est point "de l'avis de ceux qui

the mental representation is a Thing of Beauty, unique, unchangeable—the one is
>    The voice I hear this passing night,

the other is
>    The self-same song that found a path
>    Through the sad heart of Ruth.

Now let us pass from the rêverie-image as invading the region of Discourse (where it sometimes finds the ideogram an ally), and conclude this Essay with notice of the *Phaedrus* myth, and the Discourse of Diotima in the *Symposium*, where that image is to be seen reigning in its own region of Contemplation.

The outlines of the Psychology of Contemplation, or Concentration, have already, I hope, been sufficiently traced, and I now ask the reader of the *Phaedrus* myth (246 A ff.), and of Diotima's Discourse (*Sympos.* 202 D ff.), to take it that the ecstasy described in both passages, and called μανία in the *Phaedrus*, is, psychologically understood, 'concentration,' and, more especially, the concentration of the Prophet, as I have tried to distinguish him from the Artist; for the Beauty which is its object is an awful Presence compelling, rather than an attractive Personality inviting, regard.

There is a difference between the *Phaedrus* myth and the Discourse of Diotima which I consider to be of great importance, and would begin by calling attention to: that which first induces the ecstasy of the patient in the one piece differs profoundly from that which first induces it in

prétendent que Weber a noté l'une des pages les meilleures de son œuvre (la scène de la fonte des balles dans *Freyschütz*), assis au pied même de la cascade de Geroldsau, à l'heure où la lune argente de ses rayons le bassin dans lequel l'eau s'engouffre et bouillonne". L'inspiration n'a dû jaillir en lui que plus tard "avec le souvenir du lieu fantastique qu'il avait visité." Le paysagiste, ajoute Reyer, travaille sur place, "mais il est rare que le poète et le musicien traduisent, à l'instant même où elle se produit, l'impression que leur donne l'aspect d'une vallée sombre ou d'un riant paysage." . . . "Les beaux paysages, écrivait Berlioz à Richard Wagner, les hautes cîmes, les grands aspects de la mer, m'absorbent complètement, au lieu de provoquer chez moi la manifestation de la pensée. Je sens alors et ne saurais exprimer. Je ne puis dessiner la lune qu'en regardant son image au fond d'un puits."'

the other. In the *Phaedrus* myth ecstasy begins with—this must not be blinked by the admirers of Plato—with the awakening of unnatural passion, which is, doubtless, 'conquered': but the resulting so-called 'right', or pure, love is not, we must contend, to be freed, by any 'conquest' in that field, from the taint of its origin or from risk of reversion to type. No praise of its 'purity' can alter the fact that, as Aristotle holds (*E. N.* vii. 5, and Plato himself seems to agree in *Laws* 841 D), the man who has this passion, even if he conquer it, is outside the pale of human morality and immorality. That Plato should have trifled with this elementary truth of psychology and morals, if only to the extent of borrowing a word with a bad meaning in order to give it a good meaning (see *Sympos.* 211 B), is a melancholy fact, the thought of which broods over one's reading of the *Phaedrus* myth, the most brilliant piece, to my mind, in the whole range of his writings. That Plato's Vision of the Eternal Beauty, however, was the result of some erotic incident in his own life is, I think, a gratuitous supposition. The Eternal Beauty was seldom far from his sight; his vision of it was nothing exceptional, and is more naturally accounted for by the steady influence of his temperament—that 'prophetic' temperament, the psychology of which I have described and illustrated—than by any startling episode in his life. When it is assumed that the erotic experience so vividly described in the *Phaedrus* myth must have been his own, too little account is taken, it seems to me, of the fact that he was a great dramatist to whom the manners of his nation and age gave ample opportunity of observing in others the experience in question. It is true that he glorified it; but that might well be just because he knew it only as dramatist. None the less, his sympathy with it—even though we recognize the dramatic nature of that sympathy—is a painfully significant fact. What a world of difference there is between Plato's attitude and Dante's! Plato's Lovers at last get wings of the same feather in Heaven for their Love's sake;

Brunetto Latini, Dante's divine pity for whom is one of the most deeply touching things in the whole *Commedia*, walks his weary round in Hell.[1]

The ecstasy of Diotima's Discourse, on the other hand, is, notwithstanding an expression just now alluded to (*Sympos.* 211 B), the purified, or etherialized, form of natural passion.

Differing profoundly in this respect, the *Phaedrus* myth and Diotima's Discourse agree in making the Contemplation of Eternal Beauty man's chief end. This end may sometimes, we are given to understand, be realized in one intense moment of ecstasy (*Sympos.* 210 E); but more often it is achieved in detail by those who, in the pursuit of art and science, and in the conduct of their daily lives, 'remember aright' who see the Work of artist, the Theory of man of science, the Virtue of citizen, as *beautiful*, and enjoy eternal and immutable moments in the Contemplation of these objects—moments which, when they wake to the duties and pursuits of daily life, are 'remembered',[2] and make all the difference to their outlook upon life. That is, the Idea of Beauty has a regulative value; or, rather, *is the regulative value* of any Idea whatever—the value which any Idea whatever has simply as being object of Contemplation, as being, in one word, *beautiful*. Did Ideas not thus, ever and anon, rivet our attention to themselves separately by individual beauty, awaken our wonder, fill us with the awe of their real presence, they would often have difficulty in maintaining themselves as instruments of Discourse. And the Ideas with which the natural sciences work are no more independent of the strength which is thus derived from the 'Idea of Beauty' than are those which the moral sciences employ. The κλῖμαξ, as we may call it, of Diotima recognizes this fully—καλὰ σώματα, καλὰ ἐπιτηδεύματα, καλὰ μαθήματα, αὐτὸ τὸ καλόν (*Sympos.* 211 C). The End is Contemplation, as the Beginning is Contemplation. The Beginning

[1] *Inf.* xv.
[2] This is, doubtless, a case of 'affective memory': see *supra*, p. 162.

is made when some instance, seen with the eye of contemplative rêverie, shines out as *beautiful*; then, other instances are seen to have the same characteristic; then, the law of their beautiful characterization, and the laws of the characterization of other groups, are abstracted by thought—we are now in the region of Discourse, and 'on the move', but always ready to 'rest' for a moment now and then, and realize in consciousness the beauty of the laws which we are abstracting for the service of morals and science: and so, through spheres, included always in larger spheres, of connected laws, the Ascension is made, as of a κλῖμαξ of Purification, till, suddenly, the Beatific Vision bursts upon the eyes of the μύστης. After years, it may be, of laborious thinking, he attains, in one supreme moment of intuition (*Sympos.* 210 E ἐξαίφνης), to the Perfect Initiation. The object of this intuition is described in language which has puzzled and misled critics from Aristotle downwards, and evidently needs for its interpretation a psychological key which they do not possess. It is described as a Marvel, as a Thing of Beauty, as Eternal Being without generation or corruption or increase or decrease, as an Absolute without material embodiment of any kind or inherence in aught else, always abiding in Itself, with Itself (*Sympos.* 210 E ff.). In the contemplation of this Beauty man is immortal—not as individual, but as partaker of the continuous life of knowledge and noble conduct which individuals, inspired by the vision of this Beauty, from generation to generation, maintain. Thus this mortal puts on immortality. All men endeavour to eternalize themselves, in their children after the flesh, or their children after the spirit—their works, poems, laws, and such like; but the highest kind of self-eternalization is the education of each younger generation in Philosophy. Plato was a childless man; and was, moreover, as Professor Natorp suggests,[1] doubtless thinking of his own work in the Academy.

[1] p. 66.

The *Symposium* recognizes only the immortality of procreation, and of spiritual, rather than of physical, procreation. It does not recognize 'personal immortality'. Professor Natorp will have it that the *Symposium*, with its non-personal immortality, throws light back on the meaning of 'immortality' in the *Phaedo*, which he places immediately before the *Symposium*.[1] I do not think that the attempt either to reconcile, or to find important differences between, the 'immortality' of two such widely separated pieces as the *Phaedo* and *Symposium* is justified. Surely the impending death of a beloved friend, in the *Phaedo*, makes it necessary, or natural, to think of 'personal immortality'; while a non-personal immortality is quite in place in the *Symposium*, concerned, as it is, with ἔρως, the desire of procreation. The *motif* is entirely different in each Dialogue.

That ecstasy, procured by initiatory rites, was in Plato's mind when he wrote the *Phaedrus* myth and Diotima's Discourse he plainly gives us to understand; and it is the psychology of ecstasy, or concentration, as I have tried to outline it in this Essay, which gives the key to the Doctrine of Ideas as set forth in these pieces. Further, as I have shown elsewhere,[2] it was the presentment of the Doctrine in these pieces (together with the mythological presentment of it in the *Timaeus*), not the logical presentment of it, which really 'caught on'. It was the Idea for Contemplation, not the Idea for Discourse, which really 'caught on'. For the Alexandrine Neoplatonists, and for all practising Platonists, their successors, down to our own day, the Doctrine of Ideas is that set forth mythically in the *Phaedrus*,

[1] pp. 166-7. Dr. Horn, on the other hand, places the *Phaedo* after the *Symposium*: he thinks (*Platonstudien*, ii. 279) that Plato found the earthly immortality of the *Symposium* (quite a new idea which struck him) so unsatisfactory, that, in the *Phaedo* and *Republic*, he returned to his old doctrine of personal immortality. These minute inquiries, as I have said (*supra*, p. 85), detecting alterations in Plato's views from Dialogue to Dialogue, ignore the capital fact that he was a dramatist.

[2] *Myths of Plato*, pp. 475 ff.

*Symposium,* and *Timaeus*: the logical side of the Doctrine never seems to have interested people. Notably, for the two modern Philosophers, Leibniz and Schopenhauer, who have made the finest and the most original use of the Doctrine of Ideas—the one in Theology, the other in Aesthetics—and have best interpreted the secret of its perennial attractiveness, it is the Idea as object of Contemplation, not the Idea as instrument of Discourse, that matters. And Spinoza's *Res sub specie aeternitatis concipere*, too, is near akin to Plato's contemplation of the Eternal Idea, being, as Professor Höffding contends in an illuminating passage,[1] an affective and aesthetic, far more than an intellectual and scientific, attitude. It is by 'concentration', as set forth in the Fifth Part of Spinoza's *Ethics*,[2] that his μύστης attains to the sense of 'out-of-timeness', and, with it, to the sense of 'immortality': 'iam certi sumus mentem aeternam esse quatenus res sub aeternitatis specie concipit,' he says;[3] with which dictum the following pronouncement of Schopenhauer[4] bears close comparison: 'Wer nun sich in die Anschauung der Natur so weit vertieft und verloren hat, dass er nur noch als rein erkennendes Subject da ist, wird eben dadurch unmittelbar inne, dass er als solches die Bedingung, also der Träger, der Welt und alles objectiven Daseins ist.... Er zieht also die Natur in sich hinein, so dass er sie nur noch als ein Accidenz seines Wesens empfindet. In diesem Sinne sagt Byron:

> Are not the mountains, waves, and skies, a part
> Of me and of my soul, as I of them?

Wie aber sollte, wer dieses fühlt, sich selbst, im Gegensatz der unvergänglichen Natur, für absolut vergänglich halten? Ihn wird vielmehr das Bewusstsein dessen ergreifen, was der Upanischad des Veda ausspricht: Hae omnes creaturae in totum ego sum, et praeter me aliud ens non est.'

---

[1] *Philosophy of Religion*, p. 124 (Eng. transl.).
[2] *Eth.* v. 25-38.    [3] *Eth.* v. 31, scholium.
[4] *Welt als Wille und Vorstellung*, i. 213.

Let me now add, in conclusion, a few pages on the Doctrine, or Myth, of 'Recollection', by way of summarizing the results reached in the Second Part of this Essay.

The *Meno*, admittedly a Dialogue of the early period, presents the Doctrine of Ideas as a Doctrine of ἀνάμνησις, and so does the *Timaeus*, one of the latest of the series. The connexion between the Doctrine of Ideas and ἀνάμνησις is throughout present, and in the *Phaedo* and *Phaedrus* prominently present, to Plato's mind. We may hope, then, to get to the heart of the Doctrine of Ideas, to that in it which explains at once its obscurity for outsiders like Aristotle, and its perennial attractiveness for others, if we succeed in discovering the psychological meaning of ἀνάμνησις.

In ordinary cases of 'Recollection' an object now presented to sense recalls quite definitely a similar object experienced in the past, the old, as well as the new—the past, as well as the present—belonging to the 'wide-awake' world; for example, I go into a palm-house, and see there a palm-tree, which I recognize at first sight as being like one which I definitely remember having seen on a visit to the Oasis of Biskra, a visit which is part of the continuous text of my wide-awake workaday life; and such 'recognition' of the new as, in a sense, old, is always welcomed as an eminently satisfactory experience: one feels that one is 'keeping up the continuity of one's life', 'profiting by past experience', 'getting on', 'not losing one's way in the unknown'. This wide-awake 'satisfactory' recollection or recognition I would call Empirical Recollection or Recognition. But, if we consider the account of ἀνάμνησις given in the *Meno* (81), we find that it is exactly this kind of Empirical Recollection which, as δόξα, is shown to be insufficient. The Empirical Recollection in which δόξα consists must be superseded by another kind of Recollection, by that in which ἐπιστήμη consists. What, then, is it that this other kind of Recollection recalls? It recalls, the *Meno* tells us, not the particular or effect, but the universal or cause;

the 'Recollection' in which ἐπιστήμη consists is αἰτίας λογισμός—it is the successful thinking out of the causal context of a given object of sense, by bringing to bear on that object the right 'points of view', general and special. Here, although it is not, as in the case of the Biskra palm-tree, a mere particular that we 'recollect', but a 'point of view', yet we are still in the wide-awake world of Discourse, and our 'Recollection' is still 'Empirical'. We must therefore distinguish, it would appear, two kinds of 'Empirical Recollection'. But there is an ἀνάμνησις which differs *toto caelo* from this 'Empirical Recollection', whether of particular or of universal—there is a Transcendental Recollection; and it is the *Meno* itself, with the mythical setting which it gives to its strictly methodological account of ἀνάμνησις, which prepares us for it, and for an entirely new answer to the question, 'What is it, then, that we recollect?' 'On the occasion of the presentation of sensible objects resembling them, we recollect the Eternal Ideas which grow in the Supercelestial Plain of Truth—Existences without shape, or colour, or any other sensible quality.' This is Plato's answer in the *Phaedrus* myth.

How are we to describe psychologically, and explain, the experience pictured thus? That there is a real experience behind this picture of the Ideas growing in the Plain of Truth—a real experience capable of psychological description and explanation, there can be no doubt. The high-strung language of the *Phaedrus* myth is not mere rhetoric; it is honest. What, then, is the experience which it expresses? What is the object of Transcendental Recollection? It is something, we are told, which cannot be perceived by sense, something without sensible qualities. If it is not a sensible object, is it, then, a conceptual object? No, it is not a conceptual object either—it is not a universal, a general point of view, a law of nature. The Idea, merely as point of view or law of nature, could not have stirred that *amor intellectualis* with which devotees have always regarded it. It is essentially as *feeling* of some sort—feeling always ready to condense itself, as it were, round some *image* which it transfigures—that the experience of the μαινόμενος who 'recollects the Idea' must be conceived, if the perennial fascination of the Doctrine of Ideas is to be adequately accounted for. If Plato had planted his Plain of Truth with Passions and Delights, instead of with Virtues and Sciences, we might perhaps have understood him more easily when he describes its nurslings as without shape, or colour, or any of the qualities which belong to objects of sense or to their faintest images; but, even as it is, his description is not really open to misunderstanding, if reviewed in the light of present-day psychology. It is not primarily an 'object' that is 'recollected', but a feeling that is awakened, in the ecstatic experience, the psychology of which explains the *Phaedrus* picture in particular, and generally accounts for the fascination exercised by the tenet of Eternal Separate Existences behind the flux of sensibles. This tenet has, as we have seen, a large methodological significance; but its methodological significance does not account for its fascination.

There are two kinds of ἀνάμνησις, then: (1) Empirical Recollection, in which either (*a*) a similar particular is recalled, or (*b*) a general point of view is taken, a law of nature is conceived: and (2) Transcendental Recollection, in which a *feeling* is awakened by the presence of some sensible object—a feeling which is always ready to condense itself, as it were, round, to 'fringe', an *image*, so that the image becomes transfigured, becomes an object of wonder, and takes rank as archetype of the sensible object, of which it is, after all, the mental representation.

It is with what, in the present connexion, it is convenient to call Transcendental Recollection that the Second Part of this Essay has been all along concerned. Our psychological account of this variety of experience began by taking note of the distinction between Discourse and Contemplation; and it was shown that the object of Contemplation is the individual regarded as end, while particulars, regarded conveniently as instances of a law to be evolved or applied, are the objects of Discourse. In Discourse we never rest in any presented object, but always pass from it back, in recollection, to similar objects, and forward, in expectation, to a future conceived as containing objects likely to resemble those recollected in the past, the objects reviewed in the process being interesting, not in themselves, but as vehicles of some common quality serviceable for some ulterior end. But sometimes the presented object is such as to claim Contemplation *for itself*, and to exclude 'recollection' and 'expectation' of objects resembling it in the possession of some serviceable quality. A common case of such exclusion is where the object presented to sense is very familiar— either belongs to a class of objects with which one has been intimately acquainted ever since one could remember anything, such as a bird in the bush, a cloud in the sky, a rose in the garden; or else is a singular object specially connected with one's own life, such as a bit of intimately known, dearly loved landscape, or a picture which one has seen from childhood hanging in its own place. Here there is no 'Empirical Recollection'—no calling up of 'similar instances' out of an object-filled past continuous with the present moment—no bringing of a convenient point of view to bear on an object requiring interpretation. One's experience is simply that of acquiescence in the familiar present. But it is just out of such acquiescence—especially if the object be a singular object, long familiar, now seen again after lapse of time, as when the bit of intimately known, dearly loved, landscape is revisited, or one enters the room, and there is the picture on the wall just as one left it years ago —it is out of such acquiescence in the familiar present that, for some minds, a sudden flash of Transcendental Recollection is apt to lighten—recollection of the Real Landscape, which is not a landscape, of the Real Picture, which is not a picture, known, long ago, far away somewhere—and yet, see! it is here! it is 'present' in this landscape, in this picture—visibly present—for surely I *see* the landscape, the picture, before me, so altered that I cannot take my eyes off it, it is become so wonderful, so beautiful!

Naïve acquiescence in the familiar object present to sense has suddenly passed into wondering Contemplation of it; and the Contemplation has become more and more intense, till one is 'lost' in the Contemplation, and its object is 'eternalized'—the 'Eternal Idea', known long since, is revealed in the sensible object—literally *in* it. This is the ecstatic experience which finds imaginative expression in the Myth, as it must be called, of Eternal Unchangeable Ideas—existences without shape, or colour, or any other quality by which objects of sense are characterized—existences which are what objects of sense *were before they came here*—existences which are these objects not yet realized, not yet apprehended by human sense, but still abiding as 'Possibilities' in the Mind of God—so Leibniz figures them in the *Théodicée*—nurslings of the Plain of Truth, beyond the region of Space and Time—so they are described in the *Phaedrus* myth.

This 'Transcendental Recollection', this 'recollection of that which has no shape, or colour, or other sensible quality', I regard as the experience by expressing which the Doctrine of Ideas obtained, and continues to maintain, its immense vogue; and the 'value' of the experience, as an element in the Life of Art and Religion, has nothing, I take it, to fear from any psychological explanation such as that in which I have attempted to bring 'objects without shape, or colour, or any other sensible quality' into relation with such doctrines as those of 'affective states produced by arrest of sensori-motor tendencies', 'emotional memory', 'psychic dissociation', 'ideographic schemata'. 'To plead the organic causation of a religious state of mind in refutation of its claim to possess superior spiritual value is quite illogical and arbitrary, unless one have already worked out in advance some psycho-physical theory connecting spiritual values in general with determinate sorts of physiological change. Otherwise none of our thoughts and feelings, not even our scientific doctrines, not even our *dis*-beliefs, could retain any value as revelations of the truth, for every one of them without exception flows from the state of their possessor's body at the time. . . . In the natural sciences and industrial arts it never occurs to any one to try to refute opinions by showing up their author's neurotic constitution. Opinions here are invariably tested by logic and experiment, no matter what may be their author's neurological type. It should be no otherwise with religious opinions. Their value can only be ascertained by spiritual judgements directly passed upon them, judgements based on our own immediate feeling primarily; and secondarily on what we can ascertain of their experimental relations to our moral needs and to the rest of what we hold as true.'[1]

[1] Professor W. James, *The Varieties of Religious Experience*, pp. 14 and 17.

## NOTE ON MUSICAL EXPERIENCE

(See *supra*, p. 153).

The Dean of Christ Church writes to me :—'Mozart's way of composing was probably rather exceptional—at any rate there are composers whose proceedings did not resemble Mozart's in the least, so far as we can tell.' . . . 'Beethoven's melodies, however simple to all appearance, were not attained suddenly, but by successive corrections of an imperfect idea. In his note-books (which are extant) there are notes of attempts at tunes which when completed were so simple that it is difficult to understand how he can have failed to hit them off at the very first effort.[1] On the other hand, the texture of his composition is, as a rule, very much closer than that of Mozart; and one would say, looking on from outside, that it represents not merely effort at producing the melodies, but elaborate thought of a quasi-logical character in their exposition and treatment.'

With regard to what Musical Experience itself is, the Dean writes :—' There are two points I should like to mention—one is this: that musicians seem to me to be distinctive in that their language is simply emotion. . . . The world when they are thinking musically seems to be an emotional whole rather than an intellectual whole or system of laws. . . . The musician does in the way of emotion what Spinoza wanted done from the philosophical side. He sees his emotion *sub specie aeternitatis* ; but this does not mean that he defines it calmly and places it in a system, but that the whole world is swallowed up in it. . . . Again, it is possible for a musician to get his emotional stimulus from some very small circumstance. The last movement of Beethoven's last Quartett is called *Der schwergefasste Entschluss*. The movement is introduced by three phrases set to the words " Must it be ?—it must be—it must be " (Muss es sein ?—es muss sein—es muss sein). These are part, not of a tragic reflection on fate, but of a dialogue with Beethoven's cook as to some dish for his dinner. This has set up the whole emotions of the man.'

[1] See Grove's *Dictionary of Music*, art. Beethoven, p. 230, ed. 1904.

# INDEX

Academy, the, 4.
Adam, his *Republic of Plato*, referred to, 10; distinguishes 'Idea of square' and 'mathematical square', 57; on 'paradeigmatic' view of Idea taken in *Rep.*, 61; on Lotze's interpretation of Doctrine of Ideas, 109.
Aesthetic Experience, a variety of ecstasy, 151; a condition in which 'concentration' isolates an object, 135; a condition in which dream-state co-exists with, or alternates rapidly with, waking state, 141 ff.; place of rêverie-image in, 140-51; clashing of 'psychic systems' in, 148 ff.; rêverie-images of, cluster round 'prophetic' trance-image, 163 ff.; perception of 'ugliness' in, 146; μέθεξις not a difficulty for, 169; only in it are there Eternal and Immutable Archetypes, 172; sometimes 'contaminates' Plato's discursive experience, 172; illustrated from painting, 146-50; illustrated from poetry, 150-1; illustrated from music, 152 ff.; Schopenhauer on, 145-6.
'Affective Memory', 162, 194.
Algazel, 158 ff.
ἀνάμνησις, 192-6; 'empirical' and 'transcendental', 192-6; logical side of doctrine of, in *Meno*, 25 ff.; as αἰτίας λογισμός, 28; unfortunate influence of doctrine of, according to Prof. Natorp, 28; in *Phaedo*, 42, 43.
Angell, Prof. J. R., on 'affective memory', 162.
Antisthenes, 29, 35, 67.
*Apology*, 16 ff.
Apraxia, 180.

Archer-Hind, Mr., on ὑποδοχή, 104.
Aristotle, his criticism of Doctrine of Ideas, 2-5, 107 ff.; his criticism has misled subsequent expositors, 5; his misunderstanding of the Doctrine of Ideas, 75; misunderstands methodological, and is blind to aesthetic side of Doctrine of Ideas, 3-5, 129; unconscious of the experience for which Ideas are 'Things', 129; his criticism of Idea of Good, 54; his Doctrine of Substance basis from which he criticizes Doctrine of Ideas, 108 ff.; his difficulty about Universals not being Substances, 110 ff., 181-2; his Doctrine of Categories assumes Substance as given, 107; unwittingly develops and makes explicit Plato's Doctrine of Ideas, 112 ff.; his φύσις similar to Platonic παρουσία, 116; his οὐσία ἄνευ ὕλης equivalent to Plato's χωριστὸν εἶδος, 113-14; his τόποι compared with Methods of Agreement, Difference, &c., 125; his testimony for a 'Later Theory of Ideas', how to be interpreted, 121-2; at once a Logician and a Naturalist, 111; his opinion of pupils of Academy, 4.
Arnold, Matthew, quoted on the language of the Bible, 51.
Arréat, M., on experience of musician, 152 ff.; on 'affective memory', 162; on the Ideogram, 177-8; on memory, visual, auditive, and motor, 184; the imaged, not the actually presented, landscape inspires the artist, 185-6.

## INDEX

Arrest of tendencies produces affective states, 136, 147 ff.
Avicenna, 158 ff.

Baldwin, Prof., says children make 'persons' sooner than 'things', 133; on 'expectation', 135; on law of circular reaction, 140; on 'organic imitation', 170; on apraxia, 180; opposes *habit* to *interest*, 182.
Beauty, Idea of, its 'visibility' insisted on by Plato, 167; regulative value of, in *Symposium*, 188.
'Beauty perceived in an object', psychological account of, 139 ff.
Beautiful Body', the, consubstantial with the Idea of Beauty, 136.
Bergson, M., on the 'intelligible world', 39; quoted on *la durée vraie*, 78; his '*durée vraie* symbolized in Time and Space', compared with doctrine of $\dot{\upsilon}\pi o\delta o\chi\acute{\eta}$, 105; on art and hypnosis, 140-1; his *durée vraie* and musical experience, 153; his *durée vraie* and the One of Plotinus, 158.
Berkeley, distinguishes 'notion' from 'idea', 58.
Bonitz, on Ideas as Numbers, 117.
Burnet, Prof., holds that the Ideas are never represented mythically, 171.
Bury, Mr. R. G., his 'Later Platonism' referred to, 8; his *Philebus* referred to, 10; on τὰ μαθηματικά, 58; on Ideas as Numbers, 94; his view of place assigned to Ideas in *Philebus*, 99.

Campbell, his contributions to question of chronological order of Dialogues, 15.
'Categories', mathematical, logical, moral, in *Phaedo*, 43; list of, in *Theaetetus*, 66, in *Soph.*, 86; of *Theaet.*, their relation to other Ideas, 68.
Cerebral Dissociation, 144.

Charcot, Dr., referred to, 182, 184.
*Charmides*, 20 ff.
χωρισμός, 18, 41, 42, 168.
Circular Reaction, law of, 139, 140.
'Clear and distinct ideas', 58.
Coleridge, on relation of Poet's images to predominant passion, 164-5.
'Concentration', 134.
Consistency—σαφήνεια, the criterion of truth in *Phaedo* and *Rep.*, 46, 58.
Contemplation, distinguished from Discourse, 11, 130 ff.; its object the *Thing*, as individual, as end, and as beautiful, 131-3; only for it are there Eternal and Immutable Archetypes, 172-3; Plato makes a 'regulative use' of its Eternal Archetypes in Discourse, 173-4; reveals God as Person, 157; induced and maintained by artistic representation, 133-4.
*Cratylus*, 34 ff.; absence of 'Platonic Idea' from, maintained by Dr. Raeder, 35.
*Crito*, 19 f.; 'Conscience' in, 19.
Cudworth, quoted for 'essence cannot be *arbitrary*', 61.
Cunninghame-Graham, G., *Teresa*, by, referred to, 161.

Dante, on 'Light intervening between Truth and Intellect', 53; his *Paradiso*, psychology of, same as that of Doctrine of Ideas in *Symp.* and *Phaedrus*, 148; his *fulgor vivi e vincenti*, and Moslem 'Illuminative Philosophy', 159; his Mount of Purgatory, 159, 161; quoted in illustration of 'affective memory', 162; referred to in illustration of clustering of aesthetic images round prophetic trance-image, 164; and Brunetto Latini, 188.
Davies, Mr. J. Llewelyn, on Plato's Later Theory of Ideas, 8.
Descartes, his criterion of Truth, 58.
Dialectic *versus* Rhetoric, 24, 25,

## INDEX

30; as Science of the Good, 55; as *scientia scientiarum*, distinguished from a special science, 56; in *Phaedrus*, 6?.
Dialectical method, 115; account of, in *Rep.*, 54 ff., 77.
Dialectician, defined, 37.
Dialogues, earliest, importance of, for interpretation of Doctrine of Ideas, 7.
Diotima, compared with Teresa and other mystics, 158.
Discourse, distinguished from Contemplation, 130 ff.; object of, the Common Quality as means, 132-3; God is not a Person, but a System of Laws, for, 157.
Dream-state, general characteristics of, 141; coexists with, or alternates rapidly with, waking state in aesthetic experience, 141 ff.; how related to concentration, and perception of Beauty in an object, 140 ff.

Ecstasy, aesthetic experience a variety of, 151; 'prophetic', illustrated, 154 ff.; 'aesthetic' distinguished from 'prophetic', 162 ff.; M. Guyot on, 154.
εἰδῶν φίλοι, who are they?, 87.
ἐπακτικοὶ λόγοι καὶ τὸ ὁρίζεσθαι καθόλου, 15, 16; advance of Doctrine of Ideas on, 18, 19.
*Euthydemus*, 28, 29.
*Euthyphro*, 17 ff.; Prof. Natorp doubts authenticity of, 17; logical lesson of, 18.

Galton, Mr. F., on visualization of numbers, 183.
Geley, Dr., on neurones and synapses, 142.
Genius, artistic, how distinguished from Talent, 163 ff.
God, in *Timaeus*, relation of, to Idea of the Good, 101-2; in *Timaeus*, relation of, to other Ideas, 102-3; as Person revealed to Contemplation, 157.

Good, the, in Dialogues of 'Socratic Group', 18, 19, 20, 21, 22, 25; in *Gorgias*, 29-31; in the *Phaedo*, 45; in *Republic*, 49 ff.; in *Philebus*, 92, 96-100; relation of Ideas to, in *Philebus*, 57-8; as principle of scientific explanation in *Phaedo*, *Republic*, and *Philebus* respectively, 96-7; is ἐπέκεινα τῆς οὐσίας, 51; as Ideal, 53.
Good, Idea of, 115; as object of Dialectic, 55, 56; evidence for, 58; relation of, to God, 59; relation of God in *Timaeus* to, 101-2; covers the three Kantian Ideas of Reason, 58; Aristotle's criticism of, 54.
*Gorgias*, 29 ff.; relation of, to *Phaedrus* according to Prof. Natorp, 31, 32.
Grote, speaks of 'Dialogues of Search', 16; on *Protagoras*, 24; his *Aristotle* referred to, 72; on table of 'values' in *Philebus*, 98.
Guyau, M., referred to for association of affective states, 165.
Guyot, M., on prophetic ecstasy, 154.

Hartmann, Von, on the Ideas, 109; on distinction between Talent and Original Genius, 166.
Höffding, Prof., on Doctrine of Ideas, 137; on the 'permanence of value', 175; on relation between ethics and religion, 176; on Spinoza, 191.
Horn, Dr., his *Platonstudien* referred to, 15; his view of relation of *Theaetetus* to *Parmenides*, 65; places the *Sophistes* before the *Republic*, 85; on difference between *Republic* and *Sophistes*, 88-9; on 'immortality' in *Symposium*, and in *Phaedo* and *Republic*, 190.
ὁσιότης, in *Euthyphro* and *Protagoras*, 18.
Hume, on 'the eternal frame and constitution of animals',

44; referred to for association of passions, 165.
Hypnosis, 140–1.
ὑποδοχή, doctrine of, in *Timaeus*, 104–5.

Idea, the, for Contemplation, and in Discourse, distinguished, 11 ff.; for Contemplation, not that in Discourse, conspicuous in later Platonism, 190–1; in Discourse, (1) Cause, or Law, discovered in some special inquiry, (2) category of understanding employed in all inquiries, 119; not a 'universal substance', but an 'individual substance', 112; its being broken up among particulars, difficulty about, 77–8, 93; unity of, amounts to unity of Consciousness, 77–8; as 'Thing in Itself', 79; set forth as δύναμις, in *Sophistes*, 88; as 'use' or 'Final Cause' in *Cratylus* and *Republic*, 36, 60; as παράδειγμα, 102–3; 'paradeigmatic' view of, taken in *Meno*, 27; 'paradeigmatic' view of, taken in *Republic*, 61; as 'separate', 'immanent', 'paradeigmatic', 125–6; as Concept, 37; as Ideogram, 176 ff.; as Ideogram contrasted with Idea as Concept, 181; how understood by Leibniz, 109; exists as 'eternal possibility' according to Von Hartmann, 109; has 'Validity' according to Lotze, 109, 116; existence of, only 'hypothetical' according to Prof. Jackson, 109.
ἰδέα, term occurs in *Euthyphro*, 17.
Ideas, the, are 'Things' for Contemplation, but not for Discourse, 129; distinguished as of general, and of special, applicability, 9; extend over the whole ground of science, 76; five classes of, in *Parmenides*, 75; a table of, given, 122–3; as 'Categories of Understanding' already recognized by Plato in *Republic*, 34; as Numbers, 94, 116 ff.

Ideas, Doctrine of, has two sides, methodological, and aesthetic, 3; methodological side of, 6, 7, and Part I, *passim*; its methodology does not account for its attractiveness, 129; as expressing aesthetic experience, 128 ff.
Ideogram, the, in Art and Science, 177 ff.; M. Arréat on, 177–8; and Concept tend to coalesce in Plato's mind, 181–2.
Images, 'activity' of, 170–1.
Imitation, organic, 170.
Immortality, personal, proof of, in *Phaedo*, inconclusive, 47; in *Symposium* and *Phaedo* respectively, 189, 190; Spinoza on, 191.
Intelligible, relation of, to sensible in Plato, 185.

Jackson, Prof. H., on 'Plato's Later Theory of Ideas', 8, 9; rejects 'Categories' of *Theaetetus* from list of 'Ideas', 67–8; assigns Ideas to τὸ μικτόν in *Philebus*, 98; his view that existence of Ideas is only 'hypothetical', 9, 109; distinguishes εἰδητικοὶ ἀριθμοί from 'Ideas', 118.
James, Prof. W., on pictures and the mystic consciousness, 161; on 'organic causation' and 'spiritual value', 196–7.
Jowett, on Idea of the Good, 53–4; on 'chasm' between Idea and particulars, 79; on connexion between the two parts of *Parmenides*, 80.

Kant, his three Ideas of Reason covered by Plato's Idea of the Good, 58.
Ker, Prof. W. P., on Goethe's 'Platonic idea of the absolute plant', 173.
Κοινωνία εἰδῶν, 82, 83, 87.

*Laches*, 22 ff.
*Laws*, 106.
Leibniz, how he understands the Ideas, 109; his doctrine of Real

Presence in the Eucharist, 136; his Platonism concerned with the Idea for Contemplation, 191; his 'Eternal Possibilities', 160-1, 196.
Leuba, Prof., quoted, 156.
Light, simile of, in Plato, Aristotle, Fourth Gospel, Dante, 53; in ecstatic experience, 160.
Lipps, Prof., his theory of *Einfühlung*, 169.
Lotze, his interpretation of Doctrine of Ideas, 6, 109; on traditional misunderstanding of Doctrine of Ideas, 130.
Lucas, Mlle Blanche, her musical experience, 152.
Lutoslawski, Dr., his order of Dialogues, 14, 15; on date of *Euthyphro*, 17; on development of Doctrine of Ideas in Plato's mind, 32-4.

M<sup>c</sup>Dougall, Mr., on State of the Brain during Hypnosis, and 'cerebral dissociation', 141; on projection of mental images on a card, 142; on neurones and synapses, 142.
μαθηματικά, as intermediate between αἰσθητά and νοητά, 57-8, 93-4, 99, 100; Mr. R. G. Bury on, 58.
Mendelssohn, his musical experience, 153.
*Meno*, 24 ff.
μέθεξις, 45; means 'predication', 77; not a difficulty where aesthetic experience is concerned, 169.
Methods of Agreement, Difference, &c., compared with Plato's employment of Categories of Identity, Difference, &c., 123-4; compared with Aristotle's τόποι, 125.
Mill, J. S., on 'Whether Definitions are of Names or of Things', 37; on criterion of Truth, 58.
Millet, quoted, 150.
μίμησις, substitution of, for μέθεξις or παρουσία, 8, 126.
Mithraic κλῖμαξ, 161.

Moral Sciences, concepts of, marking 'values', are easily figured as Eternal Archetypes, 174.
Moslem mystics, referred to in illustration of prophetic ecstasy, 158 ff.
Mozart, his musical experience, 153.
Music, aesthetic experience in, 152 ff.; M. Arréat on aesthetic experience in, 152 ff.; Schopenhauer's Theory of, 154.

Natorp, Prof., his *Platos Ideenlehre*, referred to, 5, and elsewhere, *passim*; ignores aesthetic side of Doctrine of Ideas, 10 ff., 26; on *Phaedrus* Myth, 11; his view of *Phaedrus* as contributing to misunderstanding of Doctrine of Ideas, 62-3; thinks that Doctrine of Ideas first set forth distinctly in *Phaedrus*, 64; on Lotze's interpretation of Doctrine of Ideas, 109; on 'immortality' in *Phaedo* and *Symposium* respectively, 190; on Ideas as Numbers, 117; on ὑποδοχή, 105.
Neurones and Synapses, 142.
νοῦς ποιητικός, 53.

ὠφέλεια, distinguished from οὐσία in *Theaetetus*, 52, 66.

Painting, aesthetic experience in, 146-50.
παράδειγμα, term occurs in *Euthyphro*, 17; the Idea as, compared with the Ideogram, 179.
*Parmenides*, 68 ff.; who is the 'Young Socrates'?, 69 ff.; who is 'Parmenides'?, 71, 80; Eleatic influence in, 73, 80; five classes of Ideas in, 75 f.; relation between the two parts of, 82-4; what does the One in the Second Part of, stand for?, 81 ff.; κοινωνία εἰδῶν in, 82-3; Prof. A. E. Taylor's interpretation of, 73 ff.
παρουσία and χωρισμός, considered

in connexion with rêverie-image, 168.
Passions, association of, 165.
Paulhan, M., on aesthetic emotion, 142–3; on affective states produced by arrest of tendencies, 136, 147, 149; on 'affective phenomena', 163; referred to for association of affective states, 165.
*Phaedo*, 39 ff.; methodology of, 41 ff., 77; meaning of χωρισμός in, 41, 42.
*Phaedrus*, 62 ff.; Prof. Natorp's view of, 62–3; early date assigned to by Prof. Natorp, 63; presentation of Idea in it and in *Symposium* differs from that in other Dialogues, 65; Idea of Beauty in, 167.
*Phaedrus* Myth, 186 ff.; ecstasy of, how induced, 187; the Ideas in, 196.
*Philebus*, 92 ff.; γένεσις εἰς οὐσίαν, 95; τὸ μικτόν, what?, 95–6; relation of Ideas to the Good in, 57–8; where are the Ideas (other than the Good) placed?, 98–100; importance of *media axiomata* recognized, 93, 94, 117; table of 'values' in, 98.
Platonists, practising, 5.
Plotinus, accepts the Idea of the Good from Plato as Supreme Principle, 97; quoted, to illustrate prophetic ecstasy, 154 ff.; his Philosophy is ecstatic experience rationalized, 160; his One as Self, 157; his One as ἄμορφον εἶδος, 161.
Poetry, aesthetic experience in, 150–1.
*Politicus*, 89 ff.; measurement (1) mathematical, (2) teleological, 89, 90; ἡ τῆς γενέσεως ἀναγκαία οὐσία, 90; μέτριον of, and ἀγαθόν of *Republic* compared, 90–1.
'Pragmatic Postulates', 44-5-6.
'Pragmatism' and 'Intellectualism' in Plato's day, 100.
*Protagoras*, 23 f.
ψυχή, place assigned to, in *Sophistes*, 87–8.

'Psychic Systems', the clashing of, in aesthetic experience, 148 ff.
Psychology, importance of, for interpretation of Doctrine of Ideas, 1–13.

Qualities and Thing, 131 ff.
Queyrat, M., on *Moteurs*, 182.

Raeder, Dr., his *Platons Philosophische Entwickelung* referred to, 15; on date of *Euthyphro*, 17, 18; on date of *Phaedrus*, 64; on the stylometric test, 84; his view of the relation of *Theaetetus* and *Sophistes* to *Parmenides*, 84; on relation of *Politicus* to Plato's opinion of the Younger Dionysius, 91; his view of place assigned to Ideas in *Philebus*, 98–9.
Representation, artistic, induces and maintains Contemplation, 133, 134, 137, 138, 144.
*Republic*, 47 ff.; iii. 402 c, Zeller, Adam, and Natorp, on, 47–8; Idea of the Good in, 49 ff.; account of Dialectical Method in, 54 ff.; Doctrine of Ideas in Tenth Book of, 59 ff.; compared with *Timaeus* as to relation of God to Ideas, 61; Plato's Criticism of Art in Tenth Book of, 60.
Rêverie-image, place of, in aesthetic experience, 140–51; its bearing on difficulty of χωρισμός and παρουσία, 168; figured as *archetype* of that of which it is image, 168, 169 ff.
Ribot, M., referred to for 'concentration', 134; on 'affective memory', 162; on Schopenhauer's theory of fine art, 167.
Ritter, Constantin, referred to, 15.
Robin, M., his *Théorie Platonicienne des Idées et des Nombres d'après Aristote* referred to, 1; notes similarity of Aristotle's φύσις to Plato's παρουσία, 116; on Ideas of σκευαστά, 61–2; on Ideas as Numbers, 118.
Royce, Prof., on 'imitation', 170.

## INDEX

Santayana, Prof., distinguishes 'Concretions in existence' and 'Concretions in discourse', 131.

Schiller, Dr. F. C. S., on Plato's 'Intellectualism,' 100.

Schopenhauer, on aesthetic Contemplation, 138, 140, 145-6; his Theory of Music, 154; concerned with the Idea for Contemplation, 191.

σκευαστά, are there 'Ideas' of ?, 36 ; Ideas of, in *Cratylus*, 36-7 ; Ideas of, in *Republic*, 61 ; Ideas of, Aristotle on, 62 ; Ideas of, M. Robin on, 61-2.

'Socratic Group' of Dialogues, 15 ff.

*Sophistes*, 84 ff.; stylometric test applied to, 84 ; real purpose of, to show that 'separation' of Ideas from *sensibilia* is fatal to knowledge, 87 ; list of logical categories, 86 ; κοινωνία εἰδῶν in, 86-7; place assigned to ψυχή in, 87, 88; sets forth the Idea as δύναμις, 88.

Souriau, M., on Rêverie, 140 ; images all-important in Poetry, 151.

Spencer, his criterion of Truth, 58.

Spinoza, makes *pulchritudo* relative, 45 ; on passions of which we have formed 'clear and distinct ideas', 55 ; distinguishes *circulus* and *idea circuli*, 57 ; on criterion of Truth, 58 ; argues that there can be only *one* Universe, 60-1 ; referred to for the 'activity' of ideas, 170 ; on the conviction of 'immortality', 191 ; Prof. Höffding on, 191.

Stahr, his *Aristotelia* referred to, 72.

Stallbaum, on Ideas in *Republic* and *Timaeus* respectively, 61.

Stout, Prof., on the 'Category of Thinghood', 131.

Strong, Dr. T. B., on attitude of Plotinus to Platonic Idea of the Good, 97.

Stylometry, 14, 15, 84, 85.

Susemihl, his view of place assigned to Ideas in *Philebus*, 98.

*Symposium*, 39 ; Diotima's Discourse in, ecstasy of, what ?, 188-9 ; Idea of Beauty in, 168, 188-9 ; 'immortality' in, compared with that in *Phaedo*, 190.

Taine, quoted for the illusion of the theatre, 147.

Taylor, Prof. A. E., his *Mind* articles on *Parmenides* referred to, 10 ; his interpretation of *Parmenides*, 73 ff.; on relation between the two parts of the *Parmenides*, 84 ; on Ideal Numbers, 94, 117.

Teresa, her ecstatic experience, 160 ff.

τετράγωνον αὐτό of *Republic* 510 D, what ?, 57.

*Theaetetus*, 65 ff.; list of 'categories' in, 66 ; 'critical' position opposed to 'dogmatic' in, 67 ; ὠφέλεια distinguished from οὐσία in, 66 ; Dr. Horn's view of its relation to *Parmenides*, 65.

Thing and Qualities, 131 ff.

*Timaeus*, 101 ff.; relation of God in, to Good in *Republic*, 101-2 ; relation of God in, to Ideas other than Idea of the Good, 102-3 ; compared with *Republic* as to relation of God to Ideas, 61 ; doctrine of ὑποδοχή, 104-5.

Tocco, M., places *Timaeus* before *Parmenides*, 103.

Transcendental Feeling, 147-8.

τρίτος ἄνθρωπος, 6, 60, 69, 77, 79.

Truth, criterion of, 58 ; according to Plato, 46.

τύποι περὶ θεολογίας of *Republic*, 45.

Ugliness, in aesthetic experience, 146.

Value-judgements, 43.

Vaux, M. Carra de, his *Gazali* quoted, 158 ff.

'Virtue is Knowledge', meaning of, 120.

Visualization, Plato's tendency towards, 182-3; of 'relations', or 'ideals', 183-4; of numbers, 183.

Wonder, aesthetic, 148 ff.
Wordsworth, his 'Solitary Reaper' examined psychologically, 150-1; quoted for relation of poetic imagery to passion, 165.
Wundt, Prof., on the Beautiful, 167.

Xenocrates, referred to, 122.

'Young Socrates' of *Parmenides*, who is he?, Dr. Horn's view, 71; Prof. Natorp's view, 72-3; Mr. R. G. Bury's view, 70-1.

Zeller, identifies God and Idea of the Good, 59; his view of place assigned to Ideas in *Philebus*, 98; on contradiction involved in Aristotelian Philosophy, 112, 114-15.

OXFORD
PRINTED AT THE CLARENDON PRESS
BY HORACE HART, M.A.
PRINTER TO THE UNIVERSITY